QUICK ESCAPES®
WASHINGTON, D.C.

Help Us Keep This Guide Up to Date

Every effort has been made by the authors and editors to make this guide as accurate and useful as possible. However, many things can change after a guide is published—establishments close, phone numbers change, facilities come under new management, etc.

We would love to hear from you concerning your experiences with this guide and how you feel it could be improved and kept up to date. While we may not be able to respond to all comments and suggestions, we'll take them to heart and we'll also make certain to share them with the author. Please send your comments and suggestions to the following address:

> The Globe Pequot Press
> Reader Response/Editorial Department
> P.O. Box 480
> Guilford, CT 06437

Or you may e-mail us at:
> editorial@globe-pequot.com

Thanks for your input, and happy travels!

QUICK ESCAPES® SERIES

QUICK ESCAPES®
WASHINGTON, D.C.

24 WEEKEND GETAWAYS
FROM THE NATION'S CAPITAL

Third Edition

BY

JOHN FITZPATRICK

AND

HOLLY J. BURKHALTER

The
Globe
Pequot
Press

GUILFORD, CONNECTICUT

Photo credits: p. 4: courtesy Shenandoah National Park; p. 20: courtesy Virginia Division of Tourism; p. 31: courtesy Richard T. Nowitz/Metro Richmond Visitors & Convention Bureau; p. 44: courtesy Fredericksburg Department of Tourism; p. 57: courtesy Virginia Division of Tourism; p. 73: courtesy Tom Darden/MD Tourism; p. 83: courtesy Chesapeake Bay Maritime Museum; pp. 97, 109, 123, 134: courtesy MD Tourism; pp. 157, 184: courtesy Steve Shaluta Jr./West Virginia Division of Tourism; p. 145: courtesy David Fattaleh/West Virginia Division of Tourism; p. 169: courtesy Larry Belcher/West Virginia Division of Tourism; pp. 199, 249, 275: courtesy Pennsylvania Office of Travel and Tourism; p. 266: courtesy Fallingwater/The Western Pennsylvania Conservancy; p. 288: courtesy Delaware Economic Development Office; p. 301: courtesy Cape May Chamber of Commerce.

Cover photo © Kunio Owaki/The Stock Market
Cover design by Laura Augustine
Text design by Nancy Freeborn
Map design by Maryann Dubé

Quick Escapes is a registered trademark of The Globe Pequot Press.

Library of Congress Cataloging-in-Publication Data
Fitzpatrick, John (John Joseph)
    Quick escapes Washington, D.C. : 24 weekend getaways from the nation's capital / by John Fitzpatrick and Holly Burkhalter.—3rd ed.
        p.   cm. — (Quick escapes series)
    Includes index.
    ISBN 0-7627-0636-8
    1. Washington Region—Guidebooks. 2. Middle Atlantic States—Guidebooks. I. Burkhalter, Holly. II. Title. III. Series.
    F192.3 .F565 2000
    917.5304'42—dc21   00-042179

Manufactured in the United States of America
Third Edition/First Printing

To Grace and Jo

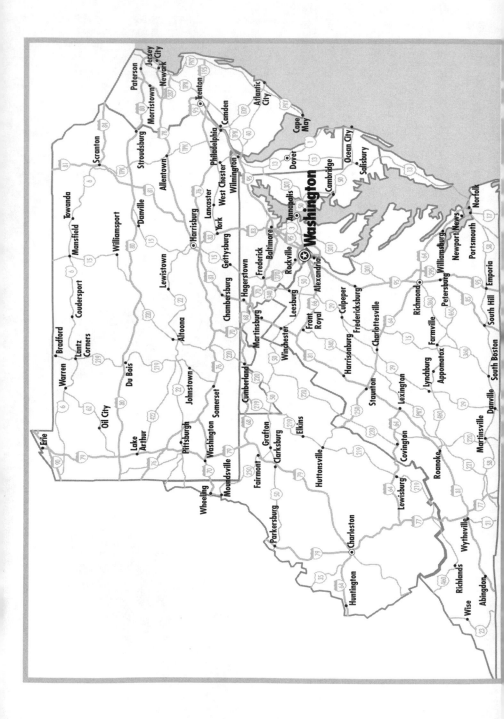

CONTENTS

Introduction ix

VIRGINIA ESCAPES.   1
1. Shenandoah National Park.   2
2. Charlottesville 16
3. Richmond. 29
4. Fredericksburg and Westmoreland County 41
5. Williamsburg 52

MARYLAND ESCAPES 69
1. Annapolis. 70
2. The Eastern Shore 80
3. Berlin, Assateague Island, Ocean City, and More 92
4. Baltimore. 103
5. Antietam National Battlefield and Catoctin Mountain. 117
6. Western Maryland. 128

WEST VIRGINIA ESCAPES 141
1. Berkeley Springs and Cacapon State Park 142
2. Elkins and Canaan Valley 154
3. Lewisburg 166
4. Pipestem State Park and the New River Gorge 178

PENNSYLVANIA ESCAPES.............. 191

1. Philadelphia 192
2. Lancaster County 208
3. Gettysburg and Hershey 223
4. Laurel Highlands............................. 235
5. Pittsburgh 244
6. Fayette County............................... 260

DELAWARE AND BEYOND ESCAPES..... 271

1. Wilmington and the Brandywine Valley............... 272
2. Bethany Beach and Rehoboth Beach 285
3. Lewes and Cape May 296

Index....................................... 309

> The prices and rates listed in this guidebook were confirmed at press time. We recommend, however, that you call establishments before traveling to obtain current information.

INTRODUCTION

There are many advantages to living in the Washington, D.C., area. One of them is that our nation's capital is located within easy driving distance of some of the most spectacular scenery and most enjoyable vacation spots in the United States.

For example, a three-hour drive east takes you to the Atlantic Ocean, where you can revel in the busy beach scene or walk for miles along the surf, alone except for the wild beach ponies. Three hours north is Pennsylvania Dutch country, where horse-drawn buggies, handheld plows, Mennonite and Amish women in somber dresses and bonnets, and handmade quilts fluttering on clotheslines are common sights. Straight west takes you to the mountains, abounding with great hikes, orchards where you pick your own apples and berries, and cozy country inns. Head south and you're in the land of Colonial and Civil War history.

All this and much more is included in *Quick Escapes: Washington, D.C.,* a narrated travel itinerary that will be useful to both locals and visiting tourists. Our twenty-four weekend escapes include a mix of urban and rural, with great dining, shopping, and sight-seeing in such cities as Philadelphia, Pittsburgh, Richmond, and Baltimore, as well as hiking in West Virginia's parks, sailing on the Chesapeake Bay, bicycling on the Eastern Shore, and beachcombing at Assateague Island.

Here's how to use this book: The chapter heading lists the activities that are included in the itinerary. When you've found an activity you're interested in, read through the whole chapter. In each chapter, we tell you what's special about the destination, explain how to get there, and describe the restaurants, lodgings, and sights that we've planned for you. Once you've made a decision on a destination for your quick escape, be sure to make reservations for lodgings, restaurants, and other activities (such as white-water rafting trips) that require them. In fact, it's always a good idea to call ahead when you're planning a jaunt: Hours of operation and prices of admission change, and restaurants change their menus or sometimes close. We've included Web addresses (when they were available) for attractions and lodgings as well as a listing of Web sites to help you plan your trip.

In planning weekend escapes, we have used the following formula:

First, we love the outdoors, and we look for backcountry roads and scenic stops whenever we can. Our general approach is to use the slower, picturesque routes on the drive out, and the straight-shot highways for the return trip home.

Second, the overnight accommodations we have selected are almost all small private inns or bed-and-breakfasts. (If you have a favorite chain motel or hotel, you can always call its toll-free number to find the location of the nearest branch.) We've avoided chain restaurants too and searched out one-of-a-kind local favorites, most of them in the moderate price range. Other Recommended Restaurants lists alternatives, some inexpensive and others more costly.

Third, we've included a mix of well-known must-sees as well as off-the-beaten-track finds of our own. For example, the Williamsburg chapter provides a detailed itinerary for seeing the best of the famous reconstructed Colonial area. But we've added some great new restaurants that most tourists don't know about, and we've also included a bike ride around lovely Jamestown Island—a pleasure that many visitors fail to take advantage of.

Fourth, most chapters include a mix of indoor and outdoor activities, from hiking, swimming, and skiing to shopping, antiquing, museum-going, and visiting historic homes and gardens. We even suggest coffee stops when you've been on your feet too long!

Fifth, in case you're staying longer than a weekend, or want a variation, each chapter includes a lengthy There's More section of additional sights and attractions. And there's a calendar of Special Events full of local seasonal and annual events, with numbers to call for precise dates and details.

Sixth, a word about restaurant prices: "Inexpensive" means less than $6.00 for lunch and coffee and less than $10.00 for dinner and a drink; "moderate" means $6.00–$15.00 for lunch, $10.00–$25.00 for dinner; "expensive" means $15.00–$30.00 for lunch, $25.00–$50.00 for dinner; "very expensive" means more than $30.00 for lunch, more than $50.00 for dinner.

Finally, we have tried to include activities that everybody will enjoy—friends, children, and grandparents. Some weekend itineraries are especially kid-friendly, such as Hershey Park in Pennsylvania, and others are obviously more adult-oriented, such as the visit to the mansions and formal gardens of the Brandywine River Valley. But every weekend includes things that everybody will like: fresh air, beautiful scenery, and great food.

Oh, yes. There's one more thing. We break for doughnuts whenever possible. Have a great time!

VIRGINIA
ESCAPES

Shenandoah National Park

SCENIC SKYLINE DRIVE

2 NIGHTS

National Park • Scenic mountain drive • Hiking
Apple orchard • Picnicking • Gourmet dining

The Shenandoah National Park in northwestern Virginia is considered by many to be among the premier national parks in America. It is, by anyone's reckoning, a national treasure.

The park sits astride the beautiful Blue Ridge Mountains, which are spectacular 365 days a year. In fall the ridge is aflame with color. In winter snow and ice glisten from every branch. In spring the budding trees turn a misty pale green, and high summer brings a dark green velvet cloak to the mountains.

You'll see exposed rock faces, tunnels of trees, high ridges dappled with light and shade, and banks of wildflowers. With its 280 square miles of forest and mountains, the park is home to some 200 species of birds, as well as deer, bobcats, bears, groundhogs, and other creatures. You're sure to see some of them on the two long hikes included in this itinerary.

Winding through the park is the beautiful 105-mile-long Skyline Drive, which offers glorious views of the Shenandoah River in the deep valley to the west and the lush piedmont terrain to the east. Much of Skyline Drive, which stretches from Front Royal on the northern end to Waynesboro on the southern end, is on top of the ridge, and you can see for miles in every direction. Every turn and twist (and there are many!) brings a new and breathtaking vista into view.

Best of all, Shenandoah National Park has more than 500 miles of trails, nearly all of them accessible from Skyline Drive. You can walk a short loop to

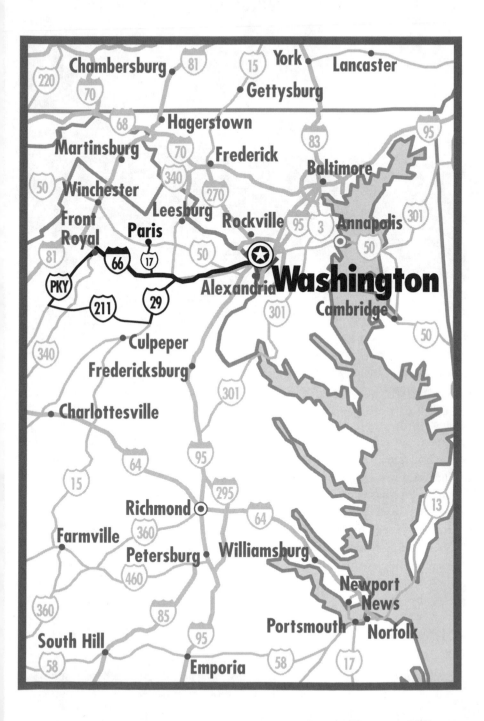

View from Buck Hollow Overlook, Shenandoah National Park

see a waterfall, or pack a picnic lunch and go the distance with a 10-mile hike. Indeed, if you wanted to, you could hike all the way down the mountain chain on the Appalachian Trail, which runs the length of the park.

This quick escape to rural Virginia takes full advantage of both the spectacular scenery of Skyline Drive and the unparalleled hiking possibilities in Shenandoah National Park. You'll dine and relax at a different country inn each evening as you watch the sun set over the Blue Ridge Mountains.

DAY 1

Afternoon

Leave late afternoon or after work on a Friday to get an early start on the weekend. Your first destination is the tiny town of Paris, Virginia, where you'll have dinner and spend the first night. Paris is about 50 miles west of Washington on

U.S. Highway 50. If you prefer, you can take Interstate 66 west about 50 miles to exit 23 and then take U.S. Highway 17 north 7 miles to Paris.

If it's late summer or early fall, consider a short detour to **Stribling Orchard** (Route 688 south; 540–364–3040), near Markham, where you can pick your own or buy already-picked apples or peaches to snack on throughout the weekend. Stribling's is easy to find from I–66. Just after you exit onto U.S. Highway 17, turn left on State Highway 55 and take it west 5 miles to Markham. (From the more scenic U.S. Highway 50, you'll have to take U.S. Highway 17 south 7 miles and State Highway 55 west 5 miles to get to Markham.) The orchard is a half mile south of Markham on Route 688; follow the signs. You can stock up on Jonathans, Red or Golden Delicious, Granny Smiths, or a half dozen other varieties of apples. You can also buy fresh peaches and nectarines, cider, jelly, honey, and baked goods for weekend picnicking and snacking, and for the drive home.

DINNER: The Ashby Inn & Restaurant, 692 Federal Street, Paris (200 yards west of the intersection of U.S. Highways 17 and 50 on State Highway 701); (540) 592–3900. The Ashby has won accolades for the beauty of the facility and the splendor of its menu, which changes daily but always includes homemade bread and desserts, beautifully prepared fresh seafood and game entrees, and produce and herbs from the inn's garden. If you go on a Friday, you can get the famous cassoulet made with white beans, lamb, duck confit, and garlic sausage. Moderate to expensive.

LODGING: The Ashby Inn is located in a tiny corner crossing of a town, and the nineteenth-century dwelling and nearby schoolhouse, which houses four extra suites, have been meticulously restored, expanded, and decorated. Antiques, worn Oriental rugs, old quilts, dark rich colors on the walls, and old prints and paintings can be found in every room. In addition, each room has a wonderful view of the surrounding countryside and mountains. Rooms are $110–$180, and the big, beautiful suites (each with its own fireplace) are $200–$250.

DAY 2

Morning

BREAKFAST: The Ashby Inn serves a full breakfast with fruit, cereal, and something luscious from the oven.

After breakfast, head for **Front Royal.** Go 7 miles south on U.S. Highway 17, then go 17 miles west on I–66 and 4 miles south on U.S. Highway 340. If you plan on picnicking, there are a half dozen places in Front Royal where you can stop and pick up provisions for a picnic lunch at the park. The best is **J's Gourmet,** 206 South Royal Avenue (U.S. Highway 340). There you can get the likes of a trout mousse with cucumber sandwich, fresh salads, sweets and savories, and a decent bottle of wine. Phone in advance (540–636–9293 or 800–742–6421) and your provisions will be ready when you arrive.

After you've picked up lunch, cross the street to **Royal Oak Bookshop,** 207 South Royal Avenue; (540) 635–7070. The Royal Oak has been in business for more than twenty-four years and has five pleasant rooms crammed with new and used books, posters, and prints. Open Monday to Saturday 10:00 A.M. to 6:00 P.M., Sunday noon to 5:00 P.M.

The northernmost entrance to **Shenandoah National Park** is on U.S. Highway 340 just south of Front Royal. Get on **Skyline Drive** there and plan on spending the entire day in the first 30 miles of the park and Skyline Drive. Both the park and the drive are open 365 days a year, weather permitting; call (540) 999–2243 for information. The entrance fee is $10 per car; save your receipt because the admission is good for a week. Admission is free if you have a $20 annual "Shenandoah Pass," a Golden Eagle Passport, a Golden Access Pass, or a Golden Age Passport.

The National Park Service personnel at the Front Royal entrance station will give you a free map, a brochure describing the park and Skyline Drive, and a publication called the *Shenandoah Overlook* that tells you the times all facilities are open and lists special events in and around the park.

Don't resist stopping at the **Shenandoah Valley Overlook** at mile 2.8. There you have a panoramic view of the Shenandoah Valley to the west and 40-mile-long Massanutten Mountain, which divides the Shenandoah River into two forks that meet near Front Royal.

Stop at the **Dickey Ridge Visitor Center** at mile 4.6 to see exhibits describing the geology, flora, and fauna in the park. If you're planning any serious hiking, you should buy a copy of the Potomac Appalachian Trail Club's *Circuit Hikes in Shenandoah National Park* or one (or more) of their detailed trail maps. Also talk with the park personnel at the visitor center. They'll help you plan a hike and let you know if any of the trails have been washed out by rain or are undergoing repair.

Across the road from the visitor center is the **Fox Hollow Nature Trail,** a short 1.3-mile loop trail that takes you past an ancient cemetery, rock fences, and the foundation rocks of several ruined buildings. Until the 1920s when the

Commonwealth of Virginia purchased the land and gave it to the federal government to create Shenandoah National Park, this area was populated by farmers. The gently sloping nature trail roughly follows the farm road the Fox family traveled to go to market before there was a paved road in the area.

As you drive south on Skyline Drive, you'll be climbing steadily for the first 20 miles or so from an elevation of about 600 feet near the entrance at Front Royal to nearly 3,400 feet at Hogback Overlook. Then the road dips up and down over Hogback Mountain, through Elkwallow Gap, over Neighbor Mountain, through a couple of hollows, up over Pass Mountain, and, finally, down again at Thornton Gap without a billboard in sight. It's as pretty a drive as you'll ever take.

Plan on stopping at several of the overlooks and waysides. There's nearly always a vista or some close-in scene worth a photograph. Remember to watch the road carefully as you drive. You'll be sharing it with hikers, bikers, deer, an occasional bear, and other rubbernecking drivers.

LUNCH: At **Elkwallow Wayside** at mile 24.1 there are tables where your can eat a picnic lunch. There's also a snack bar that sells soup, sandwiches, chips, and drinks. The snack bar is usually open weekdays 9:00 A.M. to 5:30 P.M. and weekends 9:00 A.M. to 6:30 P.M. from mid-April through early November; (540) 999–2253. Inexpensive.

Afternoon

Set aside the whole afternoon for a strenuous hike with breathtaking views; you're going to climb the **Little Devils Stairs.** Drive back north 5 miles from Elkwallow Wayside to **Little Hogback Overlook** between mileposts 19 and 20. Park there, walk north a half mile along the roadside, cross Skyline Drive, and look for a fence gate leading to the Keyser Run Fire Road going south and east down the mountain. Follow the fire road 1 mile to the Little Devils Stairs Trail; halfway there, you'll pass beneath Little Devils Stairs Overlook where cars are parked at the top of a steep cliff to your right.

When you reach the trail marked by blue blazes on the trees, leave the road, turning left (to the right is the Pole Bridge Link Trail), and descend Little Devils Stairs. The descent is quite steep; in the first mile or so of the trail, you'll go from an elevation of more than 2,600 feet to an elevation of 1,100 feet.

The "stairs" are enormous boulders and chunks of the mountain that broke off and tumbled down eons ago. You'll feel like a mountain goat as you scram-

ble from rock to rock, sliding and slipping as you go. A stream, Keyser Run, parallels the trail almost the whole way; take frequent breaks and sit on a log or a boulder by the stream to give your legs and knees a rest.

When you've reached the bottom of Little Devils Stairs after about 2 miles, you'll know you've had a hike! At that point, you will have come to the edge of the park; the boundary is marked by signs and you'll see a parking lot where hikers from outside the park leave their cars while they climb up the stairs.

Now for the moment of truth. You can turn around and climb up the Little Devils Stairs or you can walk past the parking lot to the Keyser Run Fire Road and stroll up the gravel road all the way back to Skyline Drive. Walking up the fire road adds a mile or so to the 8-mile hike, but it will be easier on your muscles. Either way, allow at least four hours for the entire circuit.

When you're "hiked out," get back in your car for a 12-mile drive south to **Thornton Gap.** Exit from Skyline Drive and Shenandoah National Park (save your receipt for admission the next day) onto U.S. Highway 211 west, and follow it 9 miles to Luray. In Luray, pick up State Highway 340 Business south and drive 6 miles. Turn left on State Route 624. After a half mile, turn right onto State Route 626 (Hawksbill Park Road). Your evening destination is a quarter mile on the right.

You will be dining and staying over at **Jordan Hollow Farm Inn,** 326 Hawksbill Park Road, Stanley; (540) 778–1759 or (888) 418–7000, www. jordanhollow.com. The inn is known for its gracious hospitality and its beautiful views of the Shenandoah Mountains. It also has a stable and offers guided horseback tours at reasonable prices.

DINNER: The Farmhouse Restaurant at Jordan Hollow Farm Inn combines traditional home-style cooking and fancy new-American cuisine with an emphasis on local produce. You can start with the likes of in-house hickory smoked rainbow trout with an herbed radish compote on a bed of wilted spinach, and follow it with grilled breasts of free-range chicken on a bed of fettuccine with a lime and summer herb vinaigrette. Moderate to expensive.

LODGING: The Jordan Hollow Farm Inn has nine guest rooms and seven luxury suites. The rooms are homey and beautifully furnished; most have fireplaces, whirlpool baths, and private porches. The suites have a two-person thermomassage spa in the bedroom and a separate sitting room/anteroom. Rates: $133–$190 a night.

DAY 3

Morning

BREAKFAST: The Jordan Hollow Farm Inn serves a big breakfast, which is included in the price of the room. It's likely to feature ham and eggs or pancakes, and fruit and fresh baked pastries. Fuel up, because you have another good hike ahead of you.

After you've breakfasted and packed up your car, reenter Shenandoah National Park at Thornton Gap and head south 20 miles to **Big Meadows.** This morning, you'll hike from Big Meadows to Camp Hoover and back, a 10-mile trek that takes in some of the loveliest features of the park, including streams, waterfalls, boulders, and spectacular views.

Park at Big Meadows Wayside just south of milepost 51. Cross Skyline Drive diagonally to Rapidan Road, a gravel service road with a chain across its entrance. As you hike down the road through the meadow and into the woods, keep your eyes open for deer, which frequently graze there. You'll also see plenty of wildflowers, and strawberries and blueberries if they're in season.

Rapidan Road descends from an elevation of more than 3,600 feet to about 2,500 feet through a series of three gentle switchbacks over a 5-mile stretch. After a mile or so, you'll pass the yellow-blazed Mill Prong Horse Trail on your right, and after another mile or so the blue-blazed Upper Dark Hollow Trail on your left; ignore both and stay on the gravel road another 2-plus miles until you reach the narrow Rapidan River and an intersecting gravel road heading uphill to the right. Follow this road up the hill 0.7 mile, crossing the bridge over Mill Prong Stream. Once you've crossed the bridge, you're at the halfway point on your hike.

You'd turn right on the yellow-blazed Mill Prong Horse Trail to head back, but before you do, take a few minutes to walk around **Camp Hoover,** a small fishing camp built as a summer retreat by President Herbert Hoover. The three buildings there are closed to the public except for two days in August when they're open for touring (see Special Events). You can, however, read the signs posted throughout the camp that describe the history of the area.

To return, take the Mill Prong Horse Trail along the stream (notice the waterfall) 0.8 mile to the blue-blazed Mill Prong Trail, which goes straight as the horse trail heads right. Follow Mill Prong Trail 1 mile and turn right onto the Appalachian Trail (marked with white blazes on the trees). Take it 1.7 miles back to Skyline Drive. Turn right and head back to Big Meadows.

LUNCH: When you complete the hike to Camp Hoover and back and you are completely hot, tired, and sweaty, cool off and have lunch at **Big Meadows Lodge.** There is a casual restaurant where you can get sandwiches and full meals at moderate prices. At Big Meadows, you can also bone up on park history, geography, and biology at the **Byrd Visitor Center** or stop in at the gift shop and pick up some Appalachian crafts.

Afternoon

After lunch, take one last scenic swing on Skyline Drive before leaving for home. You'll especially like the drive back from Big Meadows to Thornton Gap. You will be breezing through the highest points in the park, and the traffic is always lighter going from south to north.

If you still have energy to spare, just north of Big Meadows at **Dark Hollow Falls** is a 70-foot waterfall about three quarters of a mile from the parking area. And 8 miles farther north at mile 42.6 is **Whiteoak Canyon,** a popular spot near the highest point in the drive where you can take a 5-mile hike and see six waterfalls and a beautiful stand of hemlocks.

Exit from the park at Thornton Gap and return home via U.S. Highway 211 east 35 miles to Warrenton, U.S. Highway 29 north 13 miles to the interstate, and I–66 east about 30 miles to Washington.

THERE'S MORE

Horseback Riding. Shenandoah National Park has stables at Skyland; (540) 999–2210. One-hour or two-and-a-half-hour rides available; reservations necessary. Rates: $22–$40. A fifteen-minute pony ride for children is $3.00.

Washington, Virginia. Delightful village with upscale art galleries, antiques stores, cabinetmaking studios, and a pleasant museum.

Luray Caverns. Very popular commercialized natural cavern that features a one-hour tour, a huge "stalacpipe" organ that plays real music, a forty-seven-bell carillon, and a car and carriage museum. A restaurant, motel, and golf course are also on the premises. Located on U.S. Highway 211 about 9 miles west of Shenandoah National Park; (540) 743–6551 or www. luraycaverns.com. Open seven days a week year-round at 9:00 A.M.; closing time varies with the season. Admission is $14.00 for everyone over age fourteen and $6.00 for children seven to thirteen. Children six and under are admitted free.

New Market Battlefield State Historical Park. Commemorates the Civil War battle of New Market; artifacts, dioramas, and films. Located just off U.S. Highway 211, New Market; (540) 740–3132. Open daily 9:00 A.M. to 5:00 P.M. Admission is $5.00 for adults and $2.00 for children six and older; children under six are admitted free.

SPECIAL EVENTS

March. Annual Spring Arts and Crafts Show. Area artists display and sell their works in Harrisonburg. (540) 434–0005.

May. Wildflower Weekend in Shenandoah National Park. Naturalist tours and lectures, photo exhibits, and, of course, the flowers. (540) 999–3500.

May. Reenactment of the historic Civil War battle in New Market. (540) 740–3212 or (877) 740–3212.

August. Hoover Days. Camp Hoover in Shenandoah National Park is usually open to the public for two days. Tours, historical talks; refreshments for sale at the presidential retreat. (540) 999–3281.

August. Hoover and Heritage Day. Food, entertainment, arts and crafts, and games in Madison; held in conjunction with the park activities on Hoover Days. (540) 948–5121.

OTHER RECOMMENDED RESTAURANTS

Washington

The Inn at Little Washington, Middle and Main Streets; (540) 675–3800. One of the best restaurants in the country—of the "you have to go there at least once in your life" type. Menu changes daily, but everything is prepared from the freshest local ingredients; very elegant, very romantic, very expensive.

Flint Hill

Four and Twenty Blackbirds, U.S. Highway 522 and State Highway 647; (540) 675–1111. Lovely, casual-chic restaurant in an old home with fireplace, lace curtains, and antique furniture; specializes in new-American cuisine, with Italian, Thai, and Southwestern tones. Moderate to expensive.

Sperryville

Appetite Repair Shop, just off U.S. Highway 211; (540) 987–9533. Good place to get a deli sandwich, chips, fruit, and a candy bar for a picnic or for the road. Inexpensive.

Front Royal

Giuseppe's Italian Restaurant, 865 John Marshall Highway; (540) 636–2000. Traditional, family-oriented Italian restaurant serving spaghetti, lasagna, and veal dishes that are popular with locals. Moderate.

Stadt Kaffee Cafe and Restaurant, 300 East Main Street; (540) 635–8300. Traditional, family-oriented German restaurant serving sauerbraten, schnitzel, and apple strudel. Moderate.

Stanley

Best place for doughnuts: D.R. Quick Shop Bakery, East Main Street; (540) 778–1982. Your choice: glazed, cake, cinnamon . . . and they open between 3:30 A.M. and 5:00 A.M. for early birds. If they run out of doughnuts, they'll make them up fresh for you within fifteen minutes. Call ahead for large orders.

(For other restaurants, see the listings under Other Recommended Lodgings.)

OTHER RECOMMENDED LODGINGS

Shenandoah National Park

Shenandoah National Park has two lodges, one at Skyland and one at Big Meadows; (540) 743–5108 or (800) 999–4714. Both have comfortable guest rooms, great views of the Shenandoah Valley, and restaurants on the premises. Rates: $50–$165. You can also rent a rustic cabin in the park (the Lewis Mountain Cabins); cabins are set up for housekeeping but have no stoves. Rates: $59–$91. There are campgrounds at Big Meadows, Lewis Mountain, and Loft Mountain. Campsites cost $14 at Lewis Mountain and Loft Mountain and are on a first-come, first-served basis. You can reserve a site at Big Meadows ($17) by calling (800) 365–2267 and giving SHEN as the four-letter designator when prompted. Backcountry camping is permitted throughout the park; the required permit is free. There are also six locked cabins in backcountry areas of the park rented through the Potomac Appalachian Trail Club; (703) 242–0693.

Woodstock

The Inn at Narrow Passage, U.S. Highway 11, about 3 miles south of Woodstock; (540) 459–8000 or (800) 459–8002, www.innatnarrowpassage.com. Log inn that has been a stopping place for travelers for 250 years; completely restored with gleaming floors, air-conditioning, and a huge limestone fireplace. The inn has twelve guest rooms with private baths. Large country breakfast by the fire. Rates: $75–$110.

Syria

Graves' Mountain Lodge, County Road 670; (540) 923–4231, www.graves mountain.com. Hilltop lodge located about 1 mile from the pedestrian entrance at the base of Shenandoah National Park's Whiteoak Canyon Trail and Old Rag Mountain Trail, two of the park's most beautiful and popular trails. There are thirty-eight rooms in the lodge; the $66–$100 per person daily charge includes all meals. There are also eleven cabins with cooking facilities that accomodate up to fifteen people; the cabins rent for $66 to $230 a day. The dining room's fried chicken, country ham, and rainbow trout dinners are first-rate.

Washington

Bleu Rock Inn, U.S. Highway 211; (504) 987–3190 or (800) 537–3652, www. bleurockinn.com. Pleasant, rather new country inn with five guest rooms, all with private baths and balconies with views of the mountains. Complimentary afternoon sherry; orchards to stroll through before you retire. Excellent restaurant serving regional variation of new-American cuisine on premises. Rates: $125–$195.

Strasburg

The Hotel Strasburg, 213 South Holliday Street; (540) 465–9191 or (800) 348–8327, www.svta.org/thehotel. A recently renovated century-old Victorian hotel with seventeen rooms and twelve suites, some of which have Jacuzzis. The $74–$165 room charge includes breakfast.

Front Royal

Killahevlin, 1401 North Royal Avenue; (540) 636–7335 or (800) 847–6132, www.vairish.com. Antique-filled Edwardian mansion with Irish pub on the premises. All guest rooms have whirlpool baths, telephones, and working fireplaces. Large breakfasts; complimentary coffee and soda available all day. Rates: $120–$210.

Chester House, 43 Chester Street; (540) 636–8695 or (800) 621–0441, www. chesterhouse.com. Beautiful, century-old house with marble mantels, three sitting rooms, terraced garden, shady lawn. Six guest rooms (four with private baths) with flowers, mints, terry-cloth robes, fireplaces. Full breakfast served. Rates: $65–$125. Detached carriage house with bedroom, living room, dining room, kitchen, and whirlpool rents for $165–$190.

New Market

Cross Roads Inn, 9222 John Sevier Road; (540) 740–4157 or (888) 740–4157, www.crossroadsinnva.com. Clapboard Victorian with five guest rooms, all with private baths. Austrian-style hospitality includes complimentary strudel in the afternoon and beverages in the evening; full breakfast included. Rates: $55–$100.

Red Shutter Farm House, Route 1; (540) 740–4281. Old farmhouse with five spacious guest rooms; most have private baths, some have fireplaces. Family suites available. Large country breakfast; games and TV in library. Rates: $60–$75.

Sperryville

The Conyers House Country Inn and Stable, 3131 Slate Mills Road; (540) 987–8025, www.conyershouse.com. Elegant old country store made into an inn. Eight guest rooms with lovely antiques, private baths, and cozy fireplaces; full country breakfast. Seven-course, four-wine, candlelight dinner available upon reservation. A two-hour cross-country horseback ride can be arranged for $50 a person. Rates: $150–$300; dinner for two is an additional $140.

FOR MORE INFORMATION

Shenandoah National Park, Route 4, Box 348, Luray, VA 22835; (540) 999–3500, www.nps.gov/shen.

Shenandoah Natural History Association, 3655 U.S. Highway 211 East, Luray, VA 22835; (540) 999–3582.

Shenandoah Valley Travel Association, P.O. Box 1040, Dept. SNP, New Market, VA 22844; (540) 740–3132, www.svta.org.

Front Royal Visitors' Center, 414 East Main Street, Front Royal, VA 22030; (540) 635–3185 or (800) 338–2576, www.frontroyalchamber.com.

Charlottesville

A PRESIDENTIAL NEIGHBORHOOD

2 NIGHTS

Three presidential homes • University of Virginia
Antiques • Music festival • Vineyards

They were the best of friends. They rode to each other's neighboring plantations to play chess, loaned one another skilled servants, and bought each
other's furniture when one or another of them was hard up for cash. They also
succeeded each other as the third, fourth, and fifth presidents of the United
States of America.

Thomas Jefferson, James Madison, and James Monroe lived within 30 miles
of one another in the rolling foothills of the Blue Ridge Mountains. It was
quite a neighborhood. And it is your destination on this perfect weekend
escape to Charlottesville and its environs.

It is said that Charlottesville is "Mr. Jefferson's town." And, indeed, his
imprint is everywhere. Just above the city is Monticello, the plantation home
that he designed and lived in until his death. And Charlottesville itself is dominated by another of his architectural creations: the University of Virginia, considered by some to be the most beautiful college campus in America.

Yet every aspect of Jefferson's life was influenced and enriched by his
beloved neighbors, James Madison and James Monroe. Madison was the brilliant young Virginian who crafted the Constitution, as well as many of the
famous Federalist Papers, which became the basis for the form of government
America has today. He was a close political collaborator of Jefferson, as well as
warm friend, and served the third president as his secretary of state.

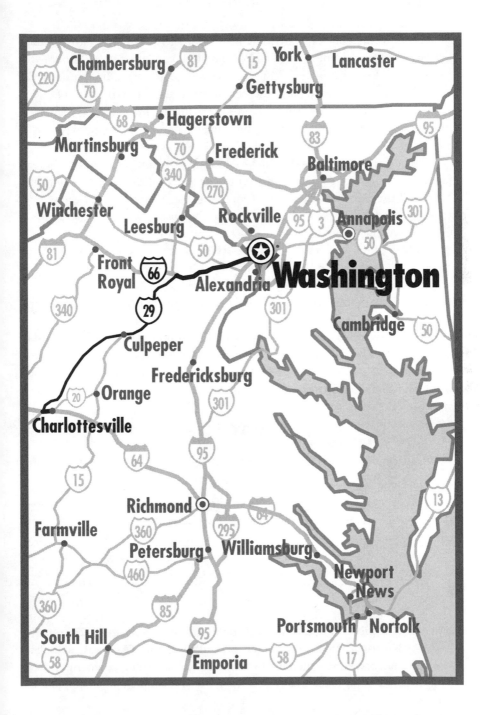

The third member of the trio, James Monroe, studied law with Thomas Jefferson and served both Presidents Washington and Jefferson as Minister to France. And it was his famous Monroe Doctrine that drew a line in the sand with Europe by prohibiting any encroachment in the Western Hemisphere.

The three friends were truly "men of the Enlightenment," and evidence of their voracious appetites for philosophy, foreign language, agricultural pursuits, engineering inventions, and most of all, public service, is everywhere.

The best way to explore their neighborhood is by touring their three great homes. Each tour offers a very different experience of the past. At Jefferson's Monticello you will see the home much as it was when he lived there. The vegetable gardens are planted with the crops he raised, and tour guides quote from his writings. A visit to Madison's ancestral home at Montpelier, by contrast, is like joining an architectural dig, where devoted historians and archaeologists are "looking for Mr. Madison" beneath the changes wrought by two centuries of subsequent owners. James Monroe's more modest Ash Lawn–Highland Plantation is not just a lovely historic home but also a working farm, as well as a favorite spot for evening concerts, plays, and operas.

Your weekend escape also includes two nights at a beautiful downtown Charlottesville inn, a sampling of the city's first-rate restaurants, a tour and wine-tasting at one of Virginia's best vineyards, a stroll through artists' workshops, and shopping for antiques.

DAY 1

Afternoon

Charlottesville is 120 miles southwest of Washington. Depending on traffic, the trip can take anywhere from two to three hours. Plan a late afternoon or after-work departure so you can get there by dinnertime. From Washington, take Interstate 66 west about 35 miles to Gainesville (exit 43). Then head south on U.S. Highway 29 for 87 miles. About 10 miles before you get to Charlottesville, begin looking for your dinner stop, which is located 1 mile past Charlottesville Airport Road. Turn left on State Highway 1520 and head east about a mile to the restaurant.

DINNER: The **Silver Thatch Inn,** 3001 Hollymead Drive (804–978–4686), has three intimate dining rooms in a house that dates back to the Revolution. (The original structure, which has been added to, was built by Hessian soldiers fighting in the war.) It is a totally charming place, and the new-American cuisine will help you unwind from the drive and begin to enjoy your weekend. The menu features several interesting dishes using the best of Virginia ingredients. You can start with an appetizer such as sauté of sweetbreads, country ham, and hazelnuts deglazed with raspberry vinegar served over baby greens, and proceed to the daily meat, seafood, and vegetarian specials. And they will be special: The roast turkey might come as pinwheels stuffed with spinach mousse, sun-dried tomatoes, and pine nuts with a tomato relish. The Silver Thatch Inn has a full-time pastry chef and is renowned for its desserts, so linger after dinner for coffee and a treat. Expensive.

After dinner, continue south on U.S. Highway 29 to town. Avoid the bypass and take Business Route 29 (Emmet Street) to Business Route 250 (West Main Street). Turn left and follow Main Street downtown to South Street, a short one-way street heading east into the historic area. Look for two yellow houses, one with a large wraparound veranda. This is your lodging for the night. Pull into the parking lot and head for the red door at the back of the larger building.

LODGING: 200 South Street Inn is indeed located at 200 South Street; (804) 979–0200 or (800) 964–7008, www.southstreet.com. The inn consists of two buildings, both of which have been completely restored. It is old-fashioned and very romantic. Many of the twenty rooms and suites have whirlpools and fireplaces; all have high ceilings and private baths, and all are furnished with English and Belgian antiques. Rates: $105–$200 a night; two-night minimum on spring and fall weekends.

DAY 2

Morning

BREAKFAST: 200 South Street Inn serves a very nice complimentary continental breakfast of fruit and rolls. Order an early-morning wake-up call and ask at the same time for a 7:00 A.M. breakfast; breakfast usually begins at 8:00 A.M., but the inn's friendly staff will be happy to accommodate you.

You need to get an early start on your first full day in Charlottesville because the lines at **Monticello** form early and only get longer. If you get there by 9:00 A.M., however, you can join a tour and enter the home with no more than a fifteen-minute wait.

Monticello is located on State Highway 53, 3 miles southeast of Charlottesville. It is perched high on a mountaintop that offers a dazzling view

Monticello, near Charlottesville

of the surrounding countryside and the Blue Ridge Mountains. Start your tour at the Monticello Visitors Center, on Route 20 South at Interstate 64; (804) 984–9822, www.monticello.org. There you can purchase tickets to enter Monticello at $9.00 for adults, $8.00 for seniors, and $5.00 for children six to eleven. Children under six are admitted free. Monticello is open daily 9:00 A.M. to 4:30 P.M. from November through February, 8:00 A.M. to 5:00 P.M. from March through October, closed Christmas. At the visitors center, you can also purchase a combined Monticello/Ash Lawn–Highland/Michie Tavern admission ticket for $18.50.

The house tour at Monticello takes about fifty minutes and offers a superb look at Jefferson and his times. Guides are clearly devoted to the preservation of his memory and proudly describe his formidable intellect (he could read in seven languages), his genius as a self-taught architect, his love of gadgets, his prowess as a horticultural scientist, and his skill as a violinist.

At the same time, there is no attempt to avoid the fact that Jefferson was also a typical slave owner, who treated the men and women he owned no better and no worse than others of the period. A separate hour-long outdoor plantation life tour provides abundant information about the lives of slaves at

Monticello, including those, like Sally Hemings, who were particularly close to the Jefferson family.

If you got an early start at Monticello, you should be able to beat the rush for lunch at historic **Michie Tavern,** just down the hill from Monticello at 683 Thomas Jefferson Parkway; (804) 977–1234, www.michietavern.com. The tavern is a beautiful eighteenth-century inn that offers its own tour. Once serving travelers on a stagecoach route in the 1780s, Michie Tavern is steeped in history. Guests who explore the house from ballroom to wine cellar will see wonderful artifacts, displays, and furnishings from the period. There's a fun General Store on the premises full of Virginia specialties for sale. Open daily 9:00 A.M. to 4:20 P.M. The tour costs $6.00 for adults and $2.00 for children six to eleven; children under six are admitted free.

LUNCH: The Ordinary at Michie Tavern offers famished guests a very hearty Colonial meal, specializing in fried chicken, black-eyed peas, and apple cobbler. Happily, the service is buffet so the wait is short, and the seating for hundreds is divided up into adjoining, wood-beamed dining rooms. The buffet lunch is $10.95, but you'll get a $1.00 discount on your Michie Tavern tour admission if you lunch there.

After lunch, a 3-mile drive east on State Highway 53, then south on State Highway 795 (follow the signs), takes you to **Ash Lawn–Highland,** the home of James Monroe, located on the James Monroe Parkway, Charlottesville; (804) 293–9539. Open daily 9:00 A.M. to 6:00 P.M. March through October, 10:00 A.M. to 5:00 P.M. November through February. Admission is $7.00 for adults, $6.50 for seniors, $4.00 for children six to eleven. Children under six are admitted free.

Ash Lawn–Highland, which is now owned by the College of William and Mary, is not as grand a structure as Monticello. But a tour there is nearly as interesting an experience as Monticello itself, and it is much less crowded.

The grounds, boxwoods, great trees, and gardens are very beautiful. The house, still under renovation, is full of Madison's things and each has a story to go with it. After the short, well-presented guided tour, take time to roam about the grounds and gardens. You'll see and hear cattle lowing in nearby meadows on the farm, and the screech of a peacock in the garden. On summer evenings, Ash Lawn–Highland is a favorite place for music and theater lovers to bring a picnic supper and enjoy opera or a concert under the stars. (See Special Events.)

Back in town, visit the **McGuffey Art Center,** 201 Second Street, NW; (804) 295–7973. At this schoolhouse turned artists' collective, you'll find forty local artists at work in their studios and galleries. The center has sculpture, fiber, clay, paintings, prints, photographs, and more, and a gift shop where the artists' works are for sale. If kids are restless, they can play in a park adjacent to the art center while their parents peruse the artwork inside. Open Tuesday to Saturday 10:00 A.M. to 5:00 P.M., Sunday 1:00 to 5:00 P.M.

A stroll through the downtown pedestrian mall on Main Street takes you past lots of interesting local shops. Be sure to stop for an ice-cream soda at **The Hardware Store Restaurant,** 316 East Main Street; (804) 977–1518. This is a really fun collection of boutique stores housed within an old converted hardware store, which has a very nice casual restaurant in it.

When you return to your inn, relax in the deep rockers on the veranda or sit in the pleasant library and sip the complimentary wine.

DINNER: Less than 2 blocks away from the inn is your dinner destination, the **Metropolitain,** 214 West Water Street; (804) 977–1043. You would never guess that this modest-looking establishment, housed in what used to be a hardware store (it's a Charlottesville thing!), is one of the town's best restaurants. The decor is severely plain, '50s retro, with the kitchen right smack in the middle of the large, square room. You can watch the chefs work their magic with the likes of pork chops and sweet potato salsa, tuna sashimi with marinated seaweed salad, and vegetarian Wellington made with portobello mushrooms. Expensive.

LODGING: 200 South Street Inn.

DAY 3

Morning

BREAKFAST: 200 South Street Inn.

After you finish your coffee, drive west on Main Street for a mile or so to the **University of Virginia** campus. The mighty Rotunda, with its brick courtyard and statue of Jefferson, dominates the center of the campus. Walk around it and enter the long greensward between the Rotunda and Cabell Hall. On each side of the park are Jeffersonian buildings, and the whole campus has a feeling of peace and dignity. The university offers free historical tours five times a day, except mid-December to mid-January. Call (804) 924–7969 to arrange one.

LUNCH: Charlottesville is full of great restaurants for Sunday brunch. One favorite is the funky **Southern Culture Cafe and Restaurant,** 633 West Main Street; (804) 979–1990. The food is wonderful, the check surprisingly small, and the atmosphere pleasant and casual. Southern Culture offers a Hangtown Fry of eggs scrambled with bacon and oysters, an Eggs Basin Street (served with tiny crab cakes), and eggs with smoked salmon. The tiled floors, comfy booths, and friendly wait staff make this a great Sunday spot. Moderate.

Afternoon

As you drive out of Charlottesville, take time to stop at **Oakencroft Vineyard,** about 3 miles west of U.S. Highway 29 on State Highway 654 (Barracks Road). You can tour the wine-making rooms and have a chat with the wine masters at the gift shop, who will urge you to try five or six different wines. Oakencroft, while not the largest vineyard in Virginia, is one of the finest; its Country White was selected by the Reagan White House for the president to take to the Gorbachev summit in 1986. Open daily 11:00 A.M. to 5:00 P.M. April through December and weekends in March; closed January and February. (804) 296–4188, www.oakencroft.com.

Your next destination is **Montpelier,** the estate of James Madison, which is located a scenic 25 miles northeast of Charlottesville on State Highway 20; (540) 672–2728. Open daily 9:30 A.M. to 4:30 P.M. April through November, 9:30 A.M. to 3:00 P.M. December through March. Admission is $7.50 for adults, $6.50 for senior citizens, and $3.50 for children six to twelve. Children under six are admitted free.

Montpelier is the least dramatic and the least seen of the three presidential estates (tourists are relatively few), but in many ways it is the most interesting of them all. It has been a museum only since 1987, and a dedicated team of archaeologists, curators, preservationists, and grounds staff are, as they put it, attempting to bring back Mr. Madison to the house.

The crux of the problem is that, because of the gambling debts of Madison's stepson, Montpelier was sold shortly after the ex-president's death in 1849. Since then, it has had six private owners, and they all felt obliged to put their own dramatic stamp on the original building. The du Ponts, for example, who owned the home for most of the last century, enlarged it to twice its size and installed elaborate Victorian furnishings and woodwork throughout. Earlier owners rampaged throughout Montpelier, moving walls, building staircases, replacing eighteenth-century mantels, and so on.

Mr. Madison and his wife, Dolley, almost got lost in the process, but today you can see the effort in progress to bring them back. A two-hour tour of the nearly empty house is absolutely fascinating. Knowledgeable guides show you the cracks and excavations that tell something about the original house and the way it was built. They call it "jogging the house's memory."

In one room, for example, the guide lovingly shows off a huge ceiling hole where the original beams (built by George and Peter, two slaves on the plantation) are still as straight and strong as when they were put in. Those beams provided the clue to where the original wall had been in 1760—and say something about the tools and talent of Madison's master builders.

And that's the way the whole tour is: a crack here, a story there. Throughout the tour, you hear the words of James Madison and learn of his enormous contribution to American government and political thought, and of the influences on his own life and thought.

After the tour, you are free to roam about the beautiful grounds and garden at Montpelier for as long as you like. It is a lovely spot, high on a hill with a stunning view of the rolling countryside around it.

When you leave Montpelier, you might want to make one last stop in the area. Take State Highway 20 back south 8 miles to State Highway 33, turn right, and follow State Highway 33 west 7 miles until it intersects with U.S. Highway 29 at **Ruckersville.** There you will find a couple of large antiques complexes, each with dozens of small stalls bursting with old stuff. The shops are a gold mine of modestly priced furniture, jewelry, books, china, silver, pictures, and all sorts of wonderful junk. You can wander to your heart's content—there's no pressure to buy. You can't miss **Greene House Shops** (804–985–6053) and **Country Store** (804–985–3649) on opposite corners of the highway intersection.

Return to Washington on U.S. Highway 29 north and I–66 east. It should take about two hours.

THERE'S MORE

Virginia Discovery Museum. Small, interactive children's museum with permanent exhibits featuring puppets, arts and crafts, computers, magnets, bees, and, of course, Thomas Jefferson. Located at the east end of the downtown mall; (804) 977–1025, www.vadm.org. Open Tuesday to Saturday 10:00 A.M. to 5:00 P.M., Sunday 1:00 to 5:00 P.M. Admission is $4.00 for adults, $5.00 for children one to twelve.

Heritage Repertory Theatre. University of Virginia's professional summer theater, which has been performing at Culbreath Theater for more than twenty years; (804) 924–3376, www.virginia.edu/~drama.

Barboursville Vineyards and Ruins. Ruined remains of a great home designed by Thomas Jefferson. Now home to a fine vineyard, located at 17655 Winery Road, Route 777, Barboursville; (540) 832–3824, www. barboursvillewine.com. Open for tastings and sales, Monday to Saturday 10:00 A.M. to 5:00 P.M., Sunday 11:00 A.M. to 5:00 P.M. Tours on Saturday only.

Canoeing and Tubing on the James River. Day or overnight trips on the James River by canoe, raft, or inner tube. Offered by James River Runners, 10080 Hatton Ferry Road, Scottsville; (804) 286–2338, www.jamesriver.com.

SPECIAL EVENTS

March. James Madison Birthday Celebration. Music and events at Montpelier. (540) 672–2728.

June–August. Ash Lawn–Highland Summer Festival of the Arts. Opera, musicals, choirs, country music on the lawns of the Monroe estate. (804) 979–0122.

July. Independence Day Ceremony at Monticello. Naturalization of new citizens, patriotic music, and speeches. (804) 980–3861.

July. Annual African American Cultural Arts Festival. Art exhibits, food, entertainment, games for kids in Charlottesville's city parks. (804) 296–4986.

October. Virginia Festival of American Film, at the University of Virginia. (804) 924–3378.

October. Monticello Wine and Food Festival. Local wineries bring their best offerings to the Boar's Head Inn for tasting. (804) 296–4188.

OTHER RECOMMENDED RESTAURANTS

Charlottesville

Memory and Company, 213 Second Street, SW; (804) 296–3539. Prix fixe dinners that change seasonally. You might start with duck and shiitake mushroom pâté followed by an entree of beef tenderloin, scallops on kalamata olive fettuccine, or lamb tenderloins with mint, garlic, and mustard on caramelized onions in Madeira. Excellent desserts. Expensive.

Blue Ridge Brewing Company, 709 West Main; (804) 977–0017. Everything from steak and burgers to white pizza to grilled duck breast and leg confit with Thai barbecue sauce in a breezy, cheery microbrewery; popular with students and faculty. Moderate.

C&O Restaurant, 515 East Water Street; (804) 971–7044. The modest exterior belies the offerings. Upstairs, the setting is formal. The downstairs "bistro" offers the same seafood, chicken, and beef dishes for $12 to $19.

Blue Bird Cafe, 625 West Main Street; (804) 295–1166. Popular, casual cafe with good pasta and sandwiches; patio dining in season. Moderate.

The Boar's Head Inn's Old Mill Room, U.S. Highway 250 West; (804) 296–2181. Regional specialties in a restored 1834 gristmill. Expensive.

Tastings, in the downtown parking garage at Fifth and Market Streets; (804) 293–3663. Restaurant and wine bar. The cuisine is traditional European and American with an emphasis on seafood and local produce. Moderate.

Best places for doughnuts: If you must eat chain-store doughnuts, there are only two brands to consider, and Charlottesville has them both. In fact, it may be the only city in the mid-Atlantic that does. So conduct your own taste test. There is a Spudnut shop at 309 Avon Street (804–296–0590), and it sells the real thing: doughnuts made with potatoes. The almost-as-good challenger, Krispy Kreme Doughnuts, has a shop at 1805 Emmet Street; (804) 923–4007.

OTHER RECOMMENDED LODGINGS

Charlottesville

Silver Thatch Inn, 3001 Hollymead Drive; (804) 978–4686, www.silverthatch.com. Very nice 200-year-old inn with seven period rooms, all with private baths and some with fireplaces. Continental-plus breakfast. Guests can use adjacent swimming pool and tennis courts. Rates: $115–$165.

The Boar's Head Inn & Sports Club, U.S. Highway 250 West; (804) 296–2181 or (800) 476–1988, www.boarsheadinn.com. Large 173-room country resort hotel complete with tennis courts, pools (indoor and outdoor), saunas, golf, and squash courts. Rates: rooms, $165–$219; suites, $350–$400.

Clifton, The Country Inn, 1296 Clifton Inn Drive (7 miles from downtown); (804) 971–1800 or (888) 971–1800. Manor house built by Thomas Jefferson's son-in-law has fourteen guest rooms and suites, all with private baths and fireplaces; swimming pool, heated spa, tennis courts. Breakfast and dinner available. Rates: $125–$450, dinner extra.

The Inn at the Crossroads, U.S. Highway 29 at State Highway 692 about 9 miles south of town; (804) 979–6452, www.crossroadsinn.com. Five guest rooms and one cottage, all with private baths. Spacious grounds with fantastic views; full country breakfast. Rates: $80–$125.

The Foxfield Inn, 2280 Garth Road; (804) 923–8892, www.foxfield-inn.com. Newly renovated five-room country B&B 8 miles from town. Fireplaces in most bedrooms; full country breakfast. Rates: $125–$160.

Scottsville

High Meadow Inn, State Highway 20 about 17 miles south of Charlottesville; (804) 286–2218, www.highmeadows.com. Superb small inn with fourteen guest rooms and fifty acres of gardens and lawns. Country breakfast and complimentary local wine in the afternoon. Rates: $90–$195. If you stay on a Saturday, you must have dinner at High Meadow's fine restaurant, which adds $45 per person to the price.

Orange

Hidden Inn, 249 Caroline Street; (540) 672–3625 or (800) 841–1253. Pleasant ten-room Victorian B&B with Jacuzzis, fireplaces, and verandas. Full breakfast; dinner available with advance reservations. Rates: $99–$169.

Willow Grove, 14079 Plantation Way; (540) 672–5982 or (800) 949–1778, www.willowgroveinn.com. Manor house in rural Orange County with five guest rooms and one suite, all with private baths; lots of antiques, acres of countryside. Willow Grove is on a modified American plan: Dinner and a large breakfast are included in the $225–$330 room price.

FOR MORE INFORMATION

Charlottesville/Albemarle Convention and Visitors Bureau, State Highway 20 South, P.O. Box 178, Charlottesville, VA 22902; (804) 977–1783, www. charlottesvilletourism.com.

Orange County Visitors Bureau, 122 East Main Street, Orange, VA 22960; (540) 672–1653, www.visitocva.com.

Richmond

OLD SOUTH, NEW SOUTH

1 NIGHT

State capitol • Historic sites • Museums
Art galleries • Fine dining • Shopping

Richmond, Virginia, with its Confederate war heroes posed triumphantly on Monument Avenue, its antebellum mansions, towering magnolias, and languid accents, is as traditionally Southern as a mint julep. At the same time, a visit to Richmond reveals sights you might not have expected from the one-time capital of the Confederacy. The new galleries and restaurants of funky Shockoe Slip and a museum that illuminates the history of Richmond are also part of this beautiful old city. A quick escape to Richmond offers visitors a great opportunity to explore both the old South and the new South in one weekend.

Richmond's landmarks tell the story of the city's extraordinary place in American history. There is the neoclassical Virginia State Capitol, designed by Thomas Jefferson, where the legislature met in 1785 and still does today. A mile or so east is Saint John's Church, where Patrick Henry made a speech that became the battle cry of the American Revolution: "Give me liberty or give me death!" The White House of the Confederacy, where its president, Jefferson Davis, lived, is here, as is the home of the nation's first female African-American banker, Maggie Walker.

Richmond is a fairly easy city to navigate, but there is an enormous amount to do and see in just a few short days. Accordingly, try to organize your visit along geographic lines, so you can explore the maximum number of attractions with a minimum of wear and tear.

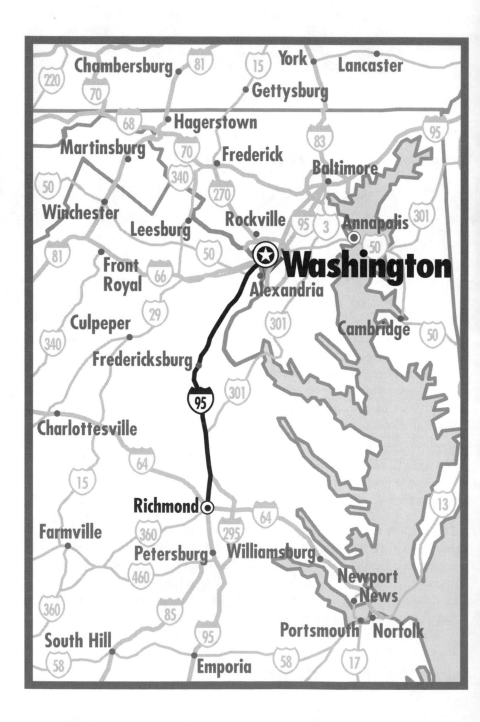

Richmond skyline

DAY 1

Morning

Richmond is about a two-hour drive from Washington on Interstate 95 heading south. An 8:00 A.M. start will get you to the Metropolitan Richmond
Convention and Visitors Bureau by 10:00 A.M. Located a mile or so from exit
78 off of I–95 (follow the signs) in an old railway station at 1710 Robin Hood
Road (804–358–5511), the visitors bureau is a good place to begin your visit
to Richmond. Guides there are friendly and knowledgeable and will give you
a map of the city with most of the sights clearly marked.

From the visitors bureau, drive into the city on Monument Avenue, which
is a tree-lined boulevard with enormous old southern mansions (with double-
and triple-decker porches) on both sides of the street. Until recently, the only
statues on Monument Avenue honored Confederate War heroes. Now, the
sports great (and Richmond native) Arthur Ashe has joined their ranks.

Monument Avenue becomes Franklin Street after a mile or so, and your
first stop should be a short one to drop off your bags at your "digs" for the

weekend—the **Linden Row Inn,** 100 East Franklin Street, (804) 783–7000 or (800) 348–7424. This lovely seventy-room hotel in a restored block of row houses belongs to the Historic Richmond Foundation, and the flawless attention to period details reflects it. The larger rooms have 12-foot-high ceilings and heavy crown molding. The guest rooms and common parlor are furnished with antiques (except for the renovated, modern bathrooms). The Linden Row Inn's $89–$179 per night rates would be reasonable even without the complimentary continental breakfast; afternoon wine, cheese, and fruit tray; and free use of the pool and gym at the nearby YMCA.

After you've dropped off your bags, drive east about 2 miles to the Church Hill area of Richmond to see **St. John's Church,** 2401 East Broad Street, (804) 648–5015. St. John's sits high on a hill in the middle of a churchyard cemetery shaded by huge trees. Some of the gravestones date back to the 1700s, and most are so old that they're crumbling.

On March 23, 1775, during a meeting of the Second Virginia Convention, Patrick Henry rose to support the raising of a Virginia militia with the words:

> Is life so dear or peace so sweet as to be purchased at the price of chains and slavery? Forbid it, Almighty God. I know not what course others may take, but as for me, give me liberty or give me death!

You can tour the inside of the beautiful church itself (which has been in use for more than 200 years) Monday to Saturday 10:00 A.M. to 4:00 P.M., Sunday 1:00 to 4:00 P.M. At 2:00 P.M. on Sundays, Patrick Henry's famous speech is reenacted.

LUNCH: Your lunch stop is located just 2 blocks south and 8 blocks east of St. John's: the **Main Street Grill,** 1700 East Main Street; (804) 644–3969. Looking like the worn old cafe it is, the Main Street Grill is nonetheless a much-loved local institution, with its chalkboard menus, black-and-white linoleum floor, kindly wait staff, and a collection of art and "curiosities" on the walls. The house specialty is the "paco," and there are several variations of this vegetarian pita sandwich stuffed with refried beans. During the lunch hour, the Main Street Grill also serves ham and turkey sandwiches, burgers, Middle Eastern fare, Tex-Mex entrees, and the occasional Hawaiian special. In the evenings, only vegetarian meals are served. Inexpensive.

The Main Street Grill is located in an area known as **Shockoe Bottom.** This area (and adjoining **Shockoe Slip**) is in Richmond's old warehouse district, which artists, restaurateurs, and small shop owners have recently discovered. While you are in the area, do a little window shopping. Worth a stop is the **Shockoe Bottom Arts Center,** 2001 Grace Street (804–643–7959), where you can wander among working painters, jewelry makers, and sculptors. Open Tuesday to Saturday 10:00 A.M. to 5:00 P.M., Sunday 1:00 to 5:00 P.M.

Afternoon

Next, drive to the downtown historic area. You can park your car at one of a half dozen parking garages in the area bounded by Seventh and Eleventh Streets and East Broad and East Clay Streets and spend the afternoon on foot. Some garages allow you to park for free if you are visiting the museum sites; ask the attendant on duty how to get your parking stub validated.

Your first destination is the **Valentine Museum,** 1015 East Clay Street; (804) 649–0711, www.valentinemuseum.com. The Valentine specializes in the economic, social, and cultural history of Richmond, and it is a fitting place to begin your historical sight-seeing. The museum prides itself on having one of the largest costume and textile collections in the nation. The tour of the adjoining 1812 **Wickham House** complements the extensive collections through an in-depth look at one family over time. Open Monday to Saturday 10:00 A.M. to 5:00 P.M., Sunday noon to 5:00 P.M. Admission for the museum and the Wickham House is $5.00 for adults, $4.00 for senior citizens and students; children under six are admitted free. (A Historical Downtown Block Ticket, which costs $15 per person for adults and children, will gain you admission to the Valentine Museum, the Museum of the Confederacy, the Maggie Walker National Historic Site, the Black History Museum and Cultural Center of Virginia, the John Marshall House, the Edgar Allan Poe Museum, the Richmond Children's Museum, and a handful of other sites.)

A short 2 blocks away is your next destination, **The Museum of the Confederacy,** 1201 East Clay Street; (804) 649–1861, www.moc.com. Open Monday to Saturday 10:00 A.M. to 5:00 P.M., Sunday noon to 5:00 P.M. Admission is $5.00 for adults, $4.00 for senior citizens, and $3.00 for students. Children under six are admitted free. For an additional $3.00 ($2.00 for students), you get a tour of the **White House of the Confederacy** next door, where Jefferson Davis lived during the Civil War. At the museum, don't expect a Confederate flag-waving tribute to the slave-owning South; instead you'll get an absorbing account of the South's role in the Civil War. Although the facility is small enough to tour in an hour or so, the collection of Civil War letters, weapons, photographs, flags, uniforms, newspapers, paintings, and documents could easily capture the attention of anyone with even a passing interest in the Civil War for much longer.

As you continue your tour of the area on foot, don't miss the **Virginia State Capitol,** located at Capitol Square about 3 blocks south of the museums; (804) 698–1788. It is as grand and gracious as you would expect. In the rotunda is the Washington statue that is said to most resemble America's first president. Outside is another statue of George Washington flanked by other famous Virginians. You can tour the capitol free of charge from 9:00 A.M. to 5:00 P.M. April through November and from 1:00 to 5:00 P.M. December through March.

Before you finish your walking tour of the downtown area, consider a stop at the **Maggie Walker National Historic Site,** 110½ East Leigh Street; (804) 780–1380, www.nps.gov/malw. Open Wednesday to Sunday 9:00 A.M. to 5:00 P.M.; donations are requested. Walker, an African-American who was paralyzed and confined to a wheelchair for much of her life, was the first woman in America to found a bank. She and her family lived in the twenty-two-room house on Leigh Street from 1904 to 1934. The National Park Service, which maintains the site, shows an inspirational ten-minute film about Walker's life and conducts guided tours of the house.

Four blocks from the Maggie Walker House is the **Black History Museum and Cultural Center of Virginia,** an expanding facility designed to display the economic, social, and cultural life of Virginia's African-Americans from Colonial times to the present. It's located on Clay Street at St. James Street, (804) 780–9093, and is open Tuesday through Saturday 10:00 A.M. to 5:00 P.M., Sunday 1:00 to 5:00 P.M. Admission is $4.00 for adults, $3.00 for senior citizens, and $2.00 for children under age thirteen.

After your afternoon of sight-seeing, head back to the Linden Row Inn for a rest before dinner and a glass of wine or lemonade in the inn's pretty little parlor.

DINNER: Dinner is at one of Richmond's (and Virginia's) best restaurants, **The Frog and the Redneck,** a bustling bistro in Shockoe Slip that offers nouvelle French cuisine and new Southern cooking side-by-side. Grilled rare tuna with an aged Parmesan butter sauce may, for example, be accompanied by "redneck caviar" (i.e., grits) or "redneck risotto" (i.e., grits). The ambience is casual, the wine list is extensive, and the prices are moderate to expensive. Located at 1423 East Cary Street, (804) 648–3764.

LODGING: Linden Row Inn.

DAY 2

Morning

BREAKFAST: Linden Row Inn.

After a light breakfast, head south on East Fifth Street a few blocks toward the James River. Your destination is the new **Canal Walk**, which parallels the river for more than a mile.

You can easily kill an hour or two strolling along the canal, enjoying the spectacular views of the James River rushing by small tree-covered islands and large boulders. Thirty-three circular bronze plaques set up at irregular intervals are chock-full of information about Richmond and the canal. The National Park Service is installing a Civil War Visitor Center along the walk, and soon to be completed are a model of a lock and an exhibit of an Underground Railroad stopover for escaping slaves.

You can also take a half-hour boat ride down the canal for $4.00 ($3.00 for senior citizens and students age five to twelve, free for younger children). Inquire at **Kanawha Cruises**, at the foot of Virginia Street; (804) 649–2800. Romantics and do-it-yourselfers can rent a small electric-powered craft (capacity six people) equipped with a picnic table and a CD player for $20–$35 an hour.

After your canal stroll, head for **Maymont,** 1700 Hampton Street (804–358–7166), a beautiful thirty-three-room mansion set on one hundred acres overlooking the James River. The grounds—which include a Japanese garden and an Italian garden, a children's farm with sheep to pet, and wildlife habitats for birds, beavers, and bison—are a free public park operated by the city of Richmond. Maymont also has a carriage collection, and a carriage ride is a pleasant way to see the grounds. Carriage rides are available when the weather is nice; a nominal fee is charged. Tours of the mansion are available by reservation; the suggested fee is $3.00 for adults and $1.00 for children. The grounds are open daily from 10:00 A.M. to 5:00 P.M.

BRUNCH: For a late Sunday brunch, there's no better place than the **Jefferson Hotel** at Franklin and Adams Streets; (804) 788–8000 or (800) 424–8014. The Jefferson, which has been around since 1895, was meticulously renovated a few years ago. Its eye-popping, navy blue–walled Palm Court Lobby has a life-size marble statue of Thomas Jefferson and a 35-foot-high Tiffany stained glass ceiling. Two flights of steps will take you to the Jefferson Rotunda, where brunch is served. The Jefferson boasts that the Rotunda, with its stained glass ceiling, dozens of wide marble pillars, dark red walls, and heavy oil paintings, was the model for the staircase setting in *Gone with the Wind,* and you can well believe it.

Brunch itself is an awesome buffet with everything from just-made omelettes to fresh seafood. There's a meat carving station, an enormous dessert table, and acres of fresh fruit and breads. Because the Jefferson brunch is so popular (on Easter they serve upwards of 700), be sure to make a reservation well in advance. Brunch, which is easily a day's worth of food, costs about $30 for adults and $17 for children.

Afternoon

After brunch, head for the **Virginia Museum of Fine Arts.** From your first sight of the 7-foot-long golden rabbit in the entranceway, you'll know this is a special museum. It has the largest art collection in the southeastern United States, including works by Monet, Renoir, Degas, and Picasso. It also has one of the best Art Nouveau and Art Deco collections in the country, a fine array of African art, a priceless Fabergé collection of jeweled eggs and other objects from the Russian court, and a gallery of "British sporting art." Your first visit will only whet your appetite for several return trips.

The Virginia Museum of Fine Arts is located at 2800 Grove Avenue; (804) 367–0844, www.vmfa.state.va.us. It's open Tuesday to Sunday 11:00 A.M. to 5:00 P.M. except on Thursdays, when it stays open until 8:00 P.M. The suggested donation is $4.00 for adults, and there is sometimes a supplemental charge for special exhibits. Don't put off stopping at the great museum shop until the end of the day, because it sometimes closes before the museum's closing time.

Follow your visit to the museum with a driving tour of Richmond's **Fan District,** a beautiful residential area of Victorian row houses located between Cary Street and Monument Avenue on the west side of town. Its large, eclectic selection of restaurants and boutiques testifies to the diversity of the Fan

District neighborhood, which is home to old money, new money, students, and much of Richmond's art community.

Or go a few blocks farther west on Cary Street to **Carytown,** where some of the best of Richmond's shops can be found in ten-plus blocks on Cary Street between Boulevard and Thompson Streets. You can find everything from antique jewelry to Latin imports to artist-designed lawn furniture to Junior League used clothing. Gifts, beads, books, flowers, galleries, espresso, antiques—if you like to wander, gawk, and shop, Carytown is for you.

At the end of your day, allow two hours for your return trip to Washington via I–95.

THERE'S MORE

John Marshall House. Restored home of America's most famous Chief Justice of the Supreme Court and the father of the concept of judicial review. Located at 818 East Marshall Street; (804) 648–7998. Open Tuesday to Saturday 10:00 A.M. to 4:30 P.M., Sunday 11:00 A.M. to 5:00 P.M. Admission is $3.00 for adults, $2.50 for senior citizens, and $1.25 for children seven to twelve; children under seven are admitted free.

Agecroft Hall. House transported from Lancashire County, England, to Richmond. It's now the site of a lifestyle museum with an interesting collection of beds and other furnishings authentic to sixteenth- and seventeenth-century England. Located at 4305 Sulgrave Road; (804) 353–4241. Open Tuesday to Saturday 10:00 A.M. to 4:00 P.M., Sunday 12:30 to 5:00 P.M. Admission is $5.00 for adults, $4.50 for seniors, and $3.00 for children.

Richmond Children's Museum. A nice stop for the three-to-twelve crowd. The *When I Grow Up* exhibit in which kids try on firefighters' and doctors' uniforms is a favorite, as is the simulated cave. Located at 740 Navy Hill Drive; (804) 693–5436. Open Tuesday to Saturday 9:00 A.M. to 5:00 P.M., Sunday 1:00 to 5:00 P.M. (Note, however, that the museum is closed weekday afternoons during the school year.) Admission is $3.00 for children, $4.00 for everyone over twelve.

Richmond National Battlefield Park. Richmond was the capital of the Confederacy, its supply center, and the site of seven major battles. Information about all the Civil War sites in the area is available at the Chimborazo Visitor Center, 3215 Broad Street, which is operated by the

National Park Service. Open daily 9:00 A.M. to 5:00 P.M. No admission charged; (804) 226–1981, www.nps.gov/rich.

Edgar Allan Poe Museum. Worth a visit just to see the Raven Room with its several dozen illustrations of Poe's most famous poem. Located at 1914 East Main Street; (804) 648–5523 or (888) 213–2763, www.poemuseum. org. Open Tuesday to Saturday 10:00 A.M. to 5:00 P.M., Sunday and Monday noon to 5:00 P.M. Admission is $6.00 for adults, $5.00 for seniors, and $4.00 for students; children under six are admitted free.

White-water Rafting. Yes, Virginia, you can white-water raft within the Richmond city limits on the James River. A two- to three-hour trip with a guide costs $25–$50 per person. Richmond Raft Company, 4400 East Main Street; (804) 222–7238 or (800) 540–7238, www.richmondraft.com.

SPECIAL EVENTS

April. Historic Garden Week. Part of a statewide series of April garden tours, but Richmond's gardens are special. (804) 782–2777 or (800) 370–9004.

June–August. Summer Music Concert Series at the Virginia Museum of Fine Art. (804) 367–8148.

July. City-sponsored Victorian Fourth of July Celebration on the park grounds at Maymont. (804) 782–2777 or (800) 370–9004.

December. Christmas Open House. Tour of historic homes in the Fan District. (804) 254–2550.

OTHER RECOMMENDED RESTAURANTS

Sam Miller's Warehouse Restaurant, 1210 East Cary Street; (804) 644–5465. Top choice for beef and seafood. Moderate to expensive.

La Grotta, 1218 East Cary Street; (804) 644–2466. Comfortable, upscale Italian restaurant in the heart of Shockoe Slip District. Moderate.

Strawberry Street Cafe, 421 North Strawberry Street; (804) 353–6860. Popular eatery in the Fan District. Long on atmosphere, with antique mirrors, stained glass, candles and flowers on the tables, and a salad bar of fresh fruit and vegetables sitting in an antique bathtub. Pasta, potpie, and pub fare. Great for lunch, dinner, or weekend brunch. Moderate.

Soble's, West Main and Robinson Streets; (804) 358–7843. Fan District cafe and bar that serves generous salads, sandwiches, and beef and seafood specialties. Patio dining in season. Moderate.

The Tobacco Company Restaurant, Twelfth and Cary Streets; (804) 782–9431. Former tobacco warehouse in Shockoe Slip district, renovated and decorated in eclectic style. Popular with locals and tourists. Contemporary Southern menu. Dancing in the downstairs club. Moderate to expensive.

Lemaire Restaurant, Franklin and Adams Streets; (804) 788–8000. The Jefferson Hotel's premier restaurant, serving Southern cuisine at its best; also great for afternoon tea. Expensive.

The Dining Room at the Berkeley Hotel, 1200 East Cary Street; (804) 225–5105. Much-better-than-average hotel restaurant with American and continental menu. Moderate to expensive.

Third Street Diner, Third and Main Streets; (804) 788–4750. Open twenty-four hours a day, seven days a week. Breakfast anytime, dinner anytime. Long waits during the lunch hour. Ideal stop for doughnuts and coffee. Inexpensive.

OTHER RECOMMENDED LODGINGS

The Jefferson Hotel, Franklin and Adams Streets; (804) 788–8000 or (800) 424–8014, www.jefferson-hotel.com. Grand old luxury hotel with refurbished guest rooms, twenty-four-hour room service and concierge, restaurants on the premises, and complimentary use of a health spa across the street. Rates: $195–$265 for rooms, $295–$575 for suites.

The Massad House Hotel, 11 North Fourth Street; (804) 648–2893. Downtown European-style hotel with sixty-four redecorated rooms, all with private baths. Rates: $48 for a room, $55 for a two-room suite.

Berkeley Hotel, 1200 East Cary Street; (804) 780–1300, www.berkeleyhotel. com. Luxury hotel in historic Shockoe Slip area of town. Fifty-five well-appointed rooms; restaurant on premises. Rates: $139–$190.

Commonwealth Park Suites Hotel, Ninth and Bank Streets; (804) 343–7300. Elegant forty-nine-suite European-style hotel conveniently located on Capitol Square. Rates: $95–$149 per suite.

The Emmanuel Hutzler House, 2036 Monument Avenue; (804) 353–6900, www.bensonhouse.com. Conveniently located B&B with four guest rooms, all with private baths (two have Jacuzzis). Lots of antiques; full breakfast served. Rates $85–$155.

FOR MORE INFORMATION

Metro Richmond Convention and Visitors Bureau, 550 East Marshall Street, Richmond, VA 23219; (804) 782–2777 or (800) 370–9004. The visitors bureau also has offices at 1710 Robin Hood Road, (804) 358–5511; at the Bell Tower near the State Capitol, (804) 648–3146; and at the airport, (804) 236–3260; www.richmondva.org.

VIRGINIA

Fredericksburg and Westmoreland County

UNSPOILED TREASURES

1 NIGHT

Historic homes • Bald eagle nesting area • Hiking
Shopping • Winery • Pick-your-own fruit farm

With Washington just hours away from the mountains to the west and the ocean to the east, some of the region's subtler pleasures go unnoticed. Take Westmoreland County, Virginia, the flat farming area between the Potomac and Rappahannock Rivers. Driving the country back roads, you'll see fields dotted with rolled hay bales, like giant shredded wheat biscuits. Quaint little towns come right up to the edge of the rivers, which are enormously wide here, on the northernmost tip of Virginia's "Northern Neck" peninsula.

A weekend escape to this area offers lots of pleasures. You'll start with a visit to Fredericksburg, which is on the way and only an hour's drive from D.C. Fredericksburg is a delightful city. It has lovely old homes, galleries and gardens, and a clutch of bookstores and craft shops.

You'll also visit the Caledon Natural Area, a wilderness park that is home to one of the largest populations of eagles in the United States. If you're lucky enough to visit during the eagles' nesting season, you can take a hike through the area with a park ranger, who will point out the great birds and their nests.

Once you reach Westmoreland County, you'll visit Stratford Hall, the ancestral home of Robert E. Lee, and stroll along the Potomac River at nearby Westmoreland State Park. You'll also stop at an excellent vineyard and a farm where you can pick fresh berries, and stay at a charming bed-and-breakfast inn on the waterfront.

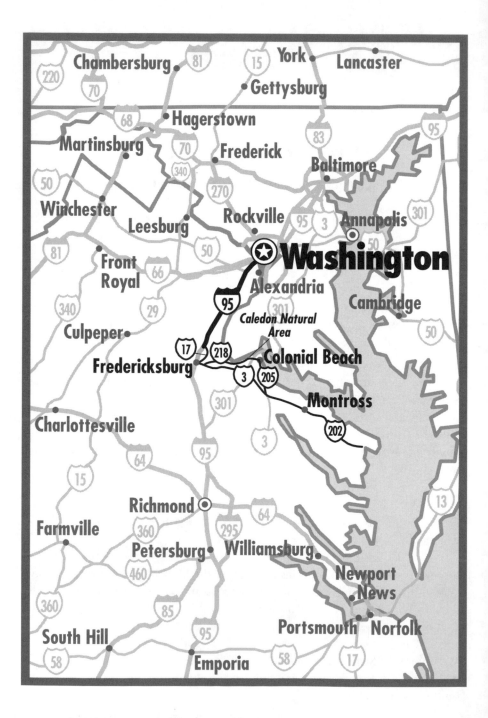

In short, there's a perfect weekend escape right under your nose; the farthest point on the itinerary is only two and a half hours away from Washington, and the crowds—by Washington standards—are tiny.

DAY 1

Morning

Leave early in the morning, so that you can spend several hours in Fredericksburg. The first 50 miles are a straight shot from Washington on Interstate 95. Take exit 133 (U.S. Highway 17 south) and drive 3 miles into Fredericksburg through Falmouth. Five blocks after U.S. Highway 1 splits off from Route 17, take a right on Germania Street, which turns into Washington Avenue after a couple of blocks.

Your first stop is **Kenmore,** the home of George Washington's only sister, Betty Washington Lewis, located at 1201 Washington Avenue; (540) 373–3381, www.kenmore.org. Kenmore is open 9:00 A.M. to 5:00 P.M. Monday to Saturday and noon to 5:00 P.M. Sunday, March through December; open weekends only in January and February. Admission is $6.00 for adults and $3.00 for students. Children under six are admitted free. A family admission is $12.50.

This lovely eighteenth-century Georgian mansion was once situated on a 1,200-acre estate reaching all the way to the Rappahannock River. Today it is in the center of residential Fredericksburg, with only a remnant (albeit a pretty remnant) of the once-great plantation surrounding it.

Washington's brother-in-law, Fielding Lewis, was an immensely wealthy man, and his wealth (as well as taste) is reflected in the beauty of Kenmore. The plaster ceilings are lavishly festooned with carved decorations; indeed, the decorative ceiling in the dining room is considered by many to be the greatest masterpiece of American plasterwork. Mantelpieces have similar lush decorations, and the pastel-painted walls and period furnishings are breathtaking. Docents conduct twenty-five-minute guided tours of Kenmore every half hour. At the end of your tour of the mansion, you're served a cup of tea and gingerbread cake, made from a Washington family recipe.

After you've been through the house, spend a little time exploring the Colonial garden, which has lots of brick paths and boxwood hedges. Also spend a few minutes strolling along **Washington Avenue** itself, which is lined with old homes.

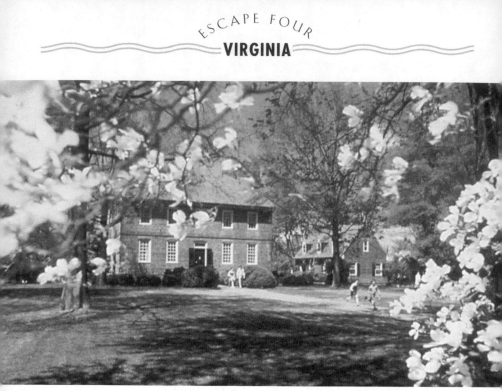

Kenmore, in historic Fredericksburg

LUNCH: Lunch is at the **Kenmore Inn,** 1200 Princess Anne Street; (540) 371–7622. The inn has no formal connection with Kenmore mansion but, like the mansion, it is an eighteenth-century building, and the dining room is full of Colonial-era furnishings. The menu is classic old Southern, including such tempters as shrimp and grits, ham and leek tart, and meat and cheese pie. Lunch prices are moderate, evening meals expensive.

Afternoon

After lunch, spend some time shopping in downtown Fredericksburg. The shops on **Caroline Street** include gift shops, upscale clothing stores, antiques shops, and new and used bookstores. You'll particularly enjoy **Riverby Books,** at 805 Caroline Street, for used, rare, and antique books, and the **Made in Virginia Store,** at 807 Caroline Street, for locally made baskets, country smoked ham, fresh roasted peanuts, and slab bacon. If you are interested in old military books and prints, you've come to the right place. There are at least three different stores on Caroline Street that sell them.

There are also interesting shops on the little side streets off Caroline. **Hanover Street,** for example, is an artists' enclave, with prints, paintings, and pottery for sale in several small studios.

When you leave Fredericksburg, drive across the bridge on State Highway 3 heading east and immediately begin looking for State Highway 218. Your next destination is about 20 miles east of Fredericksburg on Route 218, just past Fairview Beach.

Caledon Natural Area, a 2,579-acre Virginia state park (with 3.5 miles of Potomac River shoreline), is a bald eagle sanctuary. From mid-June to Labor Day you can tour some of the eagle protection areas and see the birds and their nests. For information about ranger-guided tours, phone (540) 663–3861; www.virginia.org (keyword search: caledon). You can also hike from 1 to 5 miles of interlocking marked trails through the beautiful, quiet woods. Open 8:00 A.M. until dusk. Admission to the park is free. Ranger-led tours are $5.00 a person, free for children under six.

After your hike, continue your drive east on State Highway 218 and then State Highway 205 to **Colonial Beach,** a resort community on the Potomac River for more than a century. There's swimming at the beach and several places to stop for a soda or coffee.

From Colonial Beach, drive east 6 miles on State Highway 205 and then east about 5 miles on State Highway 3 to **George Washington's Birthplace National Monument.** Located on State Highway 204 just off State Highway 3; (804) 224–1732, www.nps.gov/gewa. Open daily from 9:00 A.M. to 5:00 P.M. There you'll find Washington's birthplace site, a reconstructed eighteenth-century house, the family burial ground, a walking trail, and a pleasant picnic area right on the Potomac River. Admission is $2.00 for everyone over age seventeen.

Thirteen miles farther east on State Highway 3 is **Montross,** the county seat of Westmoreland County. Stop briefly at the old courthouse and the **Westmoreland County Museum,** which doubles as the county's visitors center. Located on State Highway 3 in downtown Montross; (804) 493–8440. The museum is open Tuesday, Thursday, and Saturday 10:00 A.M. to 4:30 P.M.

DINNER: To reach your final destination of the day, drive about 2 miles east of Montross on State Highway 3, then take State Highway 202 east another 6 or 7 miles to the **Mount Holly Steamboat Inn.**

The Steamboat Inn is a wonderful old place that has been undergoing steady renovation for the last few years, but it has been doing business since

1876. It has a bright, newly outfitted dining room with adjoining screened porches where diners can hear the water lap in Nomini Creek, a few yards away. The menu includes moderately priced meat, seafood, and pasta dishes, with regional specialties such as Chicken Shenandoah—chicken with glazed ham and sun-dried tomatoes.

LODGING: Upstairs at the inn, the eight renovated bedrooms have old-fashioned furniture and wallpaper and modern bathrooms. Prices for a stay at the Steamboat Inn are quite inexpensive, particularly considering that a hearty breakfast of eggs, bacon, and potatoes is included. Room prices range from $65 for the smallest room to $100 for a suite with a Jacuzzi in season. The inn also offers a package deal; for an additional $34, you get dinner and afternoon tea for two. Located on State Highway 202, Mount Holly; (804) 472–3336.

DAY 2

Morning

BREAKFAST: The Steamboat Inn.

After breakfast, begin your drive back to Washington, returning west on State Highway 202 and State Highway 3. Eight miles west of Montross, you'll see the signs for Stratford Hall, your first stop.

Stratford Hall Plantation, located on State Highway 214 just off State Highway 3 (804–493–8038, www.stratfordhall.org), is the birthplace of Confederate general Robert E. Lee. A tour of this enormous plantation, high on a hill overlooking the Potomac, lets you see the mansion itself, the kitchen yard, smokehouse, laundry, slave quarters, coach house stables, gardens, and more. There's an old water-powered gristmill where corn, wheat, and barley are ground (which you can buy to take home), and a nature trail along the Potomac River with spectacular views below.

A tour of Stratford Hall is enjoyable and informative. The house itself is one of the great historic mansions in the United States, with magnificent paneling, molding, light fixtures, and furnishings. Well-informed docents will take you throughout the building, from wine cellar to bedrooms, and provide cheerful commentary about life in Colonial and Civil War times. A special time to visit is in December, when Stratford Hall is decorated with evergreen, boxwood, and candles.

LUNCH: Stay at the Stratford Hall Plantation for lunch, which is a rib-sticking Southern meal of fried chicken or ham, accompanied by sweet potatoes, hot biscuits, and coleslaw. Or order a la carte from the menu, which includes soups, salads, and a wine list. Moderate.

Stratford Hall Plantation is open daily 9:00 A.M. to 4:00 P.M. except Thanksgiving, Christmas, and New Year's Day. Admission is $7.00 for adults, $6.00 for seniors, and $3.00 for children six to seventeen; children under six are admitted free.

After you leave Stratford Hall, relax for a bit at the adjacent **Westmoreland State Park,** a heavily wooded park along the Potomac. It has a clean, sandy beach, an Olympic-size swimming pool, and a number of well-marked trails for short hikes. The half-mile "beach trail" along the Potomac is particularly inviting. You just might see shark's teeth and fossils among the shells there, but leave them for other visitors. Open dawn to dusk; (804) 493–8821, www.state.va.us/~dcr/park/westmoreland.

About 8 miles west of Westmoreland State Park on State Highway 3, look for the signs for **Ingleside Plantation Vineyard,** one of Virginia's best wineries. You can tour the facility and sip award-winning wines. Don't forget to try some of the bubbly: Ingleside is one of the few Virginia wineries that make sparkling wine. Located a couple of miles south of State Highway 3 on Route 638 near Oak Grove; (804) 224–8687, www.ipwine.com. Open Monday to Saturday 10:00 A.M. to 5:00 P.M., Sunday noon to 5:00 P.M. Closed on major holidays.

A few miles farther along State Highway 3—again, look for the signs—is **Westmoreland Berry Farm and Orchard,** 2 miles west of Oak Grove; (804) 224–9171 or (800) 997–2377, www.westmoreland-berry.com. From mid-May to late October, there's something to pick at the farm, from the earliest strawberries of spring to late October's pumpkins and gourds, with cherries, raspberries, blueberries, blackberries, and apples in between. Open daily during harvest, 8:00 A.M. to 7:00 P.M.

It should take only an hour and a half to return to Washington via State Highway 3 west and I–95 north.

THERE'S MORE

Walking or Driving Tour of Historic Fredericksburg. A twenty-nine-stop historic walking or driving tour, which includes the home of George Washington's mother, Mary Ball Washington; James Monroe's law offices; the Hugh Mercer Apothecary Shop; and beautiful historic mansions, churches, and gardens. For details, brochures, and maps, contact the Visitors

Center, 706 Caroline Street, Fredericksburg, VA 22401; (540) 899–1776 or (800) 678–4748.

Fredericksburg/Spotsylvania National Military Park. Tour the site of four Civil War battles. Audiovisual presentations and museum exhibit. In the park is the Fredericksburg National Cemetery, where more than 15,000 Union and Confederate soldiers are buried. Self-guided car tours. Walking tours with park guides available in the summer and fall months. 1013 Lafayette Boulevard (U.S. Highway 1) at Sunken Road, Fredericksburg; (540) 373–6122, www.nps.gov/frsp. Open daily 9:00 A.M. to 5:00 P.M., later in the summer. Closed Christmas and New Year's Day. Admission is free.

James Monroe Museum. Includes the James Monroe Memorial Library and a large collection of Monroe's papers, possessions, and furnishings. Located at 908 Charles Street, Fredericksburg; (540) 654–1043. Open daily 9:00 A.M. to 5:00 P.M. March through November, 10:00 A.M. to 4:00 P.M. December through February. Admission is $4.00 for adults, $1.50 for students. Children under six are admitted free.

Rising Sun Tavern. Fredericksburg's first tavern now offers a historical interpretation of eighteenth-century tavern life. Located at 1304 Caroline Street; (540) 371–1494. Open daily 9:00 A.M. to 5:00 P.M. March through November, 10:00 A.M. to 4:00 P.M. December through February. Admission is $4.00 for adults, $1.50 for students. Children under six are admitted free. Note: No food or drinks are served at the tavern.

Belmont. The 1790s home of American artist Gari Melchers, Belmont is situated along the banks of the Rappahannock River and filled with artworks and antiques. Located at 224 Washington Street, Falmouth; (540) 654–1015. Open Monday to Saturday 10:00 A.M. to 5:00 P.M., Sunday 1:00 to 5:00 P.M. March through November; Monday to Saturday 10:00 A.M. to 4:00 P.M., Sunday 1:00 to 4:00 P.M. December through February. Admission is $4.00 for adults, $1.00 for students. Children under six are admitted free.

SPECIAL EVENTS

January. Open house at Stratford Hall Plantation to celebrate the birthday of General Robert E. Lee. Free admission. (804) 493–8038.

February. Open house at George Washington's birthplace near Oak Grove. Music, dance, cider, and gingerbread. Free. (804) 224–1732.

February. President's Day in Fredericksburg. Half-price admission to Washington- and Monroe-related museums. (540) 373–1776.

March. Annual Fine Arts Festival. More than 130 local artists exhibit in a juried show at the Fredericksburg Community Center during a weeklong exhibition. (540) 373–1776.

June. Annual Potomac River Festival. Fireworks and a boat parade. Colonial Beach. (804) 224–7531.

July. On July 4, Fredericksburg hosts a daylong festival with entertainment, music, games, and races. (540) 373–1776.

September. Black Arts Festival. Annual event at the Walker Grant Educational and Cultural Center in Fredericksburg features African-American arts, crafts, food, and music. (540) 373–1776.

November. Annual crafts festival at the National Guard Armory, Fredericksburg. Crafts artists from all over Virginia exhibit and sell their work. Free. (540) 373–1776.

OTHER RECOMMENDED RESTAURANTS

Fredericksburg

La Petite Auberge, 311 William Street; (540) 371–2727. Chef-owned country French restaurant; live entertainment on Friday evenings. Moderate to expensive.

Smythe's Cottage and Tavern, 303 Fauquier Street; (540) 373–1645. Colonial and contemporary American dishes served in an eighteenth-century cottage; try the ginger beef in a pot with rice. Moderate.

Sammy T's, 801 Caroline Street; (540) 371–2008. First-rate lunch and pub fare. Sandwiches, Italian dishes, soups, and salads. Lots of vegan and vegetarian choices. Extensive selection of beers. Moderate.

Bangkok Cafe, 875 Caroline Street; (540) 373–0745. Thai cuisine in the Colonial area of town. Moderate.

Goolrick's Drug Store, 901 Caroline Street; (540) 373–9878. Classic old-time lunch counter that claims to have the oldest continuously operating soda fountain in America. Perfect for a grilled cheese sandwich and an ice-cream soda. Inexpensive.

Best place for doughnuts: Paul's Bakery, 2008 Lafayette Boulevard; (804) 898–2173.

Montross

Yesterday's Family Restaurant, State Highway 3; (804) 493–0718. Steaks, chops, seafood, sandwiches; attractive setting. Moderate.

Colonial Beach

Wilkerson's Restaurant, 3900 McKinney Boulevard; (804) 224–7117. Family-operated restaurant in business since 1946. People come here for the fried or broiled seafood or for the seafood buffet. Moderate.

Kinsale

The Mooring Restaurant, at the Yeocomico Marina past the bridge, just off State Highway 608; (804) 472–2971. Steaks, seafood, sandwiches served with locally grown produce. Moderate.

L. W. Bogart's, corner of State Highways 202 and 203; (804) 472–3331. Hand-cut steaks, homemade barbecue, and burgers in an informal setting. Inexpensive to moderate.

OTHER RECOMMENDED LODGINGS

Fredericksburg

Kenmore Inn, 1200 Princess Anne Street; (540) 371–7622. Beautiful inn with twelve rooms decorated with period furniture; some rooms have fireplaces. Rates: $95–$135, including continental breakfast.

Richard Johnston Inn, 711 Caroline Street; (540) 899–7606. Elegant eighteenth-century town house converted into an eight-room B&B. Rates: $90–$145, continental breakfast served.

Selby House Bed and Breakfast, 226 Princess Anne Street; (540) 373–7037. One suite and four individual guest rooms, all with private baths; nice location. American Empire furnishings; full breakfast in the morning. Rates: $65–$125.

Dunning Mills Inn All-Suite Hotel, 2305-C Jefferson Davis Highway; (540) 373–1256. On the strip, but near the woods. Forty-four suites with full kitchens and sitting areas; great for kids. Rates: $44–$118.

Montross

Inn at Montross, 21 Polk Street; (804) 493–0573. Beautifully restored inn on courthouse square with five guest rooms, all with private baths. Gourmet restaurant (open for lunch Sunday, Monday, Tuesday, Friday; open for dinner Friday and Saturday) and comfortable pub (open Thursday, Friday, Saturday evenings) on the premises. Room rates: $85–$100, breakfast included. The restaurant is moderate to expensive.

'Tween Rivers, 16006 Kings Highway; (804) 493–0692 or (800) 485–5777, www.3n.net/tween. Nicely appointed, in-town B&B with three guest rooms, all with private baths; full country breakfast. Rates: $80–$90.

Westmoreland State Park Campgrounds, State Highway 3; (804) 493–8821. Cabins and trailer and tent sites. Restaurant in the park serves sandwiches and basic meals. Campsites are $14–$18, primitive cabins are $30, and deluxe cabins are $44–$118.

Colonial Beach

The Bell House Bed and Breakfast, 821 Irving Avenue; (804) 224-2278. Former summer home of Alexander Graham Bell is now a four-room Victorian B&B on the Potomac River; full breakfast served. Rates: $80-$125.

FOR MORE INFORMATION

Fredericksburg Department of Tourism/Fredericksburg Visitors Center, 706 Caroline Street, Fredericksburg, VA 22401; (540) 373–1776 or (800) 678–4748, www.fredericksburgva.com.

Spotsylvania Department of Tourism/Visitors Center, 4704 Southpoint Parkway, Fredericksburg, VA 22407; (540) 891–8687 or (800) 654–4118.

Westmoreland County Visitor Center, P.O. Box 996, Montross, VA 22520; (804) 493–8440 or (888) 733–9282, www.co.westmoreland.va.us.

VIRGINIA

Williamsburg

HISTORY'S ONLY HALF OF IT

3 NIGHTS

Colonial Williamsburg • Jamestown • Historic plantations
Golf • Amusement parks • Outlet shopping

Williamsburg, Virginia, is a favorite destination of Americans as well as many foreign vacationers. You can see why with just one visit. The flawlessly reconstructed Colonial town (once the capital of Virginia) is a delight with its beautiful gardens, nearly 300-year-old architecture and furnishings, and reenactments of daily life in Colonial times by staff in period costume.

Located a mere three-hour drive south of Washington, Williamsburg has so much to do and see that you'll want to make your escape an annual one. The fact is, Williamsburg offers new pleasures every single time you visit. You could easily spend a week in the Colonial area alone. Then there is the natural beauty of the land along the James and York Rivers to explore. And, if you like to shop, you've come to the right place. With hundreds of thousands of tourists visiting Williamsburg every year, shopping malls have sprung up around the outskirts of the city like mushrooms after rain.

One of the first things you'll notice when you arrive in Williamsburg is how popular it is with people of all ages. There are elderly folks in wheelchairs, young families with babies in backpacks, and energetic walkers with their handsome hounds on leashes by their side. There's plenty for school-age kids to learn and explore, and when they tire of the history lessons, the very modern Busch Gardens amusement park is nearby.

Williamsburg has some of Virginia's best restaurants and lodgings, if you're celebrating a special occasion. And for families on a budget, the area is saturated with inexpensive places to stay and eat.

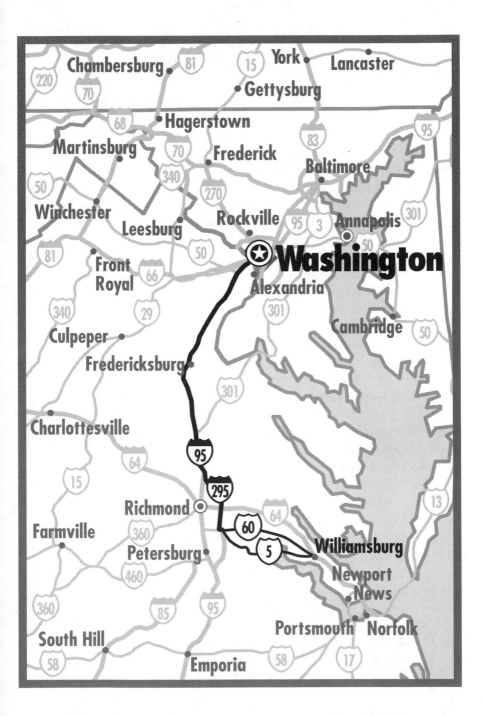

DAY 1

Morning

If you leave before 8:30 A.M., you can make it to Williamsburg in time for lunch at a fun and historic tavern, and still beat the crowds (which are huge during summer weekends). Drive to Williamsburg via Interstate 95 south, Interstate 295 (the Richmond Beltway), and U.S. Highway 60 east. Route 60 avoids the worst of the Williamsburg and beach traffic on Interstate 64, and you'll enjoy the Virginia woods and farms on either side of the road.

When you arrive in Williamsburg, follow the signs to the **Colonial Williamsburg Visitor Information Center.** There are plenty of parking places there but very few in the Colonial area itself, so leave your car at the visitors center and do your touring of the historic area on foot or on the buses that swing by in a loop around the area every twenty minutes or so.

At the visitors center you can buy tickets for those attractions that require them and see a thirty-five-minute film on Colonial Williamsburg. Be sure and pick up the publication *Visitor's Companion,* which has lots of information about special events.

A word about price: Williamsburg is priceless, but it's not cheap. General admission for adults is $30 for one day, $35 for two days, and $45 for three to five days. Children ages six to seventeen pay $18, but their tickets are good for a full week. Children under six are admitted free. Annual general admission passes are $65.00 for adults and $22.50 for children. Most of the attractions in Colonial Williamsburg are open daily from 9:30 A.M. to 5:00 P.M., although several attractions stay open later in summer months. Call (757) 229–1000 or check www.history.org if you have questions about what's open when.

LUNCH: Chowning's Tavern is part of the historic area, and it has been rebuilt to look like Josiah Chowning's 1766 tavern. Wait staff wear period costume and in the evenings entertain with songs, ballads, and games. And the menu is straight out of the past, with specialties including Welsh rabbit, game stews, and meat pies. Brunswick Stew is the top choice. Hamburgers, hot dogs, and ice cream are available in the garden from 11:00 A.M. to 5:00 P.M. Located on Duke of Gloucester Street at Queen Street; (757) 229–2141 or (800) 447–8679. Moderate.

Afternoon

After lunch, stroll through the Colonial area. There, you'll notice dozens of restored homes and shops on either side of Duke of Gloucester Street. You'll see an apothecary, blacksmith, silversmith, shoemaker, milliner, and many more shops, and in each one guides in period dress either explain their craft or actually engage in it. Be sure to stop at one of the most interesting of Williamsburg's historic sites, **Bruton Parish Church,** which has been in continuous use since 1715 and has seen a lot of history. Stroll through the old churchyard, where ancient stones mark the graves of Williamsburg's most prominent citizens.

The two major public buildings in Colonial Williamsburg are the Capitol and the Governor's Palace. Both are interesting from architectural and historical perspectives and both have hour-long guided tours.

The **Capitol,** finished in 1705, was the political center of Virginia for eighty years. There, in the House of Burgesses and in the Council, Patrick Henry, Thomas Jefferson, and others honed their oratorical and legislative skills.

The **Governor's Palace,** built in 1722, was an extraordinary achievement for Colonial days, when life was hard and houses were modest. The palace served as the home for seven royal governors and for the first two governors of the Commonwealth of Virginia: Patrick Henry and Thomas Jefferson. Make sure you walk through the formal garden (with a boxwood maze), which may be seen without a ticket.

As you wander through the Colonial town, take time to visit the side streets and byways. There are lovely gardens in back of the restored Colonial homes, sheep and horses grazing in fenced pastures, and lots going on outdoors. Outside the Magazine and Guardhouse, for example, cannons are occasionally fired. Horse-drawn carriages jingle up and down the roads, and Colonial brickmakers and ironmongers can be seen at work. Keep your eyes open for outdoor stalls, where wonderful gingerbread cookies are sold. They are perfect with a cup of hot cider on a chilly autumn afternoon.

DINNER: Plan to have dinner at **The Trellis,** a popular and highly acclaimed restaurant in the Merchants Square area featuring contemporary cuisine with a seasonally changing menu, excellent wines, and nationally famous chocolate desserts. Located near the Colonial area on Duke of Gloucester Street; (757) 229–8610. Expensive.

After dinner, you might like to sample some of Williamsburg's many evening activities. There is an excellent chamber music series at the public library, and historical musical events, plays, and dances are regularly scheduled at 7:00 P.M. and 8:30 P.M. at the Governor's Palace. There are also candlelight choral services at Bruton Parish Church.

LODGING: When you've explored Colonial Williamsburg thoroughly, head for **Williamsburg Sampler Bed and Breakfast,** at 922 Jamestown Road, approximately a mile southwest of the Colonial area. This stately brick home has four rooms filled with antiques, quilts, and cabinetwork made by the proprietress. Despite the fact that the Williamsburg Sampler has received national acclaim, it is definitely affordable. (Rooms are $100 to $150, including breakfast.) But make reservations well before your trip; the Sampler is justifiably popular. Phone (757) 253–0398 or (800) 722–1169.

DAY 2

Morning

BREAKFAST: Enjoy a "skip-lunch" breakfast of fruit, waffles, and sausage prepared by the friendly innkeepers at the Williamsburg Sampler.

After breakfast, return to Colonial Williamsburg to catch some of the exhibits and historic homes and shops that you missed on your first day in town.

Or consider as an alternative a visit to the fascinating **Abby Aldrich Rockefeller Folk Art Center,** one of the nation's top showcases for American folk art, featuring paintings, shop signs, quilts, carvings, furniture, and toys. Located on South England Street across from the Williamsburg Lodge; (757) 220–7698. Open daily except Thursday, 10:00 A.M.to 5:00 P.M.

Also interesting is the **DeWitt Wallace Decorative Arts Gallery,** a museum that displays more than 10,000 items of English and American decorative arts. Located at the corner of Francis and South Henry Streets; (757) 220–7724. Open daily, except Tuesday, 10:00 A.M. to 6:00 P.M.

You might also like to poke around the pleasant shops at **Merchants Square,** a collection of about forty locally owned and run stores selling everything from clothes and furniture and jewelry to local hams and peanuts and gourmet chocolate. Many of the shops specialize in Williamsburg reproductions, like pewter mugs and historical needlework.

LUNCH: As lunchtime nears, make your way to **The Cheese Shop,** at 424 Prince George Street in Merchants Square; (757) 220–0298. There you can

Governor's Palace

gather provisions for a picnic lunch, including great cheese, fancy salads, biscuits with thinly sliced country ham, a bottle of wine, and a selection of pastries for dessert. Inexpensive.

Then pick up your car and head for Jamestown, a fifteen-minute drive on the **Colonial Parkway.** The speed limit on the lightly traveled parkway, which stretches 23 miles from Jamestown through Williamsburg to Yorktown, is 35 to 45 miles an hour, and it's a bikers' and joggers' paradise. So take your time, drive carefully, and enjoy the splendid view of the James River. If you picked up sandwiches in town, you can picnic at one of the pull-offs along the river or at the picnic tables near the visitors center at Jamestown Colonial Historical Park.

Afternoon

Jamestown was the original landing place for Virginia's first permanent English colonists. Though the settlement did not flourish—it succumbed to Indian attacks, disease, and bad luck, and the survivors later moved to Williamsburg—Jamestown today has many fascinating remnants from those earliest times in Colonial America.

Jamestown Settlement features indoor galleries and outdoor exhibits telling the story of Jamestown. There are full-size replicas of the three ships that carried the colonists—*Susan Constant, Godspeed,* and *Discovery*—which you can board and tour. Costumed interpreters will tell you all about Pocahontas, John Smith, the Powhatan Indians, and James Fort. Open daily 9:00 A.M. to 5:00 P.M. except Christmas and New Year's Day. Admission is $10.25 for adults and $5.00 for children six to twelve; children under six are admitted free. Phone (757) 229–1607 or (888) 593–4682; www.historyisfun.org.

Jamestown Colonial National Historical Park, administered by the National Park Service, has a visitors center where you can view many exhibits on Jamestown's early life. You can, for example, see the foundation stones from the seventeenth-century buildings and the original church tower that dates to the 1640s. One particularly nice attraction is the reconstructed 1608 glass-makers' shed, where you can watch glassblowers at work making cups, pitchers, candlesticks, and vases. All the products are for sale on the premises at very reasonable prices.

One of the best ways to see Jamestown is by bicycle. (See There's More for where to rent bicycles.) What little traffic there is all goes one way in the 5-mile loop around the island. And you can see the natural beauty of marshy wet-lands or the James River from almost every vantage point. Biking or walking is a great way to see the various historic sites easily as well as see and hear the birds and other wildlife. And however you get around Jamestown Island, you won't be battling the enormous crowds that surround the Williamsburg attractions. Open daily 8:30 A.M. to 4:30 P.M. Admission is $5.00 per person but visitors under seventeen are admitted free. Senior citizens with a National Parks Golden Age Pass get in free. Phone (757) 229–1733; www.nps.gov/colo.

After you've explored Jamestown, drive to **Carter's Grove,** which is administered by the Colonial Williamsburg Foundation. Carter's Grove, an eighteenth-century plantation home, is full of artifacts and furniture from the period. In addition to providing a view of the beautiful mansion itself, a tour of Carter's Grove is an opportunity to learn a great deal about the lives of Virginia slaves during the Colonial period. Plan to tour the old slave quarters and to spend some time at the **Winthrop Rockefeller Archaeology Museum** near the premises of the slave quarters. Located on U.S. Highway 60 about 6 miles east of Williamsburg; (757) 229–1000, ext. 2973. Open Tuesday to Sunday 9:00 A.M. to 5:00 P.M. from March through Christmas.

DINNER: After you've freshened up at your B&B, drive a couple of miles east to the Kingsmill area of town for dinner at one of Williamsburg's nicest restaurants, **Le Yaca.** This innovative French restaurant is warm and inviting, with fresh flowers everywhere and a fireplace in the middle of the restaurant complete with a lamb roasting on a spit. Le Yaca specializes in lamb and seafood—try the wonderful bouillabaisse—but its appetizers and salads alone are worth the trip. Desserts, too, are spectacular. If you're really hungry, opt for the "seven-course degustation" menu. Located at Village Shops at Kingsmill, U.S. Highway 60 just east of Colonial Williamsburg; (757) 220–3616. Expensive.

LODGING: The Williamsburg Sampler.

DAY 3

Morning

BREAKFAST: The Williamsburg Sampler.

After breakfast, take your pick of the hundreds of things still available to do in the Williamsburg area. You might tour beautiful **William and Mary College,** located right next to the historic Colonial area. It is the second oldest institution of higher education in the United States. Of particular interest are the Wren Building, built in 1695 and recently restored, and the Joseph and Margaret Muscarelle Museum of Art, which contains several works by old masters; neither charges admission.

If you are interested in golf, Williamsburg has several great courses. **Kingsmill Resort's River Course** is one of the stops on the PGA tour, and its Arnold Palmer–designed **Plantation Course** is as beautiful as it is challenging. Kingsmill's **Woods Course** is also spectacular; (757) 253–3906. Colonial Williamsburg runs the **Golden Horseshoe Gold Course,** designed by Robert Trent Jones, and the **Green Course,** designed by his son Reese Jones; (757) 220–7696. **Ford's Colony Country Club** has two scenic Dan Maples–designed courses; (757) 258–4130. Also popular are the new **Colonial Golf Course** designed by Lester George and Robert Wrenn (757–566–1600) and the **Williamsburg National,** a Nicklaus Design Associates course (757–258–9642). Expect to pay $45 to $125 for eighteen holes of golf and cart rental in the Williamsburg area.

For families with children, there's **Busch Gardens,** a fabulous amusement park built around Old World European theme villages. It features more than thirty rides (including the popular Loch Ness Monster roller coaster; Quester, the world's largest flight simulator; and Escape from Pompeii, a thrill-packed boat ride during which you dodge volcanic "lava"), several Broadway and country music theaters, and kid-oriented food. It's located just off U.S. Highway 60 east of town; (757) 253–3350 or (800) 343–7946, www.busch gardens.com. The park is open weekends from late March through mid-May, daily in summer, and Friday throgh Monday during September and October. The park opens at 10:00 A.M. and closes between 6:00 P.M. and midnight, depending on the season. Admission is $35 for everyone over age six, $28 for children three to six; children under three get in free.

The Busch Gardens folks also operate **Water Country USA,** one of the largest water theme parks in the mid-Atlantic. The whole family can brave the nearly 50-foot-high Big Daddy Falls and race through white-water falls, pools, geysers, and showers in a 7-foot-wide tube. Teens and preteens love the wave pool, Surfers Bay, and the Aquazoid—a raft ride during which you careen through a pitch-dark tunnel. Little ones can play in the Rambling River or Cow–A–Bunga. Located east of town just north of I–64's exit 242; (757) 253–3350 or (800) 343–7946. Open daily at 10:00 A.M. mid-May through Labor Day and some weekends in May and September. The park closes between 6:00 and 8:00 P.M. depending on the season. Admission is $18 to $29, depending on age and time of day. At Busch Gardens and Water Country USA, multiple-day tickets and combination tickets are available.

LUNCH: A good choice for a late lunch of soup, salad, and sandwiches is **Seasons Cafe,** 110 South Henry Street; (757) 259–0018. Wooden booths, decorative trompe l'oeil walls, a family-friendly menu with delicious burgers and onion rings, and good service make Seasons a favorite. It serves a terrific Sunday brunch buffet too. Moderate.

Afternoon

Save one of your Williamsburg afternoons for shopping. Certainly the most popular shopping spot is **The Pottery,** a vast network of discount and outlet stores housed in thirty sprawling warehouses on 200 acres. The budget prices and wide selection bring busloads of shoppers looking for everything from inexpensive Christmas decorations to cookware to clothing. The best deal at The Pottery, though, is the pottery itself. Just outside the main building is an acre of terra-cotta pots and saucers in all sizes at bargain basement prices. The Pottery is located on U.S. Highway 60 west in Lightfoot, Virginia, about 5 miles from downtown Williamsburg; (757) 564–3326. Open daily except Christmas. Hours vary by season.

Other popular shopping choices include Village Shops at Kingsmill, U.S. Highway 60 east, which has pleasant art studios, boutiques, and cafes; Patriot Plaza, 3044 Richmond Road, home to Dansk, Villeroy and Boch, and other upscale outlets; Prime Outlets at Williamsburg, 5699 Richmond Road, which has more than eighty name-brand clothes, shoes, and accessory outlet stores; and the Williamsburg Outlet Mall, 6401 Richmond Road, Lightfoot, where you can find clothes, toys, home furnishings, and gift stores. Most malls and shops listed are open seven days a week and most stay open late in summer.

DINNER: If you've spent a few dollars shopping, you might appreciate a dinner stop that is easy on your wallet. An excellent choice, both for quality of the food and for value, is **Chez Trinh,** located just off Richmond Road in the Williamsburg Shopping Center, 157 Monticello Avenue; (757) 253–1888. If you haven't tried Vietnamese food yet, you're in for a treat. It's far lighter than Chinese food and not as fiery as Thai. Start with rice paper rolls (think of them as small, spicy garden salads wrapped in large, steamed rice noodles). Next tuck into a bowl of pho (beef noodle soup), the national dish of Vietnam. The list of entrees at Chez Trinh is long; particularly good are the pork with black bean sauce, the chicken with lemon herbs, and the Hanoi curry chicken. Inexpensive.

LODGING: The Williamsburg Sampler.

DAY 4

Morning

BREAKFAST: The Williamsburg Sampler.

Begin the final day of your "Colonial" escape from Washington by visiting Yorktown, the site of the final decisive battle of the Revolutionary War and the British surrender in 1781. Start at the **Yorktown Victory Center,** which is 14 miles east of Williamsburg via the Colonial Parkway; (757) 887–1775 or (888) 593–4682. The museum at the Victory Center tells the story of America's struggle for independence through exhibits, sight and sound presentations, a documentary film, and living history. Open daily from 9:00 A.M. to 5:00 P.M.

Admission is $7.25 for adults and $3.50 for children six through twelve; children under six are admitted free. (You can obtain combination tickets to the Yorktown Victory Center and the Jamestown Settlement and save a few dollars if you plan on visiting both places.)

Then tour **Yorktown National Battlefield** itself, starting at the National Park Service Visitors Center, where the land and naval battles are presented through a series of multimedia exhibits. Follow up with a self-guided tour of the battlefield or an excellent ranger-led tour during which you'll climb the redoubts and see the cannons that helped Washington and Lafayette defeat Cornwallis and his British troops. Phone (757) 898–3400; www.nps.gov/colo. Open daily from 9:00 A.M. to 5:00 P.M. Admission is $4.00 for everyone sixteen and older; everyone under sixteen is admitted free. (A seven-day multi-visit combination ticket with Jamestown Colonial National Historic Park costs $7.00.)

Once you are finished at Yorktown, head for home on the back roads for one last history lesson. Return to Williamsburg on the Colonial Parkway. Exit the Parkway on State Highway 199 heading west toward Richmond. After a couple of miles, you'll reach State Highway 5, also heading west, which follows the James River to Richmond. A drive along Route 5 will allow you to visit one of the historic James River plantations, several of which are located about 30 miles west of Williamsburg.

LUNCH: Halfway to Richmond, just past Charles City, there's a great lunch stop on the north side of State Highway 5: **Indian Fields Tavern.** This attractively restored farmhouse serves traditional Virginia dishes in a pair of dining rooms and on a porch overlooking fresh herb and wildflower gardens. The Smithfield ham and the crab cakes are excellent. Even if you settle for a sandwich, ask for some of the homemade Sally Lund bread on the side; slather it with butter and it will serve as dessert. Located at 9220 John Tyler Highway; (804) 829–5004. Moderate.

Afternoon

You next stop is **Berkeley Plantation,** just west of Indian Fields Tavern. This 1726 mansion overlooking the James River was the home of Benjamin Harrison, a signer of the Declaration of Independence and three-time governor of Virginia. Benjamin Harrison's son, William Henry Harrison, became the ninth president of the United States, and his great-grandson Benjamin served as the twenty-third president.

Some think that Berkeley's real claim to historic fame is that it is the place where bourbon was invented and first distilled in 1621. Other firsts include the first Thanksgiving, celebrated at Berkeley Plantation on December 4, 1619. Move over, Plymouth Rock: Some two years before the Pilgrims arrived in Massachusetts, a party of settlers landed at Berkeley and proclaimed a day of thanks, to be "yearly and perpetually kept holy as a day of thanksgiving to Almighty God." And in 1862 "Taps" was composed at Berkeley by General Daniel Butterfield while Union forces were camped out there.

The house tour at Berkeley is informative and amusing. In addition to the priceless furniture, you'll see another first—the cloth "Tippecanoe and Tyler Too" campaign buttons distributed by William Henry Harrison in his successful presidential campaign.

After your house tour, take time to walk through Berkeley's beautiful boxwood gardens and visit the gift shop. There are several interesting Colonial and Civil War mementoes for sale. Berkeley is located on State Highway 5 near Charles City; (804) 829–6018, www.berkeleyplantation.com. Open daily 9:00 A.M. to 5:00 P.M. Admission is $8.50 for adults, $6.50 for teenagers, and $4.00 for children six to twelve; children under six are admitted free.

After your stop at Berkeley, continue on State Highway 5 west to I–295 north and then I–95 north to Washington. It should take you less than three hours to return to Washington.

THERE'S MORE

James River Plantations. In addition to Berkeley Plantation, there are several other plantations along State Highway 5 worth a visit. Sherwood Forest Plantation, once the home of President John Tyler, has the nation's longest frame house; (804) 829–5377. Westover is considered by many to be the nation's premier example of Georgian architecture. The grounds are open to the public year-round, but the house is open only for five days in April during Virginia's Historic Garden Week; (804) 829–2882. Shirley Plantation, a beautiful eighteenth-century Queen Anne building with a unique flying staircase, has been in the same family for nine generations and is the oldest plantation in Virginia; (804) 829–5121. Admission is charged at each plantation. For more information visit www.jamesriverplantations.org.

Used Books. For a real treat, seek out Bookpress, an off-the-beaten-track shop selling out-of-print and rare books and beautiful antique prints, maps, and drawings. Located at 1304 Jamestown Road; (757) 229–1260.

America's Railroads on Parade. More than 4,000 square feet of automated toy trains, hands-on exhibits, and railroad art. Located in the Village Shops at Kingsmill, U.S. Highway 60 east; (757) 220–8725. Open daily 10:15 A.M. to 5:00 P.M. Admission is $5.00 for adults, $2.50 for children and teenagers, free for children under three. Family admission is $12.

Bicycle Rental. Bikes Unlimited, 759 Scotland Street (757–229–4620), and Bikesmith of Williamsburg, 515 York Street (757–229–9858), both rent bikes for $10 to $15 a day.

SPECIAL EVENTS

April. Historic Garden Week. Statewide garden show. In Williamsburg there are special tours of the gardens in the historic area. (757) 253–0192.

May. Jamestown Landing Day. Celebrates the founding of America's first permanent English colony. (757) 253–4838 or (888) 593–4682.

July. Independence Day. Patriotic speeches and fife and drum music followed by fireworks. (800) 447–8679.

October. Occasion for the Arts, Merchants Square. Invitational arts and crafts show, Virginia's oldest. (757) 220–1736.

October. Yorktown Day. Memorial ceremonies and parade on the 19th to commemorate the British surrender that ended the Revolutionary War. (757) 898–3400.

December. Grand Illumination in Williamsburg. Kicks off a series of eighteenth-century-style holiday celebrations in the Colonial area. (800) 447–8679.

OTHER RECOMMENDED RESTAURANTS

The Cascades, 104 Visitor Center Drive; (757) 229–2141. The choice for Sunday brunch in Colonial Williamsburg if you want everything from eggs to fried chicken; also great for dinner. Moderate.

The Williamsburg Lodge Bay Room, South England Street; (757) 229–2141. Excellent salad bar for lunch, a Friday and Saturday evening seafood buffet, and a popular Sunday brunch from 9:00 A.M. to 2:00 P.M. Moderate to expensive.

Giuseppe's Italian Cafe, 5601 Richmond Road; (757) 565–1977. Bright, cheery, and casual. Pasta, smoked chicken antipasto, individual pizzas, fantastic lentil soup. Inexpensive to moderate.

Old Chickahominy House, 1211 Jamestown Road; (757) 229–4689. Plantation-style breakfasts and lunches featuring country ham and bacon. Antiques and reproductions for sale on premises. Moderate.

A Good Place to Eat, Merchants Square; (757) 229–4370. Just what it claims to be if you happen to want a hot dog or a hamburger and a soda. Inexpensive.

New England Grill, 6925 Richmond Road; (757) 220–2910. Friendly and casual restaurant that offers fresh seafood choices including live lobster at moderate prices.

Cities Grille, 4511-C John Tyler Highway; (757) 564–3955. New-American and traditional entrees, extensive wine list, and friendly bistro ambience make this a favorite of locals. Moderate.

Berrett's Seafood Restaurant and Raw Bar, 199 South Boundary Street; (757) 253–1847. Merchants Square restaurant with full meals inside, seafood, salads, and sandwiches at the patio raw bar. Moderate.

The Whaling Company, 494 McLaws Circle (just off Highway 60 east near Busch Gardens); (757) 229–0275. Traditional and contemporary seafood dishes in a pub setting. Moderate.

Padow's Hams and Deli, 1258 Richmond Road; (757) 220–4267. Huge deli-style sandwiches, potato salad, coleslaw, ice-cream sodas. Eat in or takeout. Inexpensive.

Coach House Tavern, 12602 Harrison Landing Road, Charles City, (804) 829–6003. Highly regarded restaurant on the grounds of Berkeley Plantation. Wait staff in period dress serve what may be the best food between Richmond and Williamsburg. Moderate to expensive.

Best place for doughnuts: Williamsburg has two dozen pancake houses but no true doughnut bakery. Either do what most people do and settle for a "short stack," or head for Ukrop's Supermarket, where the doughnuts are quite good. Located in the Monticello Marketplace, west of town on Monticello Avenue extension; (757) 564–0455.

OTHER RECOMMENDED LODGINGS

Magnolia Manor, 700 Richmond Road; (757) 220–9600 or (800) 462–6667, www.magnoliamanorwmbg.com. Elegant three-suite B&B close to town. In the morning, after you nosh on homemade cinnamon buns, you'll be served a huge breakfast on china, crystal, and sterling silver that might include shirred eggs with apple-cured bacon and hash browns, or cranberry/pecan pancakes and fresh sausage. Rates: $145–$195.

Williamsburg Manor Bed and Breakfast, 600 Richmond Road; (757) 220–8011 or (800) 422–8011. Beautiful Georgian Manor near historic area with antiques, oriental rugs, guest parlor, garden, six guest rooms with private baths. Large country breakfast served. Rates: $95–$150. The optional gourmet dinners prepared on the premises get rave reviews.

Applewood Bed and Breakfast, 605 Richmond Road; (757) 229–0205 or (800) 899–2753, www.wiliamsburgbbandb.com. Four-room Georgian B&B with canopy beds and private baths. Full breakfast and afternoon refreshments are included in the $90–$150 tariff.

Colonial Capital Bed and Breakfast, 501 Richmond Road; (757) 229–0233 or (800) 776–0570, www.cobb.com. Colonial B&B with five guest rooms with private baths. Patio, deck, screened porch, wood-burning stove in guest parlor; full breakfast and afternoon tea. Rates: $68–$150.

The Homestay, 517 Richmond Road; (757) 229–7468 or (800) 836–7468, www.williamsburg-virginia.com/homestay. Downtown B&B with three rooms with private baths. Full breakfast includes fresh fruit and home-baked bread or muffins. Guests have access to bicycles to get around town or explore Jamestown. Rates: $60–$100.

Fox and Grape Bed and Breakfast, 701 Monumental Avenue; (757) 229–6914 or (800) 292–3699. Two-story Colonial with pleasant wraparound porch and four rooms with private baths close to the Colonial area. Generous breakfasts in the decoy-decorated dining room. Rates: $84–$100.

Williamsburg Inn and Colonial Houses, Francis Street, in Colonial area; (757) 229–1000 or (800) 447–8679, www.history.com. There are more than 230 rooms at the inn or in small houses run by the Colonial Williamsburg Foundation. All are well appointed and a nice alternative to standard motel fare. Rooms in the inn are $180 to $350; Colonial Williamsburg also operates the Williamsburg Lodge ($100–$245), the Governor's Inn ($67–$90), and Williamsburg Woodlands ($59–$130); rooms in the Colonial houses range from $99 to $275.

Quarterpath Inn, 620 York Street; (757) 220–0960. Motel with 130 rooms located near the Colonial area. Phones, TV, swimming pool. Rates start at $35 off season, $75 in the summer.

Williamsburg has dozens of independent and chain hotels and motels. Nearly all of them, including the Williamsburg Lodge, Inn, and houses run by the Williamsburg Colonial Foundation, belong to the Williamsburg Hotel and Motel Association. You can call the association at (800) 999–4485 (www. williamsburghotel.com), and the staff there will make a reservation for you in your preferred style of accommodation and price range. Summer rates are sometimes expensive, but off-season rates are very reasonable in Williamsburg, with weekend rates often as low as $30 to $40 a night in chain motels.

FOR MORE INFORMATION

Colonial Williamsburg Foundation, P.O. Box 1776, Williamsburg, VA 23187; (757) 229–1000 or (800) 447–8679, www.history.org.

Williamsburg Area Convention and Visitors Bureau, P.O. Box 3585, Williamsburg, VA 23187; (757) 253–0192 or (800) 368–6511, www. visitwilliamsburg.com.

MARYLAND

ESCAPES

Annapolis

CITY ON THE BAY

---

1 NIGHT

State capitol • Historic sights
Sailing • Shopping • Jazz

Many Washington area residents don't think of Annapolis, which is a scant 30 miles away, as a weekend escape. But the best way to see Annapolis is to stay over for a night or two and sample a few of its many delights; it could be on another continent for all its differences from Washington.

A beautiful, historic port city on the Chesapeake Bay, Annapolis dates back to the seventeenth century. In fact, it was once the governing center of the colonies, where the Continental Congress met in 1783 and 1784. On a weekend visit there, you can see the beautiful capitol building (now the state capitol of Maryland) where the Treaty of Paris, which brought the Revolutionary War to an official close, was ratified.

Though no longer a major commercial port, Annapolis is still very much a water town. Hundreds of sails bob and glide in the bay, fresh-seafood restaurants line the narrow streets, and midshipmen from the U.S. Naval Academy stroll about in their crisp white uniforms. Your weekend escape to what some call the sailing capital of the world includes a two-hour sail on the bay, a walking tour of the historic area, great shopping and dining, a night of jazz, and an overnight in a centrally located inn just a block from City Dock.

After sampling Annapolis's many attractions, you'll be tempted to make it an annual weekend escape.

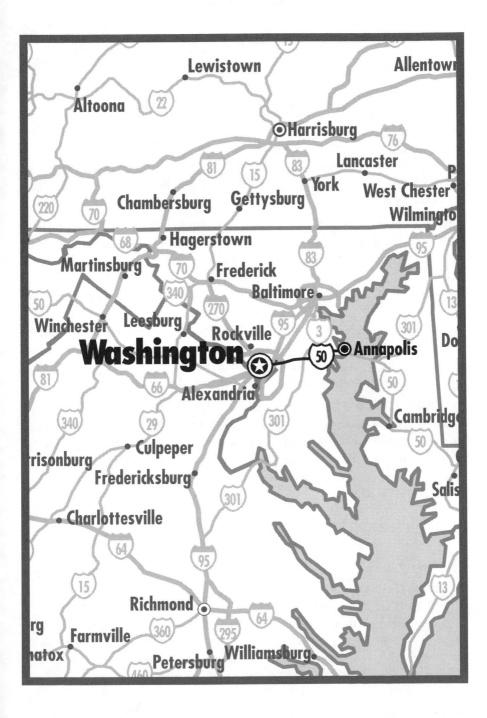

DAY 1

Afternoon

Start your weekend right after work, and drive to Annapolis in time for dinner. That way you'll get a jump on the beach crowds, who clog the highway on Saturday morning and can turn the easy forty-five-minute drive into an hours-long nightmare.

Annapolis is 30 miles east of Washington on U.S. Highway 50. Take exit 24 and follow State Highway 70, Roscoe C. Rowe Boulevard, south into the heart of town.

DINNER: Dinner your first night in Annapolis is at **Middleton Tavern Oyster Bar and Restaurant,** located in the heart of the historic district where Randall Street meets City Dock at 2 Market Space; (410) 263–3323. Dark, cool, decorated with nautical prints and paraphernalia, the Middleton Tavern serves classic shore fare, fresh pasta, and steaks. Try the smoked bluefish hors d'oeuvre first. Moderate to expensive.

After dinner, walk up Main Street to Church Circle to the **King of France Tavern,** 16 Church Circle (410–263–2641), where well-known jazz and blues performers appear regularly. For years, the King of France has been the "special" place to go in Annapolis on Friday and Saturday nights, and it still is.

LODGING: **Gibson's Lodgings,** located at 110 Prince George Street just a block from City Dock (410–268–5555), is actually three separate buildings, two of which are old Annapolis homes. Each building has a clutch of gorgeous period rooms full of antique furniture. There is off-street parking available and a pretty garden courtyard where a continental breakfast is served in the morning. Rates: $79–$139.

DAY 2

Morning

BREAKFAST: Gibson's Lodgings.

After breakfast, walk along the City Dock to **Pusser's Landing,** located on the water right in front of the Marriott Hotel. There you'll make reservations for a 4:00 P.M. sail on the schooner *Woodwind,* a beautiful yacht modeled after the century-old fast wooden schooners built to sail on the Chesapeake Bay; (410) 263–7837, www.schooner-woodwind.com.

Annapolis Harbor

Then stroll over to the **Historic Annapolis Foundation Museum Store and Welcome Center** (formerly the Victualling Warehouse Maritime Museum) to pick up brochures and maps. For $5.00 you can rent an audio-cassette to guide you on a walking tour of historic Annapolis. None other than Walter Cronkite will talk you through the ninety-minute, 1½-mile tour. Open daily 10:00 A.M. to 5:00 P.M. Located at 77 Main Street; (410) 268–5576, www.annapolis.org.

Highlights of the walking tour include Maryland's capitol, the **Maryland State House.** This pretty redbrick building has a wooden dome (the largest wooden dome in America) with the distinct look of a lighthouse. Inside are a giant sailing ship, the 1788 *Federalist;* a gorgeous rotunda; and beautiful marble house and senate chambers. Notice the quaint, tiny desks where the legislators sat. Located at State Circle; (410) 974–3400. Open daily except Christmas 9:00 A.M. to 5:00 P.M. Tours at 11:00 A.M. and 3:00 P.M.

Near the capitol on College Avenue is beautiful **St. John's College,** the third oldest in the nation. St. John's, founded in 1696, is a "great books" school with a rigorous, classical reading regimen. (On a less serious note, the school's official sport is croquet, and you can often see students practicing on the lawns.) On the campus is the **Mitchell Art Gallery,** open Tuesday to Sunday noon to 5:00 P.M. and Friday 7:00 to 8:00 P.M. Phone (410) 626–2556 for the gallery, (410) 263–2371 for the college.

The tour will also take you through the lovely residential neighborhood around the capitol. You'll walk brick streets and sidewalks and see spectacular Georgian architecture, such as the magnificent **William Paca House and Garden,** 186 Prince George Street; (410) 263–5553.

A tour of the garden and inside of the home of three-term governor of Maryland (and signer of the Declaration of Independence) William Paca is an extra $7.00 and it's worth it. You'll see a perfectly restored Colonial mansion, with its bright, sky-blue walls and ceilings. Period furnishings have been meticulously added, depicting life at the time of the American Revolution. Outside is the stately five-acre garden, with boxwoods lining the paths, a fish-shaped pond, and a little stream. Open Monday to Saturday 10:00 A.M. to 4:00 P.M. and Sunday noon to 4:00 P.M. March through December; open Friday to Sunday during January and February. Tours are offered on the half hour.

LUNCH: When you've turned in your audiocassette, walk back to the capitol and around the circle until you get to **Harry Browne's** at 66 State Circle; (410) 263–4332. This quiet, dark, lovely spot has an interesting menu with a variety of sandwiches, salads, and soups, as well as fancy beef, chicken, lamb, and seafood entrees. Moderate to expensive.

Afternoon

After lunch, take advantage of the fact that you are right in the nicest shopping area of Annapolis. A three-block stroll down the narrow, brick **Maryland Avenue** as it radiates from State Circle yields dozens of attractive shops where you'll find antiques, crafts, jewelry, prints, and gifts. Note particularly the **League of Maryland Craftsmen** at 54 Maryland Avenue (410–626–1277), which has a great selection of beautiful locally made wooden bowls, blankets, glass, and other crafts. The **Aurora Gallery** just up the street at 67 Maryland Avenue (410–263–9150) has jewelry, glass, prints, and sculpture.

If you're interested in more shopping, head back to **City Dock,** a bustling commercial area right on the water. Here the shopping is less interesting, with mall chain stores predominating, but there are lots of people and boats to watch. Stop at **Fawcett's Boat Supplies** at 110 Compromise Street (410–267–8681) for all things nautical, including gadgets, clothes, shoes, and maps. Most Annapolis shops are open on Sundays as well as weekdays.

For an afternoon cup of coffee, check out **City Dock Cafe** at 18 Market Space; (410) 269–0969. This small espresso bar also sells gigantic chocolate chip cookies, scones, and other pastries.

A few minutes before 4:00 P.M., you'll need to be back at Pusser's Landing and ready to board the schooner *Woodwind*. This large yacht can take up to forty-eight passengers. Once you're all settled and comfortable, the *Woodwind's* friendly crew starts up a small engine and navigates the ship away from the dock. Within a few minutes, the crew members ask for volunteers to run up the sails, and then, magically, the engine is cut, the sails billow, and the *Woodwind* almost silently glides into open water "like swans asleep," as the poet James Elroy Flecker put it.

Your two-hour sail will take you into the bay, and the crew will be glad to give you a turn at the wheel while explaining some sailing basics. They'll also offer free sodas and snacks, and beer and wine for a small fee. Special cruises are offered, including a "Race Watch," a microbeer tasting cruise, and runs with live entertainment aboard. The basic cruise costs $24 for adults, $22 for seniors, and $12 for children under twelve.

Note: If you want to spend more of the afternoon strolling and shopping, the schooner *Woodwind* also has a "sunset sail" from 6:30 to 8:30 P.M. at $27 for adults, $25 for seniors, and $15 for children under twelve. After the evening cruise, you can even spend the night on board in a tiny, double-berth stateroom complete with hot shower and a big breakfast at a cost of $200 for two people.

After your sail, cross over the short bridge on Compromise Street to **Eastport,** which has a distinctly different personality from the busy commercial activity of Pusser's Landing and City Dock. Here the pace is slower and the tourists fewer, and the area has more the feel of a working port.

DINNER: Have dinner at **Carrol's Creek Cafe,** a pleasant, casual restaurant with a medium-priced menu of excellent American entrees. The cafe offers a full menu but specializes in seafood. Among the most popular offerings are cream of crab soup, baked rockfish, and grade-one grilled tuna. Fabulous desserts such as rasberry tarts and mocha crème brûlée are made on the premises. Carrol's Creek Cafe also provides a great view of the water, historic

Annapolis, the sailboats, and the sailors. Located at 410 Severn Avenue in the Eastport section of Annapolis; (410) 263–8102. Moderate to expensive.

When you're finished for the day, return to Washington via U.S. Highway 50.

THERE'S MORE

United States Naval Academy. Tours lasting about an hour and a half depart from Ricketts Hall at the Naval Academy. Brochures are available for self-guided tours as well. You can see the beautiful Beaux Arts Chapel (where Revolutionary War hero John Paul Jones is buried), and lots of naval memorabilia and artifacts at the Academy Museum on campus. Tours are by reservation only, Monday to Saturday 10:00 A.M. to 3:00 P.M., Sunday 12:30 to 2:30 P.M. Tours include a fifteen-minute introductory film and involve about a mile of walking. The visitors center is located near Gate 1 on King George Street; (410) 263-6933, www.nadn.navy.mil.

Banneker-Douglass Museum of Afro-American Life and Culture. Museum with exhibits on the African-American experience in Maryland. Exhibits, lectures, and films are available in the museum's impressive facility, the 1874 Mount Moriah African Methodist Episcopal Church. Located at 84 Franklin Street; (410) 974–2893. Open Tuesday to Friday 10:00 A.M. to 3:00 P.M., Saturday noon to 4:00 P.M. No admission charged.

Hammond-Harwood House. National Historic Landmark eighteenth-century home, designed by William Buckland. Located at 19 Maryland Avenue; (410) 263–4683. Open Monday to Saturday 10:00 A.M. to 4:00 P.M., Sunday noon to 4:00 P.M. Admission is $5.00. Buckland also designed the famous **Chase-Lloyd House** at 22 Maryland Avenue, which is now a home for elderly women; (410) 263–2723. The ground floor of the Chase-Lloyd House is open to the public Monday to Saturday 2:00 to 4:00 P.M. March through December. Admission is $2.00. Both the Hammond-Harwood House and the Chase-Lloyd House have exquisite interior and exterior details.

Cruises. Chesapeake Marine Tours and Charters, Slip 20, City Dock, offers a variety of cruises, including ferry rides on the Severn River, yacht trips to St. Michaels (with a stop there for some great seafood), and special theme cruises, including a lighthouse tour and ecological tours to observe nesting birds. The basic tour is $6.00 for adults and $3.00 for children. (410) 268–7600.

MARYLAND

SPECIAL EVENTS

May. Annapolis Waterfront Arts Festival. Annual crafts and maritime festival with food and music at City Dock. (410) 268–8828.

July–August. Annapolis Rotary Crab Feast. World's largest. (410) 841–2841.

August–October. Maryland Renaissance Festival in Crownsville. Gala reenactment of sixteenth-century English festival with food and entertainment draws thousands. Weekends only during fall. (410) 266–7304 or (800) 396–7304.

September. Maryland Seafood Festival at Sandy Point State Park. Large variety of seafood dishes, with Maryland crab particularly highlighted. Music and entertainment. (410) 268–7682.

December. Christmas Lights Parade. Dozens of sailboats and yachts, festooned with lights, parade through Annapolis Harbor and Spa Creek, to the delight of spectators. Much Christmas caroling on deck. (410) 263–0415.

OTHER RECOMMENDED RESTAURANTS

Treaty of Paris Restaurant, 16 Church Circle; (410) 263–2341. Top-of-the-line gourmet American and French dishes in a lovely eighteenth-century inn. If you're splurging, try the four-course dinner. Expensive. The King of France Tavern at the same location serves soups, salads, and sandwiches at moderate prices.

Buddy's Crabs and Ribs, 100 Main Street, second floor; (410) 626–1100. A boisterous eatery with a young crowd and moderately priced menu. Emphasis on seafood and ribs, salads, and sticky desserts like brownie sundaes and caramel apple pie. Sunday brunch buffet is a bargain at $7.95.

Cafe Normandie, 185 Main Street; (410) 263–3382. Small, pretty, country-style French restaurant, offering appetizers like baked Brie and pâté, a wonderful charcuterie, seafood, veal, and crepes, and desserts worth saving room for. Moderate to expensive.

Papazee's Authentic Thai Cuisine, 257 West Street; (410) 263–8424. Casual Thai restaurant with excellent seafood hot pot, crispy fish, and flounder smothered in hot chili sauce. Moderate.

Garry's Grille, 914 Bay Ridge Road; (410) 626-0388. Bright and cheery Eastport area restaurant where you can get a great salad, sandwich, and coffee or chai tea for lunch. Excellent for breakfast as well. Moderate.

49 West Coffeehouse, 49 West Street; (410) 626-9796. A favorite for light vegetarian dining and lingering over coffee, European-style, with a newspaper. Live entertainment. Moderate.

Ram's Head Tavern, 33 West Street; (410) 268–4545. Popular pub with microbrewery on premises. Sandwiches, specials, and two dozen brands of beer on tap. Moderate.

Lewnes' Steakhouse, Severn Avenue at Fourth Street in Eastport area of town; (410) 263–1617. Family-run restaurant serving traditional steak and lobster dinners. Moderate to expensive.

Best place for doughnuts: City Dock Bakery in the Market House at City Dock; (410) 269-6361.

OTHER RECOMMENDED LODGINGS

William Page Inn, 8 Martin Street; (410) 626–1506 or (800) 364–4160, www.willampageinn.com. Five-room bed-and-breakfast furnished with antiques and period reproductions; fireplace in common room. Full breakfast. Rates: $115–$185.

Jonas Green House, 124 Charles Street; (410) 263–5892. Early eighteenth-century home in the historic district with three guest rooms, one with private bath. Children and pets welcome. Rates: $85–$135.

Historic Inns of Annapolis, 58 State Circle; (410) 263–2641 or (800) 847–8882. Includes three popular inns in the State Circle area: the Maryland Inn, the Robert Johnson House, and the Governor Calvert House. Together, they have a total of 124 rooms and suites. Rates: $119–$289 for rooms; $149–$459 for suites, which have Jacuzzis, kitchenettes, and living rooms.

Chez Amis Bed and Breakfast, 85 East Street; (410) 263–6631 or (888) 224–6455, www.chezamis.com. Charming B&B that was once a corner grocery store. The four guest rooms all have quilts, brass beds, interesting antiques, and private baths; full breakfast served. Rates: $105–$130.

Annapolis Accommodations is a commercial service that will make reservations at Annapolis hotels and B&Bs for individuals, large groups, or conferences. Located at 66 Maryland Avenue; (410) 280–0900 or (800) 715–1000, www.stayannapolis.com.

Bed and Breakfast of Maryland is a commercial service that will make reservations at Maryland inns and B&Bs. (202) 518–6066 or (800) 736–4667, www.bbmaryland.com.

FOR MORE INFORMATION

Annapolis and Anne Arundel County Conference and Visitors Bureau, 26 West Street, Annapolis, MD 21401; (410) 280–0445, www.visit-annapolis.org.
For more information visit www.hometownannapolis.com.

MARYLAND

The Eastern Shore
WATER, WATER, EVERYWHERE

1 NIGHT

Maritime museum • Boutique shopping • Biking
Fine dining • Bird-watching by boat

Water, water, everywhere—in rivers, streams, marshes, and the mighty Chesapeake itself—defines the ecology and the economy of Maryland's Eastern Shore of the Chesapeake Bay. The level, lush green lowlands of eastern Maryland are home to millions of waterbirds: Canada geese winter here, and other migratory birds stop over on their way south. As for the human inhabitants, almost everybody who lives in the Eastern Shore's quiet little fishing towns seems to be involved with water one way or another. A two-day visit to the Eastern Shore is a delightful opportunity for you to relax in and around the water too.

With the great Choptank River and the lesser Miles, Tred-Avon, and Wye Rivers, as well as countless creeks and streams flowing into the bay, boats seem to be almost as plentiful as cars in the area. Sturdy fisherfolk still ply their trade, hauling in the oysters, crabs, and fish. Sailboats bob on the bay and in the rivers, and children and old men with fishing poles hunker in solemn lines by the water's edge. Tourist boutiques offer beautiful hand-carved duck decoys, and dozens of restaurants serve up some of the best seafood in America.

This weekend in the bay area includes a popular tourist destination (the Chesapeake Bay Maritime Museum) in St. Michaels, a tiny town of Victorian B&Bs, boutique shops, and restaurants. It also gives you the opportunity to spend some time with the great herons, loons, egrets, geese, and wild ducks that frequent the area.

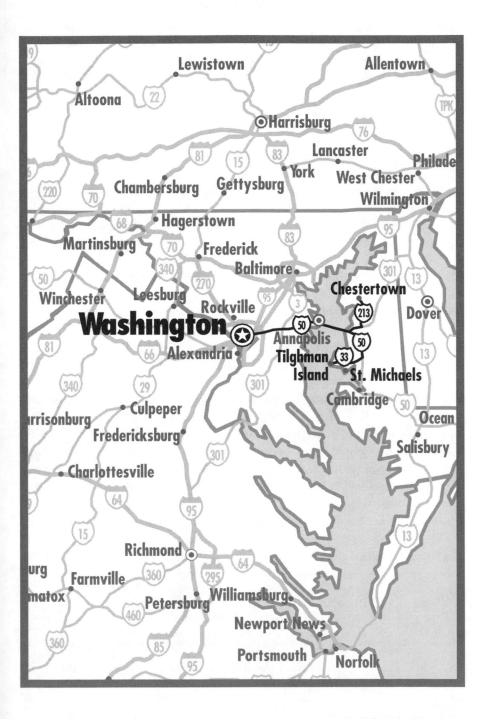

Pick a brilliant spring, summer, or fall weekend for this special quick escape from Washington, because you'll want to spend just about all your time outdoors, and on the water.

DAY 1

Morning

The Eastern Shore is only about 80 miles from Washington, D.C., but beach traffic in the summer can sometimes turn the trip into an hours-long proposition. If you can, get an early start to beat the rush. The route there is simple: Follow U.S. Highway 50 east from Washington over the Bay Bridge and you're on the northern tip of the Eastern Shore.

After you cross the Bay Bridge, continue east on U.S. Highway 50 a little over 25 miles, then take the Easton Parkway (State Highway 322) 2 or 3 miles to State Highway 33 west. Within fifteen minutes, you'll be in the quaint and beautiful town of **St. Michaels.**

Your first destination in St. Michaels is the **Chesapeake Bay Maritime Museum,** an eighteen-acre "museum campus" with several displays of Maryland maritime history. It's located on the main road (Talbot Street) right on the bay in St. Michaels; (410) 745–2916, www.cbmm.org. Open daily 9:00 A.M. to 7:00 P.M. except during the winter months, when it closes at 4:00 P.M. Admission is $7.50 for adults, $6.50 for seniors, and $3.00 for children six through seventeen. Children under six are admitted free.

Nearly everyone's favorite stop at the museum is the beautiful, restored nineteenth-century "screwpile" lighthouse, one of the last three cottage-type lighthouses in existence. The lighthouse's winding staircases, tiny and neat rooms, cunning housekeeping arrangements, and 360-degree view of the harbor and the Chesapeake Bay from 40 feet off the ground will make you yearn to live in it yourself. (In fact, the museum offers an evening program about life in the lighthouse, complete with dinner, on summer evenings.) Other displays at the museum are devoted to decoys, ancient fishing craft, bay history, and ship repair.

LUNCH: Amble next door for lunch at **The Crab Claw,** a tourist-friendly, casual restaurant specializing in seafood and burgers. If you get there before noon you might snare an outdoor table along the water. The Crab Claw's prices are reasonable: Burgers are $5.00–$7.00, and seafood platters are in the $12–$18 range. Located at Navy Point in St. Michaels; (410) 745–2900. Open March through mid-December.

Hooper Strait Lighthouse at Chesapeake Bay Maritime Museum

Afternoon

After lunch, take an hour to stroll through St. Michaels, which has more than a mile of tempting shops and boutiques lining **Talbot Street.** This is the place to pick up an ice-cream cone or an espresso and cruise the strip for antiques, jewelry, gifts, crafts, nautical prints, and decoys. If you're a real shopper, an hour won't be long enough!

When you're finished shopping, rent a bicycle or a tandem at **Town Dock Marina,** 305 Mulberry Street, just a block off of Talbot Street; (410) 745–2400. Bikes rent for $4.00 an hour or $16.00 for the whole day. (Bike rentals are also available on Tilghman Island from Island Treasures, Wharf Road, 410–886–2058, for approximately the same rates.)

The Eastern Shore's flat terrain is ideal for biking, and most of the roads in the area have wide shoulders set aside for bikers. You can bike west on State Highway 33, and if you go to the end of Tilghman Island, you'll have made a 30-mile round-trip. Or you can bike east on State Highway 33 to Easton and back, a 20-mile round-trip. Both are pleasant jaunts.

But the best bike ride in the area is a 20-mile round-trip that takes you from St. Michaels to Oxford and back, with stops in Bellevue and Oxford and a ferry ride across the Tred-Avon River. Take State Highway 33 east from St. Michaels about 4 miles to Bellevue Road. Then head south another 5 miles until you reach Bellevue. The hills are gentle and there's very little traffic to distract you from the beauty of the countryside.

In **Bellevue** you can grab a soda before boarding the **The Oxford-Bellevue Ferry,** the nation's oldest continuously operating ferry service. Although it can take only six cars at a time, plenty of pedestrians and bikers can be accommodated. The ferry is in operation Monday to Friday 7:00 A.M. to 9:00 P.M., Saturday and Sunday 9:00 A.M. to 9:00 P.M., June 1 through Labor Day. The rest of the year, the ferry runs weekdays from 7:00 A.M. to sunset, weekends from 9:00 A.M. to sunset. The ferry ride takes about twenty minutes and costs $3.00 round-trip for cyclists and $8.00 for a driver and car; pedestrians and additional car passengers pay 50 cents. (410) 745–9023.

When you disembark, spend some time biking around the tiny town of **Oxford,** one of the oldest and prettiest towns in the state. Oxford's tree-lined streets, stately old homes, churches, and lovely riverside park make it a perfect place for a picnic, or a lazy afternoon watching the sailboats on the river. There are also a number of quaint shops with antiques, gifts, tourist trinkets, baked goods, and bike supplies available.

After touring Oxford, retrace your bike route back through Bellevue to St. Michaels. If biking is not for you, consider a one- to two-hour walking tour through St. Michaels. **St. Mary's Square Museum,** near the corner of Talbot and Mulberry Streets (410–745–9561), publishes a brochure outlining a thirty-stop historical walking tour of St. Michaels, which likes to call itself "the town that fooled the British" because, during the War of 1812, its residents hoisted lanterns to the masts of ships and the tops of trees, forcing the British ships' cannons to overshoot the town. The museum itself is only open Saturday and Sunday from 10:00 A.M. to 4:00 P.M. from May through October, but you can pick up the brochure at most tourist attractions.

After your bike ride or walking tour, retrieve your car and head for **Tilghman Island,** 15 miles west of St. Michaels on State Highway 33, where you'll dine and spend the night. Tilghman Island is still very much a working fishing village on an island surrounded by the Chesapeake Bay, the Choptank River, and Harris Creek. You'll enjoy the drive down the island and the less-touristy atmosphere there.

DINNER: Join locals and visitors for dinner at **Harrison's Chesapeake House,** in operation since the 1890s and renowned for its seafood. The service at Harrison's is friendly, the seafood tantalizingly fresh, the coffee strong, and the side dishes (including mashed potatoes, excellent coleslaw, potato salad, and warm rolls) are served "family style" in large platters set in the center of the table. Entrees include crab cakes, of course, as well as fried clams, the fresh catch (which might be sea trout, flounder, or bluefish), and oysters. For dessert, the lemon chess pie is a standout. There is also an outdoor crab bar if you're in the mood for fresh steamed crabs. Located at Wharf Road, Tilghman Island; (410) 886–2121. Moderate.

LODGING: **The Tilghman Island Inn** is located at 21384 Coopertown Road, just 2 blocks west of Knapps Narrows Bridge; (410) 886–2141 or (800) 866–2141, www.tilghmanisland.com/tii. This twenty-room resort has a tennis court, pool, croquet court, fishing, biking, docking facilities, and a gourmet dining room overlooking the water at Knapps Narrows. Rooms are modern and lovely and are filled with local original art, which is for sale. Rates: $95–$160.

DAY 2

Morning

BREAKFAST: The Tilghman Island Inn's breakfast offerings include eggs, bacon, scrapple, biscuits and muffins, and waffles with bananas Foster topping. Moderate.

Following breakfast, take a few minutes to visit **Captain Dan Vaughn's Decoy Shop,** at 21536 Mission Road on Tilghman Island. It's 1 block west and about 5 blocks south of the Tilghman Island Inn. The sweet smell of cedar chips in the workshop where he handcrafts his decoys is worth a stop even if you're not in the market and, when you've seen his beautiful wooden ducks and loons, you might change your mind.

Afterward, conduct your own search for the real thing on the waterways of the Eastern Shore with the help of **Island Kayak,** at the same address, (410) 886–2083, www.island-kayak.com. If you've made an advance arrangement, you will be taken kayaking or rowing to see waterfowl along the shore. An early-morning jaunt provides an opportunity to see—besides ducks and loons—great blue herons, egrets, and ospreys wading, fishing, and diving. Bald eagles are also

frequently sighted in the area. The best time to see the waterbirds is spring and summer, but September and October, when the birds begin to migrate, offer other pleasures—wild geese fly overhead, and the foliage is glorious.

You don't have to be an experienced kayaker or rower to join in exploring the Tilghman Island shore area for waterfowl; Island Kayak offers courses in both activities. A two- to three-hour nature outing costs $45 a person.

If you want a less strenuous water jaunt, drive back to St. Michaels and snare a seat on the 180-passenger **Patriot,** which is berthed at the Chesapeake Bay Maritime Museum. The *Patriot* cruises the Miles River, a beautiful tributary of the bay. On your one-hour outing, you'll see plenty of local and migratory birds and watermen at work harvesting crabs or tonging for oysters. Phone (410) 745–3100; www.patriotcruises.com. Cruises depart St. Michaels at 11:00 A.M., 12:30, 2:30, and 4:00 P.M. April through October. Cost: $9.00 for adults, $4.00 for children under twelve.

After your water adventure, head back east on State Highway 33 and State Highway 322 (the Easton Parkway) to U.S. Highway 50 west. Follow it northwest and begin your exploration of the northern tip of the Eastern Shore.

About 8 miles north of Easton on U.S. Highway 50, you'll see a sign for **Wye Oak State Park,** and it's definitely worth the short side trip. There you can see the oldest white oak in the United States, which happens to be the state tree of Maryland. The giant Wye Oak stands right next to the road in a minute state park. Although the tree is protected by a wood fence, if you lean just right you can get a photograph of yourself next to the 400-year-old beauty. While you're there, be sure to see the restored Old Wye Church, circa 1721, just behind the oak. Located on Old Wye Mills Road (State Highway 662) 3 miles west of U.S. Highway 50; (410) 820–1668.

There are two additional good reasons for taking the short detour to visit Wye Oak. Just before you reach the oak tree on State Highway 662 is **Orrell's Maryland Beaten Biscuits,** which bakes and ships more than a half million of these Eastern Shore delicacies a year. Orrell's sells directly to the public only on Tuesdays andWednesdays, but you can find the biscuits in area supermarkets. Phone (410) 822–2065.

On Saturday and Sunday from mid-April through mid-November, **Wye Gristmill** (410–827–6909) is open to the public from 10:00 A.M. to 4:00 P.M.; on weekdays the hours are 10:00 A.M. to 1:00 P.M. On the first and third Saturday of the month, you can watch them grind the grain. But you can purchase freshly ground wheat, rye, buckwheat, and corn meal every day, and your taste buds will thank you.

As you leave Wye, take State Highway 404 west (you'll actually be traveling north) 1 mile to State Highway 213 north and follow it about 25 miles to **Chestertown,** the county seat of Kent County and one of the most delightful towns on the Eastern Shore.

LUNCH: It's worth a visit to the **Imperial Hotel,** 208 High Street (410–778–5000), just to see the beautiful, dark green plaid dining room. But don't be daunted by the elegant surroundings: Dinner may be elegant and expensive, but lunchers are likely to be wearing boating shorts, and prices are an affordable $8.00–$10.00 for crab melt sandwiches or grilled steak salads.

Afternoon

After lunch, take a walking tour of old Chestertown. Walking tour brochures are available at most hotels and shops or at the Kent County Office of Tourism at 400 South Cross Street; (410) 778–0416. Many of Chestertown's gorgeous old homes and buildings date back to the eighteenth century. The walking tour will take you about two hours. Among the top attractions are the circa 1747 **Customs House** on Water Street, with its Flemish Bond brickwork, and the **Geddes-Piper House,** a beautifully restored and beautifully furnished mansion that serves as the headquarters of the Historical Society of Kent County. Both are open to the public. Most of the houses on the tour are privately owned and are open for viewing only once a year during Chestertown's annual Candlelight Walking Tour. You can, however, enjoy gazing at the architecture of the 200-year-old gems that housed the wealthy local merchants and get a peek at many of the splendid gardens.

The recently restored **White Swan Tavern** at 231 High Street (410–778–2300) dates back to 1733. This old jewel has been lovingly polished and filled with period furniture and furnishings to museum-like perfection. You can tour the building and refresh yourself with afternoon tea, which is served from 3:00 to 5:00 P.M. George Washington himself had tea there. Indeed, Chestertown is justly proud of its "tea party" history. Five months after the Boston Tea Party, in May of 1774, the citizens of Chestertown boarded a British ship and threw both tea and crew members into the Chester River.

If you decide to stay over an extra day on the Eastern Shore, you can take a 110-mile driving tour of Kent County the next morning. Tour instruction brochures are available from the Kent County Office of Tourism. On the driving tour, you'll see wildlife refuges, pituresque villages, two or three small museums, and Washington College, one of the ten oldest colleges in America.

To return to Washington from Chestertown, take State Highway 213 south about 20 miles, U.S. Highway 301 south about 5 miles, and U.S. Highway 50 west about 50 miles. It will take you more than ninety minutes.

THERE'S MORE

Boat Rentals. St. Michaels Town Dock Marina, Mulberry Street; (410) 745–2400. Full range of services for boaters, including overnight dockage, motel rooms, showers, swimming pool, marine store, and ice, as well as powerboat rentals.

Cruises. A two-hour sail on the ***Rebecca T. Ruark,*** the oldest skipjack on the Chesapeake Bay (built in 1886!), is available for $30 a person. Phone (410) 886–2176; www.skipjack.org.

Easton. You can while away a couple of hours with a walking tour of some of the sights of downtown Easton. Make sure to stop at the **Historical Society Museum** at 25 South Washington Street; (410) 822–0773. Open Tuesday to Saturday 10:00 A.M. to 4:00 P.M., Sunday noon to 4:00 P.M. Admission to the exhibits in the three galleries is $4.00. Also worth seeing are the two-century-old Talbot County Courthouse at the corner of Washington and Dover Streets, the Academy of the Arts at 106 South Street, and the Third Haven Friends Meeting House at 405 South Washington Street.

Fishing. Harrison's Chesapeake House and Sports Fishing Center on Tilghman Island has the largest privately owned fishing fleet on the Chesapeake. Harrison's will take you out for striper, bluefish, Spanish mackerel, and sea trout at a rate of $75 a person for eight hours of fishing. Phone (410) 886–2121; www.chesapeakehouse.com.

SPECIAL EVENTS

May. Chestertown Tea Party Festival. Reenactment of the boarding of the Brigantine *Geddes* and the dumping of its stores of tea into the Chester River. (410) 778–0416.

June. Antique and Classic Boat Show, Chesapeake Bay Maritime Museum. (410) 745–2916.

August. Oxford Regatta. Three days of sailboat racing, food, and entertainment. (410) 226–5730.

September. Annual Candlelight Walking Tour of the historic district of Chestertown to benefit the Historical Society of Kent County. (410) 778–3499.

October. Tilghman Island Day. Skipjack races, boat docking contests, auction, music, and seafood, of course. (410) 886–2677.

October. Mid-Atlantic Small Craft Festival, St. Michaels. Kayaks, canoes, rowing shells, and sailing skiffs show their stuff. Workshops, races, and kids' activities. (410) 745–2916.

November. Waterfowl Festival, Easton. Exhibition of more than 500 wildlife artists. Includes retriever demonstrations and seminars. Proceeds go toward waterfowl conservation efforts. (410) 822–4567.

OTHER RECOMMENDED RESTAURANTS

Oxford

Robert Morris Inn, 312 Morris Street; (410) 226–5111. Excellent seafood and classic American dishes. Dining room overlooks the Tred-Avon River. Moderate to expensive.

St. Michaels

208 Talbot, 208 North Talbot Street; (410) 745–3838. Contemporary menu, daily specials, delightful ambience. Moderate.

Town Dock Restaurant, 125 Mulberry Street; (410) 745–5577 or (800) 884–0103. Casual, crowded eatery with outside bar and grill; good choice for seafood. Moderate.

Poppi's, 207 North Talbot Street; (410) 745–3158. Breakfast, lunch, hand-dipped ice cream. Inexpensive.

Best place for doughnuts: Richardson's Country Store, State Highway 33 just east of St. Michaels; (410) 745–2209.

Easton

Washington Street Pub, 20 North Washington Street; (410) 822–9011. Good choice for deli sandwiches, burgers, pizza, chili, and drinks. Inexpensive to moderate.

Tidewater Inn, 101 East Dover Street; (410) 822–1300. Gracious dining room serving Eastern Shore specialties. Moderate to expensive.

OTHER RECOMMENDED LODGINGS

Tilghman Island

Chesapeake Wood Duck Inn, Gibsontown Road at Dogwood Harbor; (410) 886–2070 or (800) 956–2070, www.woodduckinn.com. Formerly a boardinghouse and bordello, now a lovely six-room Victorian B&B, furnished with antiques, which serves a full gourmet breakfast. Rates: $135–$215 in season.

Harrison's Chesapeake House Country Inn, Wharf Road; (410) 886–2121, www.chesapeakehouse.com. Pleasant waterfront inn catering to families and sports anglers; large country breakfast served. Rates: $95–$105.

Chestertown

White Swan Tavern Bed and Breakfast, 402 High Street; (410) 778–2300, www.chestertown.com/whiteswan. Lovely, completely renovated 200-year-old tavern with four guest rooms and two suites, all with private baths. All guests get continental breakfast, afternoon tea, and a complimentary fruit basket. Rates: $110–$185.

Imperial Hotel, 208 High Street; (410) 778–5000, www.chestertown.com/imperial. Restored Victorian hotel with thirteen luxurious rooms and suites, all with private bath, air-conditioning, and cable TV. Rates: $125–$200.

Oxford

Robert Morris Inn, 312 Morris Street; (410) 226–5111, www. robertmorris inn.com. Romantic eighteenth-century inn with thirty-five rooms. Most have porches and water views. Rates: $110–$250.

St. Michaels

The Inn at Perry Cabin, 308 Watkins Lane; (410) 745–2200 or (800) 722–2949, www.perrycabin.com. Exquisite forty-one-room inn decorated in Laura Ashley fabrics. Rates: $195–$515, including full breakfast and afternoon tea. Restaurant on the premises: prix fixe dinners for $70 a person.

Barrett's Bed and Breakfast Inn, 204 North Talbot Street; (410) 745–3322, www.barrett.com. Five-room B&B in an 1860s home; beautifully decorated, full breakfast. Rates: $170 to $230.

The Parsonage Inn, 210 North Talbot Street; (410) 745–5519 or (800) 394–5519. An 1880s brick Victorian with eight guest rooms, all with air-conditioning and private baths. Full breakfast; free use of bikes. Rates: $100–$185.

Harbour Inn and Marina, 101 North Harbor Road; (410) 745–9001 or (800) 955–9001, www.harbourinn.com. A forty-two-room luxury hotel along the water; includes harborside pool and bar, and the Lighthouse Restaurant. Bicycle rentals and workout room available. Rates: $99–$449.

Easton

Tidewater Inn, 101 East Dover Street; (410) 822–1300 or (800) 237–8775, www.tidewaterinn.com. Elegant inn with Old World charm; 113 beautifully appointed rooms. Air-conditioning, fireplaces, pool, restaurant on premises. Rates: $120–$275.

FOR MORE INFORMATION

The Talbot County Visitors Bureau, P.O. Box 1366, Easton, MD 21601; (410) 822–4606 or (888) 229–7829, www.talbotchamber.org.

Chesapeake Bay Maritime Museum, P.O. Box 636, St. Michaels, MD 21663; (410) 745–2916, www.cbmm.org.

Kent County Office of Tourism, 400 South Cross Street, Chestertown, MD 21620; (410) 778–0416, www.kentcounty.com.

St. Michaels Business Association, P.O. Box 1221, St. Michaels, MD 21663; (800) 660–9471, www.stmichaelsmd.org.

For more information visit www.tilghmanisland.com.

MARYLAND

Berlin, Assateague Island, Ocean City, and More

BEST BEACHES AND TOWNS

2 NIGHTS

*Atlantic Ocean • Boardwalk amusement park • Shopping
Barrier island nature preserve • Wildlife museum*

The Maryland shore of the Atlantic Ocean is full of delights and contrasts. In this weekend escape you browse the elegant little town of Berlin (where the 1940s-era theater now houses a coffee bar, bookshop, and gallery of top-quality art for sale) and stay in a luxurious restored mansion, with Victorian furniture in every room and a full-course gourmet breakfast in the morning. You also get to spend a day at Ocean City—where you'll ride the water slides and roller coasters, eat greasy funnel cakes and cotton candy, and toss balls to win a stuffed bear at a gaudy, joyous carnival on the boardwalk. Combine that with dinner at one of the region's finest restaurants and a day at a peaceful and unspoiled oasis of natural beauty at the Assateague Island National Seashore, where there's just you, the white sand beach, the wild ponies, and the Atlantic Ocean, and you'll have a truly memorable minivacation.

DAY 1

Morning

Get an early morning start from Washington, D.C., for a three-hour drive to Berlin, Maryland. Follow U.S. Highway 50 east from Washington for about

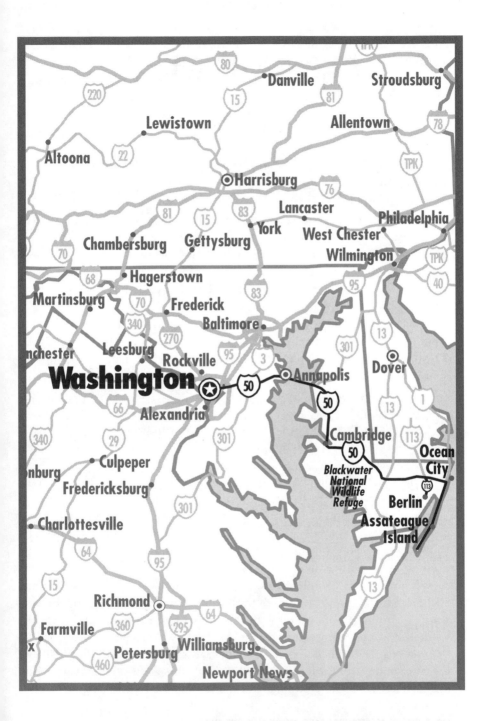

140 miles. Eight miles short of the ocean, turn south on U.S. Highway 113 and you'll be in Berlin (accent on the first syllable) within five minutes.

Your immediate destination is the **Merry Sherwood Plantation,** a recently restored mansion that is now a bed-and-breakfast a couple of miles south of Berlin on U.S. Highway 113 at 8909 Worcester Highway; (410) 641–2112 or (800) 660–0358, www.merrysherwood.com. The owners spent two years restoring this old prize, and their love for Victorian furnishings is apparent the minute you step into the foyer and the grand ballroom, where you'll see 14-foot ceilings, chandeliers, velvet furniture, paintings, carved plaster molding, and bronze statuary.

Each of the eight guest rooms at the Merry Sherwood is different, and all are lovely. Some have their own marble bathrooms, and those on the second floor have working fireplaces. The architectural details and the decorations throughout the mansion delight you with every door you open. Rates: $150–$175 a night during the summer and $100–$125 a night from October through May.

Once you've left your bags and taken a turn around the plantation grounds, head back to **Berlin** for a look around. Be sure to visit the **Globe Theatre,** a beautifully restored theater that has been turned into an upscale community center. Located at 12 Broad Street, Berlin; (410) 641–0784. Open weekdays 8:00 A.M. to 6:00 P.M., Saturday 10:00 A.M. to 6:00 P.M., Sunday 11:00 A.M. to 5:00 P.M.

The little theater—its old-fashioned iron seats painted lipstick pink—is still in use and local artists, including folksingers, jazz musicians, and storytellers, appear regularly.

What's more, the Globe's management has opened up the space around the theater for selected shops and stores, including a wine and cheese shop and an upstairs gallery selling exquisite handmade jewelry, sculpture, oil and watercolor paintings, and polished wooden bowls. Follow your nose downstairs and you'll come across the Globe's coffee bar. Pick up a cup of their best and a snack to hold you over until lunch, and prepare to hit the road.

Ocean City is a 10-mile drive east from Berlin via U.S. Highways 113 and 50. Ignore the strip and head south for the public parking lots near the **boardwalk.** Begin your walk up through the amusement parks and arcades at the south end of the boardwalk, and prepare to enjoy every bit of it. Where else can you buy five tasteless T-shirts for $10, have a funnel cake, candy apple, and bag of caramel corn for lunch, and win an appalling stuffed animal by throwing baseballs just right? And then you can lose it all on a gut-flinging "carny" ride like the "Viking Ship," which rocks you back and forth until you're nearly upside down and shrieking for mercy. You'll love it.

LUNCH: Have lunch on the Ocean City boardwalk. The possibilities here are legion.

Afternoon

There are two main amusement parks at Ocean City: **Trimper's Rides of Ocean City** at Boardwalk and South First Street (410–289–8617) and the **Jolly Roger Amusement Park** at Thirtieth Street and Coastal Highway (410–289–3477). Trimper's is open from 1:00 P.M. to midnight weekdays and noon to midnight weekends. A "wristband special" permitting unlimited rides before 6:00 P.M. costs about $12. The Jolly Roger is open daily from 2:00 P.M. to midnight. Its afternoon special costs about $13.

The Jolly Roger also operates **Splash Mountain Water Park,** which has ten water slides. There, kids (if they're under 42 inches tall) can spend happy hours shooting down the labyrinth of curves, bumps, and incredibly long descents on their inner tubes, propelled by streams of water until they go flying into a pool of water. Then they climb to the top and do it again. And again. Open 10:00 A.M. to 9:00 P.M. A four-hour pass costs $12. Located at 2901 Philadelphia Avenue; (410) 289–6962.

Teenagers seem to be drawn to the arcades full of video games on the boardwalk. If you dare to venture in, you'll feel like you're in Dante's Inferno or, at a minimum, a Mad Max movie. The noise is incredible, the games assault your eyeballs, and the kids have a ball.

Don't think that Ocean City is just for big kids and lunatics. There is a section of rides for little children set aside within the arcade facade, near the south end of the amusement park. Here, tiny kids can enjoy gentle carousel rides and slow-moving cars, protected from the hubbub of the carnival going on outdoors.

Ocean City is a scene. It's a little like a county fair on fast-forward, set right on the ocean. One of the things you must do is buy a big bucket of **Thrashers** french fries, douse them with vinegar and salt, stick a straw into a long glass of lemonade, and park yourself on a bench and just watch the people go by. There are halter-topped and muscle-shirted couples with arms around each other and tattoos rippling. There are older couples holding hands and remembering the carnivals of their youth. There are proud parents snapping pictures of their three-year-olds on the carousel ponies. And there are the shrieks of older kids as they go flying by on the Tilt-a-Whirl or roller coaster.

But not all of Ocean City is boardwalk. When you've had your fill, take a stroll out to the beach—about a hundred yards away—and get your feet wet in the Atlantic Ocean.

DINNER: Another Ocean City trademark is its large selection of restaurants, most specializing in seafood. Try one of the fresh fish specials at the **Angler Restaurant,** a sixty-year-old mainstay at the beach, and they'll throw in a complimentary hour-long scenic cruise. Located at 312 Talbot Street; (410) 289–7424. Moderate.

LODGING: Merry Sherwood Plantation.

DAY 2

Morning

BREAKFAST: The Merry Sherwood. Have some piping-hot coffee, fruit, home-made bread and rolls, and an omelette or quiche to start you on your way.

After breakfast, drive into Berlin and pick up a picnic-lunch-to-go at the **Raynes Reef** lunch counter, at the corner of South Main and Broad Streets; (410) 641–2131. This old-time classic, complete with stools along the counter and ice-cream sodas, will pack you some submarine sandwiches and bags of chips for a picnic lunch at the beach. Stop at the drugstore across the street and pick up lots of bottled water, sunblock, and, above all, insect repellent.

Your destination today is **Assateague Island National Seashore,** which you reach by driving 3 miles east of Berlin on State Highway 376 and about 5 miles south on State Highway 611 to the Verrazano Bridge, which crosses over to Assateague Island. This lovely spot is only 10 miles from Ocean City, but it could be on another planet. When you reach Assateague, be sure to stop at the **Barrier Island Visitor Center,** which has exhibits, an aquarium, maps, and publications. It is located just north of the Verrazano Bridge; (410) 641–1441, www.nps.gov/asis.

Assateague is a barrier island, with clean Atlantic surf, rolling dunes, and scrubby forests of dwarf pines, bayberry trees, tall grasses, and wildflowers. Because it is owned by the National Park Service, it has absolutely none of the urban sprawl, concessions, and billboards that have marred so many of the East Coast beaches. Assateague is a national treasure, kept safe and pristine for you and the wild ponies who share the island.

The wild ponies of Assateague and the neighboring island of Chincoteague are well known to any youngster who has read *Misty of Chincoteague,* the

Wild ponies at Assateague Island National Seashore

beloved Marguerite Henry novel about an island pony. At the visitor center you can learn much more about the famous horses, which are said to be descended from a herd left on the island in the 1700s by Eastern Shore planters. Beware: The ponies bite and kick, and feeding them is prohibited.

Assateague offers primitive camping but little else, so once you've parked your car and lugged your picnic provisions out to the sand, you can find yourself virtually isolated within a few hundred yards of the parking area. Lay out your blanket, and settle in for the day.

LUNCH: Picnic at the beach.

Afternoon

More fun at the beach, but a word to the wise—bring lots of ultra-strong sunblock and rub it everywhere. Also, the mosquitos and flies on the island, once you've left the water's edge, are legendary. They'll carry you off if you haven't slathered on repellent.

Assateague is as idyllic a spot as you'll ever find. Plan to spend the full day here. When you're ready to get out of the water, take one or all of three short

nature walks that explore the unusual foliage on the island, including wind-stunted trees and bushes. Don't forget your camera. The ponies, as well as small deer, are liable to pop up anywhere!

Back at the Merry Sherwood, treat yourself to a long soak or shower, then drive into Berlin for a fine gourmet meal.

DINNER: The **Atlantic Hotel,** 2 North Main Street (410–641–3589), has an award-winning kitchen that serves up tasty seafood, poultry, and meat dishes with style. The dining room is exquisite, set with crystal, china, and crisp linen, and the service is attentive. In addition to the staples you'd expect at a very good seafood restaurant, the chef here prepares daily specials such as grilled swordfish steak topped with crab imperial and caper sauce. Follow that with any of the excellent desserts and you have the perfect meal. Expensive.

LODGING: The Merry Sherwood.

DAY 3

Morning

BREAKFAST: The Merry Sherwood.

On your last day in the area, sleep in at the Merry Sherwood, then drive to the beach one last time for a walk along the waves or a quick dip. If you swim or sunbathe at Ocean City, there are public bathhouses on the Boardwalk at North First Street and at Wicomico Street so you can shower and change. On Assateague Island, you can rinse off and change at the rest rooms at the campgrounds.

Plan your route home so that you drive through **Snow Hill,** about 12 miles south of Berlin on U.S. Highway 113. It's full of beautiful old houses with spacious lawns; locals like to boast that the whole town is a walking tour.

LUNCH: Stop for lunch at the **Snow Hill Inn** at 104 East Market Street, Snow Hill. If you haven't had your fill of crab cakes, make that your choice; they're memorable here. Reservations recommended; call (410) 632–2102. Moderate.

Afternoon

Begin your trip home by driving 18 miles northwest from Snow Hill on State Highway 12 to U.S. Highway 50. The two roads meet at **Salisbury,** which is worth a visit. A particularly good reason for stopping is the **Ward Museum of**

Wildfowl Art, a museum of duck decoys and more. It is said to feature the world's largest collection of bird carvings, and many of them are for sale. Located at 909 South Schumaker Drive; (410) 742–4988. Open Monday to Saturday 10:00 A.M. to 5:00 P.M., Sunday noon to 5:00 P.M. Admission is $7.00 for adults, $5.00 for seniors, $3.00 for students; children under five are admitted free.

This is a great area for bird lovers, and you must stop at the **Blackwater National Wildlife Refuge,** located 12 miles south of U.S. Highway 50 near Cambridge. To get there, take State Highway 16 south 7 miles and State Highway 335 south 5 miles. Phone (410) 228–2677.

This beautiful 17,121-acre park is a marshy, wooded refuge for migratory birds and a haven for at least three endangered species, including the Delmarva fox squirrel. A 5-mile loop drive includes eleven stopping points where the birds can be viewed, including nesting spots for bald eagles. (There are said to be sixty to one hundred of the great birds in the refuge.) At any moment, a large, stately family of ducks or geese might parade across the road and, during the summer months, red-winged blackbirds dive and swoop as the great, long-legged fishing birds (including egrets and herons) wade on their spindly legs through the marsh.

Stop your car (or better yet, do the loop on bike or foot) so you can hear the chorus of birdcalls in the refuge. The refuge offers a bike map with 20- and 25-mile designated rides. Some people think early morning is the best time to see the birds, but just before sundown is great as well.

From the park retrace your route on State Highways 335 and 16 to U.S. Highway 50 west. It will take you two hours to make the 90-mile drive back to Washington.

THERE'S MORE

Parasailing. O.C. Parasail, located at the Talbot Street Pier in Ocean City (410–723–1464, www.ocean-city.com/parasail), offers short 400- to 1,500-foot-high rides for $40–$70.

Sailing. You can rent a sailboat for $30–$40 an hour or $90–$120 a day at Sailing, Etc., 4605 Coastal Highway, Ocean City; (410) 723–1144. Lessons are $15 an hour. You can also rent kayaks, sailboards, and in-line skates.

The *Sea Rocket*. The *Sea Rocket,* an enormous speedboat (150 passengers), offers a fifty-minute ride on the ocean and along Assateague Island for pony watching. Wear casual clothes. Rates: $10.00 for adults, $8.00 for senior citizens, $5.00 for children four to eleven; children under four ride free. Located at Talbot Street Pier; (410) 289–5887, www.oceancity. com/boatrides.

Planet Maze. Rainy-day fun for kids of all ages at indoor high-tech play arena. Located at 3305 Coastal Highway; (410) 524–4386, www. planetmaze.com. Open year-round from 9:00 A.M. to midnight.

SPECIAL EVENTS

April. Ward World Championship Wildlife Carving Competition. Decoy carving in Ocean City. (410) 742–4988.

June. Village Fair in Berlin. Arts and crafts, live entertainment, museum tours, bathtub races, a lawn mower parade, food, games. (410) 641–4775.

August. White Marlin Open. Hundreds of anglers and thousands of spectators flock to the white marlin capital of the world to watch contestants compete for more than $800,000 in prize money. (410) 289–9229 or (800) 626–2326.

September. Sunfest. Ocean City celebrates the end of summer in late September with food, games, arts and crafts, kite flying, and music. (410) 289–2800.

OTHER RECOMMENDED RESTAURANTS

Ocean City

Reflections Restaurant and Wine Bar, Sixty-seventh Street and Oceanside; (410) 524–5252. Dress for dinner. Nicely prepared and presented continental and local cuisine. Try one of the specialties cooked tableside. Moderate to expensive.

Hobbit, Eighty-first Street and the bay; (410) 524–8100. Casual year-round dining with pub atmosphere; fresh seafood, beef, veal. Moderate.

Jonah and the Whale, Twenty-sixth Street and Oceanside; (410) 524–2722. All-you-can-eat seafood buffet that has been an Ocean City mainstay for more than twenty years. Moderate.

English's Family Restaurant, Fifteenth Street and Philadelphia Avenue; (410) 289–7333. Local chain featuring bargain breakfast and dinner buffets; good for families. Inexpensive to moderate.

Best place for doughnuts: Dip'n Donuts Layton's Family Restaurant, 1601 Philadelphia Avenue; (410) 289–6635.

For additional restaurants in the area, see Delaware Escape Two (page 285).

OTHER RECOMMENDED LODGINGS

Berlin

Atlantic Hotel, 2 North Main Street; (410) 641–3589 or (800) 814–7672, www.atlantichotel.com. Hundred-year-old Victorian luxury hotel known up and down the coast for its charm, hospitality, and kitchen. Sixteen rooms with private baths; complimentary continental breakfast. Rates: $65–$165.

Snow Hill

Snow Hill Inn, 104 East Market Street; (410) 632–2102. Victorian B&B with three guest rooms, all with private baths; complimentary wine in rooms, continental breakfast. Rates: $75 on weekends, $50 on weekdays.

The River House Inn on the Pokomoke River, 201 East Market Street; (410) 632–2722. Nice country-inn atmosphere located in town; five rooms in the main house plus a river cottage. Full breakfast with menu selections; afternoon wine. Rooms are $100–$120; the cottage is $175.

Chanceford Hall Bed & Breakfast Inn, 209 West Federal Street; (410) 632–2231. Eighteenth-century house with four large, nicely furnished guest rooms. Sun porch and lap pool available for guest use; full breakfast served in the dining room. Rates: $150–$180.

Ocean City

An Inn on the Ocean, 1001 Atlantic Avenue; (410) 289–8894 or (888) 226–6223. Year-round B&B on the ocean with six guest rooms; all have private baths, televisions, VCRs, and air-conditioning. Free use of bicycles and beach equipment; continental breakfast. Rates: $125–$275.

Atlantic House, 501 North Baltimore Avenue; (410) 289–2333, www.atlantichouse.com. Seventy-year-old Victorian house with eleven guest accommodations ranging from an apartment to bedrooms with shared baths. Air-conditioning and cable TV; full breakfast. Rates: $50–$225.

Talbot Inn, located at the Talbot Street Pier; (410) 289–9125 or (800) 659–7703, www.ocean-city.com/talbotinn. Year-round bayside motel with forty-five efficiency units; cable and microwaves. Rates: $28–$98, depending on the season.

Inlet Lodge Motel, 804 South Boardwalk; (410) 289–7552 or (800) 294–6538, www.ocean-city.com/inletlodge. Family-friendly motel with thirty-six rooms, all with cable TV, air-conditioning, telephone, and private bath. Convenient to the boardwalk; coffeeshop on the premises. Open April through October. Rates: $70–$80.

Dunes Motel, on the beach at Twenty-seventh Street; (410) 289–4414, www.ocean-city.com/dunes.htm. Ocean-front motel with 103 rooms and suites; most have a view of the ocean. Rooms are $50–$150; suites, $70–$200.

Assateague Island

Assateague National Seashore Campgrounds, National Seashore Lane; (410) 641–3030 or (800) 365–2267, www.nps.gov/asis. Only the 800 number takes reservations. Forty-nine bayside sites and 104 oceanside sites; rest rooms but no hookups. Camping costs $14 a night.

Assateague State Park, Route 611; (410) 641–2120. The campground has 179 sites with rest rooms and hookups. Rates start at $20.

For additional lodgings in the area, see Delaware Escape Two (page 285).

FOR MORE INFORMATION

Ocean City Convention and Visitors Bureau, 4001 Coastal Highway, Ocean City, MD 21842; (410) 289–2800 or (800) 626–2326, www.ococean.com.

Worcester County Tourism Bureau, 113 Franklin Street, Snow Hill, MD 21863; (410) 632–3110 or (800) 852-0335, www.skipjack.net/le_shore/visitworcester.

For more information visit www.ocean-city.com and www.oceancity.org.

MARYLAND

Baltimore

A NEIGHBORLY CITY

2 NIGHTS

Aquarium • Harborplace • Old markets
Museums • Gardens • Ethnic dining

Less than an hour's drive from downtown Washington, Baltimore is a city with great things to see, do, and eat, with a personality all its own. It has an enormous indoor farmers' market, an eighteenth-century cobbled street neighborhood along the wharf, a stunning aquarium—the largest in the United States—and the Orioles ballpark. Baltimore has ethnic neighborhoods, ancient churches, front stoops, art galleries, crab cakes, bookshops, beer, and a lot more.

Astonishingly, many Washingtonians haven't become acquainted with their nearby neighbor to the northeast. But all it will take is one visit to turn you into a confirmed Baltimore fan. This three-day itinerary packs in the highlights of the city, including some of its best-known tourist attractions, like Harborplace and the National Aquarium, as well as longtime favorites of Baltimore locals, like the Woman's Industrial Exchange lunchroom and tea shop, the gorgeous Peabody Library, and Marconi's, a classy, old-fashioned Italian restaurant. All these attractions can be sampled in a weekend trip from Washington, and you'll only have scratched the surface.

DAY 1

Morning

Baltimore is about 40 miles northeast of Washington via Interstate 95 or the Baltimore-Washington Parkway (State Highway 295). Leave Washington as

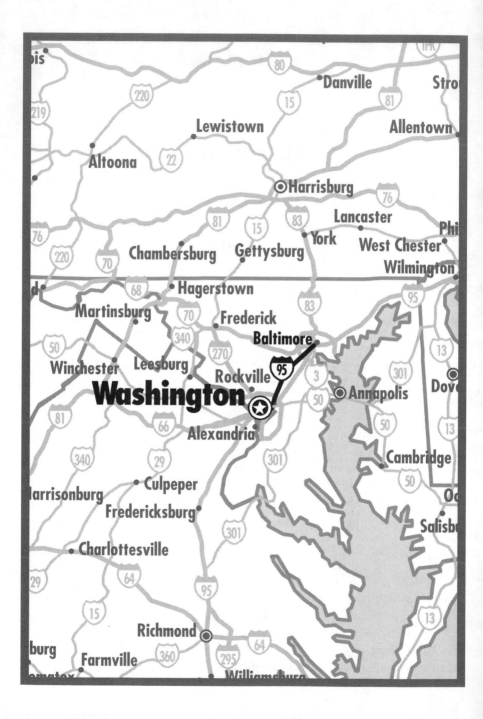

soon as possible after "the dawn's early light" and drive directly to **Fort McHenry,** located at 2400 East Fort Avenue; (410) 962–4290, www. nps.gov/fomc. Open daily 8:00 A.M. to 8:00 P.M. June through August, daily 8:00 A.M. to 4:45 P.M. September through May. Admission is $5.00 for adults; children under seventeen are admitted free.

Fort McHenry is where Francis Scott Key saw the U.S. flag flying after a British attack during the War of 1812 had failed. Key then penned his famous poem *The Star-Spangled Banner,* which—when set to music—became our national anthem in 1931. A replica of the original 30-by-42-foot, eighty-pound flag is on display at Fort McHenry. Many Washingtonians will recognize it; the original is on display at the Smithsonian's National Museum of American History. Exhibits and a movie at the Fort McHenry Visitor Center dramatically tell the whole story.

Next, head for the city's famous **Lexington Market,** at the corner of Lexington and Eutaw Streets; (410) 685–6169, www.lexingtonmarket.com. Open Monday to Saturday 8:30 A.M. to 6:00 P.M. Lexington Market brings you nose to nose with the cuisine of brawny Baltimore, from raw oysters to Italian cannoli. It is the oldest continuously operating meat, fish, and produce market in the United States. The original building—parts of which dated to 1803—burned down, alas, and the present structure, a large redbrick warehouse, was erected on the site in the 1950s. But there are still dozens and dozens of vegetable, bakery, meat, and fish stands threaded by narrow passageways, and smelling to high heaven.

Lexington Market is evidence of Baltimore's polyglot nature. There's an Irish butcher in his blood-smeared apron next to a Korean grocer, with a Jewish deli just across the way, and everybody calling out "May I help you?" as you walk by.

While you're at the market, look for **Polock Johnny's Sausage** stand, **Park's Fried Chicken** (which sells delicious deep-fat-fried chicken livers), **Konstant's Candy,** and the dozen or so fresh produce stands. Best of all, there are the fish markets, teeming with Maryland's bounty: oysters, crab, and fish of all kinds.

LUNCH: A favorite among the fish markets is **Faidley's;** (410) 727–4898. Make it your first choice for lunch. In addition to counters full of fresh seafood to take home, Faidley's has a raw bar where you can stand and gulp down raw oysters. There's also a lunch counter selling fish sandwiches; shrimp, clam, and scallop baskets; and such "sides" as greens, macaroni salad, pickled beets, and coleslaw. And, oh yes, they make the best crab-cake sandwiches in Maryland. Moderate.

Lexington Market is also an ideal spot for doughnut lovers. Among the half dozen stalls offering fresh doughnuts is **Berger's Bakery** (410–727–3685), which has been in business for more than three decades.

Afternoon

After lunch at Lexington Market, you'll spend a few hours in one of the most beautiful art galleries in the United States. The **Walters Art Gallery,** located at 600 North Charles Street on historic Mount Vernon Square, has a splendid collection of medieval and Islamic art, old master paintings, and Renaissance sculpture, plus a collection of Asian art in the attached Hackerman House.

Modeled after Italian Renaissance and baroque palace designs, the main museum building is a work of art itself. The collection is displayed in curved, light-filled hallways and tiny, dimly lit galleries, with spotlights shining on the treasures. The paintings are displayed in three ballrooms, with lush rose, blue, and gold brocade walls, and the sculptures stand in a two-story Renaissance central court.

Attached to the gallery by walkways, the Hackerman House, an 1850s mansion, exhibits the gallery's collection of Japanese, Chinese, Korean, and Indian ceramics, sculpture, calligraphy, and prints. The house itself is exquisite, with curving staircase, soaring rotunda, and lavishly carved ceilings. Don't miss the wood-paneled and brocade-walled Peach Bloom Library, where priceless Japanese ceramics and Chinese jade are on display. The Walters Gallery is open Tuesday to Friday 10:00 A.M. to 4:00 P.M., Saturday and Sunday 11:00 A.M. to 5:00 P.M. Admission is $5.00 for adults, $3.00 for seniors and college students, and $1:00 for children six to seventeen; children under six are admitted free. Phone (410) 547–9000, www.thewalters.org.

A good place for afternoon coffee or tea is the **Woman's Industrial Exchange,** 333 North Charles Street (410–685–4388), located 3 blocks south of the museum in an 1815 building with Flemish brickwork, marble stoops, and wrought-iron railings. Open Monday to Saturday for breakfast and lunch. Lunch (fresh-made soups, thick sandwiches, and old-fashioned desserts) stops at 2:30 P.M., but the gift shop and bakery stay open until 3:00 P.M. Established after the Civil War as a place for women to sell handiwork, the little shop is still a place to buy crafts and linger over a cup of coffee or tea. You'll feel that you've been transported to a British tearoom that is the opposite of fancy; the setting is spare, the thirty-some tables are set far apart, and conversations are hushed. It's been a favorite of locals for more than a century.

--456115 CLOSED UNTIL 8:50AM
AMERICAN EXPRESS   20.48
XXXXXXXXXXXXXX004   XXXXX
Total-Credit Card 20.48
Tax   1.18
Subtotal   19.31
1 HOT BEV   1.09
1 SUB HASH BR $ 0.69
1 SUB HASH BR $ 0.69
STANDARD # EGGS
1 SMKHOUSE SAU   4.89
STANDARD # EGGS
1 SMKHOUSE SAU   4.89
STANDARD # EGGS
1 SMKHOUSE SAU   4.89
1 HOT BEV   1.09
1 HOT BEV   1.09

CUG16'04 8:30AM
3:3 2/1   2 1 3-7   OCT 3

JASON KIM K
YORK, PA
Cracker Barrel Store #195

While you're on North Charles Street, spend a little time walking in the pleasant **Mount Vernon neighborhood,** which has brick streets, magnolia trees, upscale shops, and inviting park benches.

At the intersection of North Charles Street and Monument Street is the **Washington Monument,** a 178-foot-tall marble column begun in 1815, the first monument erected to honor George Washington. If you're willing to climb the 220-plus steps, you'll have a dizzying view of the downtown area. Phone (410) 396–0929. Just northeast of the monument is the **Mount Vernon Methodist Church,** a green-stone Gothic tower that's worth a visit.

Be sure to stop in at the **Peabody Musical Conservatory's Library** at 17 East Mount Vernon Place; (410) 659–8197. Even if you're not a music scholar visiting the library to examine the original manuscripts by Beethoven or Handel, you'll enjoy the six-tiered main hall with its enormous skylight. It's what every library wishes it looked like. Open weekdays 9:00 A.M. to 3:00 P.M. Admission is free.

When you're done, you can sit on a bench in the narrow strip of grassy park that stretches east of the Washington Monument and listen to music drifting out of the windows of the nearby conservatory—America's first music academy, and locals would say its finest.

Then walk 3 blocks south to the corner of Mulberry and Cathedral Streets, where you'll see the **Basilica of the Assumption,** which is the oldest Roman Catholic cathedral in the United States. Designed by Benjamin Latrobe, who also helped design the U.S. Capitol, the basilica is justly famous for its stained glass windows. Open daily 9:00 A.M. to 4:00 P.M.; (410) 727–3564.

Walk a couple of blocks west on Mulberry Street to Howard Street, turn right, and head north, and you'll find **Antique Row,** a 2-block section of Howard Street between Read and Madison Streets that includes more than two dozen antiques shops, with everything from estate jewelry and rare children's books to furniture and vintage clothes.

DINNER: Baltimore has many excellent restaurants, but a perfect pick for every visit to town is **Maison Marconi,** a local institution. With its tuxedo-clad waiters, crystal chandeliers, and old-fashioned menu featuring such scrumptious standbys as lamb chops with mint jelly, soft-shell crabs, and first-rate aged steaks, Marconi's is an elegant classic that hasn't changed much since it was founded in 1920. Whatever you order, ask for creamed spinach and a chopped-and-tossed-at-your-table salad on the side. And for dessert, everybody seems to know that they should order the ice cream with hot fudge. It comes with your own huge, private bowl of hot fudge. Located at 106 West Saratoga; (410) 727–9522. Open Tuesday to Saturday. Reservations necessary. Moderate to expensive.

LODGING: You'll spend the night at the **Admiral Fell Inn,** 888 South Broadway; (410) 522–7377 or (800) 292–4667, www.admiralfell.com. This beautiful inn started out as a seaman's hostel along the wharf and is now an eighty-room European-style hotel in the heart of Fell's Point. All the rooms are decorated with Federal period furnishings, and the Admiral Fell offers complimentary afternoon tea and continental breakfast. Rates: $160–$199 for rooms, $219–$399 for suites.

DAY 2

Morning

BREAKFAST: Admiral Fell Inn.

After breakfast, take the water taxi ($4.50 for adults, $2.00 for children ten and under for a day pass) to **Inner Harbor,** Baltimore's restored waterfront area. Head directly to one of the city's greatest attractions, the **National Aquarium,** at Pier 3, 501 East Pratt Street; (410) 576–3800, www.aqua.org. Open daily 10:00 A.M. to 5:00 P.M.; until 8:00 P.M. on Fridays and most days during the summer. Admission is $11.95 for adults, $10.50 for seniors, $7.50 for children three to eleven; children under three are admitted free.

Particularly on weekends, it's a good idea to get to the aquarium early because they sensibly limit the flow of the crowd, which generates long lines and often means buying a ticket for later in the day. (You can also order tickets for a specific time slot by telephoning Ticketmaster at least a day in advance and paying by credit card. Call 202–432–7328 or 410–481–7328.)

The aquarium is an appropriately grand building for its extraordinary collection of 5,000-plus creatures. The first thing you'll see when you enter is an immense central pool, which is visible from each of the building's four floors. Sharks, stingrays, and a mammoth sea turtle swim silently through the pool and are endlessly fascinating to watch. There's a "please touch" exhibit, where kids can hold a starfish, and there's also an Atlantic coral reef. On the top floor is an Amazonian rain forest, complete with waterfalls, heavy mist, tree sloths, and tropical birds.

Baltimore's Inner Harbor

But everybody's favorites at the aquarium are the dolphins. The Marine Mammal Pavilion, housed in an adjoining building, has an enormous pool and bleachers that seat hundreds who come to see the dolphins at play. An educational show teaches kids and adults about marine conservation and passes on interesting information about the dolphins, but the graceful creatures themselves are the stars. At the clap of a trainer's hands, the dolphins dive, race, flip, and jump, and they seem as affectionate as puppies when they swim back to the trainer for a congratulatory rubdown. (Note: Ask for show times at the counter when you pick up your tickets.)

Outside, it's just a short stroll over to the **Harborplace** shops and restaurants, the indoor mall and food court that draws thousands of visitors. The shopping, for the most part, is dominated by the big mall chains. You'll probably end up eating some greasy food at a stand-up counter, but, like everyone else, you'll love it. Harborplace is located at 200 East Pratt Street; (410) 332–4191, www.harborplace.com.

LUNCH: If you didn't succumb to temptation at the Harborplace french fry and fudge shops, take the water taxi back to Fell's Point for lunch at **Jimmy's Restaurant,** 803 Broadway; (410) 327–3273. This favorite of Baltimore natives features sandwiches and blue plate specials like meat loaf and pork chops, which you can eat while you sit at a table with a red-and-white-checked tablecloth and watch the neighborhood stroll by. Inexpensive.

Afternoon

After lunch, walk off the calories with a tour of **Fell's Point.** This marvelous wharf neighborhood dates from 1726, and is older than Baltimore itself. It has a combination of cobblestone and brick streets, old warehouses, jazz clubs, front stoops, 1850-era stained glass house numbers, and lots of personality. On Fells Point Square, you can buy fresh pretzels and lemonade and sit on benches.

The shops ringing the area are a fun mélange of junk stores, antiques shops, galleries, bookstores, and coffeeshops. Don't miss the **China Sea Marine Trading Company** right along the wharf at Ann Street, which sells ship salvage, hardware from obsolete ships, sailor caps, scrimshaw, and lots of other curiosities. Next door at 905 South Ann Street is **Japonaji,** which has Japanese art, books, antiques, screens, jewelry, and much more. Also interesting is the **Art Gallery of Fell's Point** at 1716 Thames Street, which features works by Maryland artists, and **P.J.'s Place,** at 1704 Lancaster Street, which has a year-round Christmas room and great souvenirs. Be sure to walk through the **Broadway Market,** where you can get a cup of coffee and a pastry to tide you over until dinner. The market is located on Broadway between Lancaster and Fleet Streets. Nearly all Fell's Point shops are open seven days a week.

After being on your feet all day, you'll want to take advantage of the Admiral Fell Inn's complimentary afternoon tea before dressing for dinner.

DINNER: An excellent choice is **Helmand,** an Afghan restaurant with tasty, meal-size appetizers, including leek-filled pasta with mint and yogurt sauce and pastry shells stuffed with beef and onions and smothered with peas and carrots. Entrees include char-grilled rack of lamb, and baby eggplant stuffed with spinach. Save room for the ice-cream dessert served with figs, dates, and mango. Helmand is one of those rare finds where you can get a four-star dinner, including dessert, for less than $20. Located at 806 North Charles Street; (410) 752–0311. Open for dinner only.

If you are interested in evening entertainment, you can choose from the following: The Baltimore Symphony performs at the **Joseph Meyerhoff**

Symphony Hall (1212 Cathedral Street, 410–783–8000); the Baltimore Opera Company performs at the **Lyric Opera House** (140 West Mount Royal Avenue, 410–494–2712); concerts and recitals are held at the **Peabody Conservatory of Music** (1 East Mount Vernon Place, 410–659–8124); plays are staged at the **Morris A. Mechanic Theater** (Baltimore and Charles Streets, 410–625–4230); and the **Baltimore Orioles** play at Oriole Park at Camden Yards (Camden and Eutaw Streets, 410–685–9800).

LODGING: Admiral Fell Inn.

DAY 3

Morning

BREAKFAST: Admiral Fell Inn.

After a leisurely breakfast, drive to the **Baltimore Museum of Art,** located at Art Museum Drive and North Charles Street (at Thirty-first Street); (410) 396–7100, www.artbma.org. Open Wednesday to Friday 11:00 A.M. to 5:00 P.M., Saturday and Sunday 11:00 A.M. to 6:00 P.M. Admission is $6.00 for adults and $4.00 for seniors; students and everyone under eighteen are admitted free.

This fabulous museum is Maryland's largest. It is home to the world's second largest collection of Andy Warhol's work, an enormous collection of decorative arts (with period rooms outfitted with precious furniture, china, and paintings), and the Cone Collection, with more than a hundred paintings and sculptures by Matisse, Picasso, Renoir, Cézanne, van Gogh, and Gauguin. As if that weren't enough, the Baltimore Museum of Art also has hundreds of pre-Columbian, African, and Oceanian works of art, and new exhibitions are coming and going all the time.

LUNCH: It's your last meal in town, and you haven't yet been to a diner. Try **Paper Moon Diner,** a real, twenty-four-hour-a-day Baltimore diner just a few blocks south of the museum. You can, of course, get meat loaf, but you can also get meatless burgers and sweet-potato fries. Located at 227 West Twenty-ninth Street; (410) 889–4444. Inexpensive.

Afternoon

Your last adventure in the area is a trip about forty-five minutes north of Baltimore to visit the **Ladew Topiary Gardens,** located at 3535 Jarrettsville

Pike, Monkton; (410) 557–9570. To get there from Baltimore, take Interstate 83 from downtown to the Beltway (Interstate 695). Head east to exit 27, then drive 14 miles north on State Highway 146 (Dulaney Valley Road). Ladew is open Monday to Friday 10:00 A.M. to 4:00 P.M., Saturday and Sunday 10:30 A.M. to 4:30 P.M. mid-April through October 31. Admission for the house and gardens is $12.00 for adults, $11.00 for seniors, and $4.00 for children.

Said by the Garden Club of America to be "the most outstanding topiary garden in America," the estate and grounds of Harvey Smith Ladew actually offer many more delights than the whimsical carved shrubs that are its claim to fame. A tour of the home is a must; Ladew was an extraordinarily eccentric man as well as talented painter and collector, and the house is strewn with trompe l'oeil paintings. Everyone loves the Oval Library he built for an over-size desk he imported from England.

But save the bulk of your time for the gardens. There you can wander for hours, which is what it will take to see it all. You will be enchanted with the hedges, including the famous "fox hunt," with boxwood horses, riders, and dogs chasing a boxwood fox across the lawn. In addition to the long alleys of topiaries, the gardens include an enormous crystal pool, a teahouse, a croquet court, and a rose garden. Harvey Smith Ladew also planned and planted many garden "rooms"—hedge-enclosed areas filled with shrubs, vines, and flowers. For example, there is the pink garden, planted to bloom with pink color from earliest spring to late fall, and the white garden, with thirty-five species that bloom in white throughout the growing season.

When you've finished your tour of the gardens, return to Washington via State Highway 146 south, I–695 (the Baltimore Beltway), and I–95 or State Highway 295 (the Baltimore-Washington Parkway). The drive will take you about ninety minutes.

THERE'S MORE

Baltimore Zoo. Fourteen major animal exhibits including lions, elephants, hippos, reptiles, and birds. Druid Hill Park; (410) 396–7102, www. baltimorezoo.org. Open daily 10:00 A.M. to 4:00 P.M. Admission is $9.00 for adults, $5.50 for senior citizens and children two to fifteen; children under two are admitted free.

Maryland Science Center. Hands-on science museum that includes the Davis Planetarium and a 50-foot IMAX theater; an afternoon's worth of fun for kids. Located at 601 Light Street; (410) 685–2370, www. mdsci.org. Open weekdays 10:00 A.M. to 5:00 P.M., weekends 10:00 A.M. to 6:00 P.M. Admission is $10.50 for adults and $9.00 for senior citizens and children four to twelve; children under four are admitted free.

Babe Ruth Birthplace and Baltimore Orioles Museum. A small museum devoted to the Babe, complete with a film and lots of memorabilia. Also the official museum of the hometown Orioles. Located at 216 Emory Street; (410) 727–1539 or (800) 435–2223, www.baberuthmuseum.com. Open daily 10 A.M. to 5:00 P.M.; 10:00 A.M. to 7:00 P.M. during the Orioles' home games. Admission is $6.00 for adults, $4.00 for senior citizens, $3.00 for children five to sixteen, free for children under five.

Jewish Museum of Maryland. This museum and archive operated by the Jewish Historical Society of Maryland is the largest institution in America devoted to regional American Jewish history. Located at 15 Lloyd Street; (410) 732–6400. Open Tuesday to Thursday and Sunday noon to 4:00 P.M. Admission is $4.00 for adults and $2.00 for children twelve and over; children under twelve are admitted free.

Lovely Lane Church and Museum. Stanford White–designed church that is the mother church of Methodism in the United States. Unique circular sanctuary with domed ceiling that makes for wonderful acoustics. 2200 St. Paul Street; (410) 889–1512. Open Monday to Friday 9:00 A.M. to 3:00 P.M. No admission charge.

B&O Railroad Museum. Collection of railroad cars of every type exhibited in a railway roundhouse. Kids can even scramble onto some of the old engines. Located at 901 West Pratt Street; (410) 752–2490, www.borail.org. Open daily 10:00 A.M. to 5:00 P.M. except for major holidays. Admission $6.50 for adults, $5.50 for seniors, $4.00 for children three to twelve, free for children under three.

Baltimore Maritime Museum. The museum houses the U.S.S. *Torsk,* a World War II submarine, and the lightship *Chesapeake,* a floating lighthouse. Located at Pier III, Inner Harbor (Pratt Street); (410) 396–3453. Open daily 11:00 A.M. to 6:00 P.M., extended hours in the summer. Admission is $5.50 for adults, $4.50 for seniors, $3.00 for children five to twelve, free for children under five.

SPECIAL EVENTS

May. Preakness Horse Race. Second jewel in racing's Triple Crown for three-year-olds at Pimlico Race Course; parades and other events. (410) 542–9400.

June–August. Concert series at Ladew Topiary Gardens. Bluegrass, big-band music, bagpipes, steel bands, country and western, and more. (410) 557–9570.

July. Fourth of July Celebration. Fireworks, music, food, and entertainment at the Inner Harbor. (410) 837–4636 or (800) 282–6632.

July. Artscape. Food, music, and display of works by local artists. (410) 396–4575.

October. Fell's Point Fun Fest. Bands, beer, arts and crafts, music of all kinds. (410) 675–6756.

OTHER RECOMMENDED RESTAURANTS

Germano's Trattoria, 300 South High Street; (410) 752–4515. Little Italy favorite for more than twenty years. Pleasant dining room; great bread, al dente pasta, osso buco, Tuscan specialties. Moderate.

Hampton's, 550 Light Street; (410) 234–0550. Enjoy four-star new-American cuisine overlooking the Inner Harbor. Many consider it one of America's top restaurants. Expensive.

Azeb's Ethiopian Restaurant, 322 North Charles Street; (410) 625–9787. New Mount Vernon favorite serving traditional Ethiopian chicken, beef, and vegetable dishes that you eat with enjera, the thin, spongy bread that also doubles as plate and silverware. Moderate.

Cafe Viet, 800 North Charles Street; (410) 332–1554. Mount Vernon–area Vietnamese restaurant featuring spring rolls, rice paper rolls, pho, sataylike pork and chicken, and more adventuresome fare. Inexpensive.

Charleston, 1000 Lancaster Street; (410) 332–7373. Highly touted; New Southern menu includes seafood, Cajun specialties, wild-boar chops, greens, grits, and great desserts. Moderate to expensive.

Obrycki's Crab House, 1727 East Pratt Street; (410) 732–6399. Tops for no-frills, order-by-the-dozen steamed crabs. Moderate.

Bertha's, 734 South Broadway; (410) 327–5795. Famous for its mussels, afternoon tea, jazz, and bumper stickers. Moderate.

Bombay Grill, 2 East Madison Street; (410) 837–2973. Try the tandoori chicken with a tongue-scalding side order of stir-fried okra and onions. Moderate.

Kawasaki, 413 North Charles Street; (410) 659–7600. Casual Japanese restaurant with more than forty offerings of sushi and sashimi. The teriyakis are also great. Moderate.

OTHER RECOMMENDED LODGINGS

The Inn at Henderson's Wharf, 1000 Fell Street; (410) 522–7777 or (800) 522–2088, www.hendersonswharf.com. Century-old former tobacco warehouse converted into a thirty-eight-room English country–style inn in Fell's Point; landscaped courtyard; continental breakfast. Rates: $125–$189, depending on room size and season.

Clarion Hotel at Mount Vernon Square, 612 Cathedral Street; (410) 727–7101 or (800) 292–5500. Renovated European-style hotel in Mount Vernon neighborhood has 103 beautifully decorated and furnished rooms. Rates: $130–$190.

Scarborough Fair, 1 East Montgomery Street; (410) 837–0010, www.scarborough-fair.com. Six-room B&B near the Inner Harbor; all rooms have private baths, some have fireplaces and whirlpools. Library, afternoon refreshments, off-street parking; full breakfast served. Rates: $119–$149.

Ann Street Bed and Breakfast, 804 South Ann Street; (410) 342–5883. Charming eighteenth-century house in Fell's Point restored in Colonial style. Three guest rooms with private baths and fireplaces; pleasant garden; full breakfast. Rates: $85–$95.

Abercombie Badger Bed and Breakfast, 58 West Biddle Street; (410) 244–7227, www.badger-inn.com. Nicely furnished fifteen-room mid town inn. All rooms have air-conditioning, private baths, and phones; continental breakfast served. Rates: $105–$145.

Celies's Waterfront Bed and Breakfast, 1714 Thames Street; (410) 522–2323 or (800) 432–0184, www.bbonline.com/md/celies. Large new house with seven nicely furnished guest rooms and a rooftop deck; some rooms have whirlpools and fireplaces. Rates: $136–$220.

Biltmore Suites, 205 West Madison Street; (410) 728–6550. Eighteenth-century building converted to a bed-and-breakfast inn with twenty-eight guest rooms, many of them suites. Breakfast is fruit, cereal, coffee, and muffins or bagels. Rates: $109–$149.

FOR MORE INFORMATION

Baltimore Area Visitors Association, 100 Light Street, 12th Floor, Baltimore, MD 21202; (410) 659–7300 or (800) 343–3468, www.baltimore.org.

Antietam National Battlefield and Catoctin Mountain

A WEEKEND FOR CHILDREN AND ADULTS

1 NIGHT

Civil War battlefield • Children's museum
Hiking • Swimming • Boating • Zoo

It seems ironic that the Civil War's bloodiest battles were fought in such a beautiful region of the United States. Near Frederick, Maryland, are rolling, wooded hills, fields of corn, and quiet towns that witnessed some of the most significant events in American history.

Maryland's Antietam National Battlefield is the highlight of this weekend visit. It brings the past to life, with lectures, tours, war relics, and an excellent film reenacting the epic battle between Union and Confederate troops in which more people were killed and wounded than on any other single day of the Civil War. One historian describes the guns of Antietam "slashing at rows of men and corn," and as you walk through the battlefield you can imagine what it must have been like.

North-central Maryland offers many nooks and crannies to explore; this itinerary includes some of particular interest to children. In addition to Antietam, which will fascinate adults and kids alike, you'll enjoy picnicking and swimming at Catoctin Mountain and Cunningham Falls Parks, a visit to a zoo with small animals to pet, and a trip to a children's museum in Frederick.

All this and more is included in a 200-mile driving loop through Maryland's gorgeous countryside, with forests, wildflowers, old stone fences, and the misty mountains looming everywhere.

DAY 1

Morning

Start your morning by packing a picnic lunch and hitting the road by about 9:00 A.M. Your first stop is in **Frederick,** about 45 miles northwest of Washington on Interstate 270.

When you reach Frederick, don't be deterred by the strip-mall feel to the outskirts of town. Follow the signs to Historic Frederick and you'll be rewarded by a serene, nineteenth-century town with old brick buildings, antique stores, and grand old homes.

While in Frederick, plan to spend an hour or so at **The Children's Museum of Rose Hill Manor Park.** Rose Hill Manor is the historic home of Thomas Johnson, Maryland's first elected governor. The estate is now an interactive children's museum set in a forty-three-acre park, where kids are asked to "please touch" some of the exhibits.

Rose Hill's kindly volunteers teach little people something about what America was like 200 years ago by letting them play with replicas of antique toys and dress up in old-fashioned aprons and hats. They'll be asked to "find the bathroom" in antique rooms where chamber pots lurk beneath beds, and in the restored kitchen they can handle the homemade pigfat soap and nineteenth-century tools. They can help spin and weave in one room, pick out their favorite "car" in the shed housing twenty-five restored carriages and sleighs, and try out the antique rope bed in the 150-year-old log cabin on the property. Located at 1611 North Market Street, Frederick; (301) 694–1646. Open Monday to Saturday 10:00 A.M. to 4:00 P.M., Sunday 1:00 to 4:00 P.M., April through October, and the same hours weekends during November; closed December through March. Admission is $3.00 for adults and $2.00 for seniors and children three through seventeen. Children two and under are admitted free.

If you didn't pack a picnic lunch at home, you can pick up food to go in Frederick at **The Deli,** 55 East Patrick Street (301–663–8122), or **Beans and Bagels,** 49 East Patrick Street (301–620–2165). Both places have sandwiches, salads, soft drinks, and coffee.

From Frederick, drive about 15 miles west on Alternate U.S. Highway 40 to Boonsboro and then about 6 miles west to Sharpsburg on State Highway 34.

LUNCH: Stop en route to eat your lunch at **Washington Monument State Park,** which is about halfway to Boonsboro on Alternate U.S. Highway 40. There are picnic tables and a playground very near the parking lot.

After lunch, take a ten-minute walk up to the monument itself, which the citizens of Boonsboro erected in a single day in 1827 in honor of George Washington. It was restored in 1933 by the Civilian Conservation Corps. The oddly shaped building (rather like a great, stone milk bottle) commands a panoramic view of the valley below and the Blue Ridge Mountains beyond, which you can see even better by climbing up the interior stairway to the top. Phone (301) 791–4767.

Afternoon

The afternoon is devoted to an exploration of **Antietam National Battlefield,** which is one of the National Park Service's many great historic treasures. The battlefield is located just north of Sharpsburg on State Highway 65; (301) 432–5124, www.nps.gov/anti. Open daily 8:30 A.M. to 6:00 P.M., until 5:00 P.M. in winter. Admission is $2.00 a person, $4.00 for a family.

Here, on just a few acres of hills and cornfields, 12,410 Confederates and 10,700 Federal troops were killed or wounded in a single day, September 17, 1862. While the battle itself was not a definitive victory for either side—both sides might be said to have lost, given the massive casualties—Antietam was significant in that the North's failure to convincingly defeat General Lee's army prolonged the war by many months. At the same time, the Confederates' failure to hold the area was important in that it caused Great Britain to postpone recognition of the Confederacy, which was under consideration at the time.

Begin your tour at the visitors center. There you can pick up a map of the battlefield and watch an excellent orientation film. With a background of Civil War songs and quotes from actual soldiers' letters, the film reenacts the battle of Antietam (or the battle of Sharpsville, as the Confederates called it).

Be sure to visit the small museum at the lower level of the visitors center. It includes a collection of artifacts from the battle, including weapons, uniforms, letters, photographs, and medical equipment. It also has an interesting display of quotations from those who participated in the battle. Consider this from one of the soldiers: "The consuming passion in the breast of the average man is to get out of the way . . ." Union Major Joseph Hooker wrote, "It has never been my fortune to witness a more bloody, dismal battlefield."

But the highlight of the park is the battlefield itself. You can take a self-guided 6- or 7-mile tour by bike, foot, or car. Each site is carefully labeled with signs describing the battle in detail, and you can rent a tape recorder and cassette that walks you through every phase of the battle. Better, go on an hour-and-a-half tour with a Park Service guide. These Interior Department employees are exceptionally knowledgeable, friendly, and eager to share their love of Civil War history.

The Park Service also offers an extensive range of lectures and presentations at the headquarters that both adults and children will find mesmerizing. Pick up a schedule of ranger programs on the day you visit—there will be three or four different programs throughout the day, including specialized lectures and tours on such topics as "A Soldier's Perspective" or the use of artillery in the Civil War.

When you have completed your visit to Antietam, turn back to Hagerstown, where you'll dine and spend the night. Your dinner destination is about 14 miles from Antietam. You can reach it by driving north on State Highway 65 to Hagerstown and then heading west on Wilson Boulevard to Virginia Avenue (U.S. Highway 11). Turn south and the restaurant is a couple of blocks away on your right.

DINNER: Junction 808, 808 Noland Drive at Virginia Avenue, Hagerstown (301–791–3639), is a family-run and family-oriented restaurant serving '50s-style main dishes and sandwiches kids will love.. Inexpensive; for example, a hamburger with fries and soda is $3.25.

To find your resting place for the night, return to Wilson Boulevard and drive east a few blocks to Downsville Pike (State Highway 632). Follow it south a few miles to your lodgings.

LODGING: Lewrene Farm B&B, 9738 Downsville Pike, Hagerstown; (301) 582–1735, www.virtualcities.com. Lewrene Farm is a century-old farmhouse on a 125-acre working farm with chickens, peacocks, and cattle nearby. It has six spacious guest rooms, two of which combine to make a suite. All rooms have poster or canopy beds; three of the rooms have private baths. Children are welcome. Rates: $55–$115 a night.

DAY 2

Morning and Afternoon

BREAKFAST: Enjoy the pancakes, sausage, and homemade applesauce at Lewrene Farm. In season, you might also get sweet corn on the cob, picked that morning at the farm.

After breakfast, head for Catoctin Mountain, which you reach by driving 4 miles north on State Highway 65 to Hagerstown, 7 miles east on State Highway 64 to Smithburg, and 5 miles east on State Highway 77 (Foxville Road) to the parks.

There are two adjoining parks located on Catoctin Mountain: **Catoctin Mountain Park,** administered by the National Park Service, and **Cunningham Falls State Park.** The parks, which are in a 6,000-acre forest preserve, offer wilderness hiking, camping, horseback riding, and swimming. Start at the visitors center at Catoctin Mountain Park and pick up a map. With more than 25 miles of marked trails, there is a hike for everybody, from thirty minutes of easy walking to a six-hour round-trip of strenuous scrambling.

In spring and fall, Catoctin offers orienteering courses, but the classes fill up quickly, so reserve early if you're interested. Other activities you can enjoy at the parks are scenic drives, snowshoeing, cross-country skiing, canoeing, sailing, and swimming. So pick your pleasure and relax for the day at the "park of presidents." (Camp David is located within Catoctin Mountain Park but is not available for touring.)

LUNCH: There are two snack bars at Cunningham Falls State Park. One is located at the swimming area at Hunting Creek Lake, the other near the falls. Both have sandwiches and ice cream.

While you're there, be sure to see the spectacular waterfall, the largest in Maryland. You can take a long hike and end up at the falls, or go there directly from your car on a wheelchair-accessible 200-yard trail.

The parks are open dawn to dusk, except for campers. The phone number for Catoctin Mountain Park is (301) 663–9388, www.nps.gov/cato. For Cunningham Falls State Park, phone (301) 271–7574.

Leave time at the end of the afternoon for one final activity. Just 3 miles south of the parks is **Catoctin Wildlife Preserve and Zoo,** U.S. Highway 15, Thurmont; (301) 271–3180, www.cwpzoo.com. Open 9:00 A.M. to 6:00 P.M. from May through September, 10:00 A.M. to 5:00 P.M. in April and October; closed November through March. Admission is $9.95 for adults and $6.75 for kids two to twelve; children under two admitted free.

Here, many of the animals are outdoors and have plenty of space to roam. There are also a few cages of wild animals, including a tiger and a grizzly bear. For the most part, though, animals and visitors alike seem to be pleased. A peacock struts about on the same paths as the people, and emus, deer, and other creatures graze happily in a large enclosure. There is an aviary full of bright parrots, a baboon cage, and an alligator pool.

Canoeing in Cunningham Falls State Park

The best thing about the zoo park, though, is the petting area where you can enter a large pasture and pet and snuggle the animals to your heart's content. There is a 575-pound tortoise, a potbellied pig, goats, and sheep. But the most affectionate of all are the pygmy goats from Africa. These darling creatures (the young stand no more than 18 inches high) will come thundering toward you the minute you enter their pen and frisk about joyfully when you scratch their ears. Even the tiniest child (or the oldest adult) will want to pat them.

DINNER: After an afternoon of hiking and swimming, an all-you-can-eat dinner seems just right. Go where everybody who visits the area eventually ends up: the **Cozy Restaurant,** 103 Frederick Road (State Highway 806) about 5 blocks from U.S. Highway 15, Thurmont; (301) 271–7373.

You sort of have to see the Cozy to believe it. In the first place, it's anything but cozy. With room after adjoining room, the Cozy can feed more than 700 people in a pinch. And when is the last time you ate at a restaurant that has its own newspaper? You might call it "the diner that ate Thurmont."

Consider the food: For starters, there's always fried chicken, meat loaf, fried fish, ham, mashed potatoes, macaroni salads, and dozens of other home-style dishes at reasonable prices. (Kids under twelve can get a chicken drumstick dinner with unlimited trips to the salad and dessert bars for $3.99.) The dessert bar is enormous; there are eighteen different kinds of pie alone. Also there's a separate ice-cream parlor, a darkly lit bar, and a bakery. Pinball machines line the hallways, and there are lots of trinkets for sale. The trinkets have expanded to the Cozy's cluster of stores across the street. Needless to say, kids and tourists of every description adore the place, and they come here by the busload.

The 60-mile drive back to Washington via U.S. Highway 15 and Interstate 270 will take you just over an hour.

THERE'S MORE

Covered Bridges. There are two covered bridges very near Thurmont. The 40-foot-long Roddy Road Covered Bridge is located just north of Thurmont on Roddy Creek Road less than a mile from U.S. Highway 15. The 90-foot-long Loy's Station Covered Bridge is a few miles west of town on Old Frederick Road just off State Highway 77 east. A third bridge, the 101-foot-long Utica Mills Covered Bridge is located on Old Frederick Road southwest of Thurmont.

Used Books. Wonder Book and Video, the largest used bookstore in the Washington-Baltimore area (with more than 300,000 books and thousands of used comic books), is located at 1306 West Patrick Street (U.S. Highway 40 west) in Frederick; (301) 694–5955. Open Monday to Saturday 10:00 A.M. to 10:00 P.M., Sunday noon to 10:00 P.M.

Antiques. Frederick, Emmitsburg (22 miles north of Frederick on U.S. Highway 15), Middletown (8 miles west of Frederick on U.S. Highway 40), and New Market (10 miles east of Frederick on State Highway 144) have some of the best antiques in the state of Maryland. Particularly recommended are the shops on West Main Street in New Market.

Crystal Grottoes Cavern. Maryland's only commercial underground cave. Located at 19821 Shepardstown Pike near Boonsboro; (301) 432–6336. Open daily 9:00 A.M. to 6:00 P.M. from March through September, 11:00 A.M. to 5:00 P.M. October through February. Admission is $8.50 for adults, $4.50 for children eleven and under.

Family Recreation Park. Large commercial park with picnic area at 21036 National Pike, Boonsboro (6 miles east of Hagerstown on U.S. Highway 40—not Alternate Route 40). It also has a snack bar, miniature golf, driving range, batting cages, go-carts, and lots of other attractions for children. Phone (301) 733–2333. Open daily noon to 11:00 P.M. in season.

SPECIAL EVENTS

May. Memorial Day Parade and Ceremony. Oldest Memorial Day parade in the nation. Antietam National Battlefield. (301) 432–8410.

June. Strawberry Festival. Antique car show, crafts, square dancing, and lots of strawberries at the Cozy Village in Thurmont. (301) 271–4301.

June. Frederick Festival of the Arts. Juried art exhibits along the Carroll Creek Promenade in downtown Frederick. (301) 694–9632.

September. Battle Anniversary Weekend at Antietam National Battlefield Park. Annual event features battlefield encampments, special walking tours, and a Saturday night torchlight tour for which reservations are necessary. (301) 432–5124 or (800) 228–7829.

October. Fall Festival at Rose Hill Manor. Hay rides, antique tractor and horse pull, children's games. (301) 694–1650.

October. Catoctin Colorfest. Arts and crafts fair in Thurmont. (301) 271–4432.

November–December. Maryland Christmas Show. More than 500 artists and craftspeople and thousands of customers fill seven buildings and numerous tents at the Frederick County Fairgrounds in Frederick. (301) 898–5466.

OTHER RECOMMENDED RESTAURANTS

Frederick

Di Francesco's Ristorante, 26 North Market Street; (301) 695–5499. Fresh pasta, casual setting. Moderate.

The Province Restaurant, 129 North Market Street; (301) 663–1441. Elegant but casual restaurant with new-American menu in downtown Frederick. Moderate.

Brown Pelican, 5 East Church Street; (301) 695–5833. Fine dining in downtown Frederick; veal, seafood, and daily specials. Moderate.

Boonsboro

Old South Mountain Inn, 6132 Old National Pike; (301) 432–6155. This beautiful and capacious restaurant, situated in a 250-year-old building, has a contemporary menu in a Colonial setting. Ask for a seat in the garden room, with an excellent view of the surrounding countryside. Moderate to expensive. If you happen to be in the area on Sunday morning, the all-you-can-eat brunch (including casseroles, round of beef, eggs, waffles, pastries, fruit, and more) is a mere $13.95.

Thurmont

Mountain Gate Family Restaurant, 133 Frederick Road; (301) 271–4373. Breakfast, lunch, and dinner buffets. Also full menu with dinner specials and sandwiches. Moderate.

Best place for doughnuts: Busy Bee Bakery, 410 Frederick Road, Thurmont; (301) 271–4100. Open at 4:00 A.M. for early birds.

For additional listings, see Maryland Escape Six (page 128) and Pennsylvania Escape Six (page 260).

OTHER RECOMMENDED LODGINGS

Sharpsburg

Piper House Bed and Breakfast, located in Antietam National Battlefield on State Highway 65; (301) 797–1862. The Piper House was used as a battlefield headquarters by Confederate General James Longstreet during the battle of Antietam and as a field hospital where wounded soldiers from both sides were treated thereafter. Now it is a pleasant B&B with three bedrooms furnished with antiques, and modern bathrooms. Children must be ten or older. The $85–$95 tariff includes a full breakfast.

Inn at Antietam, 220 East Main Street, Sharpsburg; (301) 432–6601. Restored country Victorian nicely furnished with antiques; four guest suites with private baths. The wraparound porch with swings and rockers is a great place to relax. Full breakfast served. Rates: $110–$135. A fifth, extra-large suite (1,000 square feet) rents for $150–$175 a night.

Thurmont

Cozy Country Inn, State Highway 806 just off U.S. Highway 15, Thurmont; (301) 271–4301, www.cozyvillage.com. Standard motel with twenty-one newly remodeled rooms, some with Jacuzzis. Fine for families; presidential aides and the national press corps staking out Camp David often stay there too. Rates: $45–$150.

Bluebird on the Mountain, State Highway 550 north of Thurmont near Cascade; (301) 241–4161 or (800) 362–9526, www.bbonline.com/md/bluebird. Century-old manor house with five guest rooms, all with private baths; some rooms have Jacuzzis and fireplaces. Rates: $95–$125.

Catoctin Mountain National Park (301–663–5895) has a fifty-one-site, wooded, no-reservation campground. Sites rent for $12; cabins rent for $40 and up. Cunningham Falls State Park (301–271–7574) has 180 campsites that rent for $13–$23.

Keedysville

Antietam Overlook Farm, Keedysville; (301) 432–4200 or (800) 878–4241, www.innbook.com/inns/antietam. Mountaintop country inn with a four-state view. All of the inn's six rooms have antiques, fireplaces, and garden baths; full country breakfast. Rates: $115–$165.

For additional listings see Maryland Escape Six (page 128) and Pennsylvania Escape Six (page 260).

FOR MORE INFORMATION

Tourism Council of Frederick County and Frederick Visitors Center, 19 East Church Street, Frederick, MD 21701; (301) 663–8687 or (800) 999–3613, www.visitfrederick.org.

Antietam National Battlefield and Cemetery, Box 158, Sharpsburg, MD 21782; (301) 432–5124, www.nps.gov/anti.

Hagerstown/Washington County Convention and Visitors Bureau, 16 Public Square, Hagerstown, MD 21740; (301) 791–3246 or (800) 228–7829, www.marylandmemories.org.

MARYLAND

Western Maryland

HEADING WEST ON THE NATIONAL PIKE

2 NIGHTS

Back-roads drive • Mountain crafts community • Shopping
Country stores • Old inns and hotels • C&O Canal

This weekend escape is a driving trip in western Maryland that lets you travel in time as well as space. You'll take the interstate to Frederick, Maryland, then pick up the National Pike and follow it as far as Grantsville. You'll exchange the chain hotels, the fast-food franchises, and the four lanes of whizzing cars on the interstate for a back-roads route that is nearly deserted in places.

Your drive will take you by ancient stone fences and emerald green forests and fields, and through quaint little towns that time seems to have passed by. Best of all, you'll get to experience a bit of American history while you're at it.

The National Pike is really four roads in one place, built over one another as the country's needs grew and changed. Starting out as an Indian trail winding up and down hills and through the Allegheny Mountains, it grew to be a gravel post road for travelers in Colonial times, and the section between Cumberland, Maryland, and Wheeling, West Virginia, was the first road financed by the federal government. The advent of the automobile brought paved roads, three lanes in places, but still narrow and winding as they snaked their way through the mountains of western Maryland.

The most recent chapter in the story of the National Pike was the development of the Interstate Highway System in the 1950s. Now it almost seems that the small communities that grew up and thrived along the National Pike in its heyday have been forgotten in the noisy race to progress on the nearby interstate. But there is still lots to explore, from the distinctive National Pike

mile markers that you can still see here and there, to the crafts and music of Appalachia, which are much in evidence in this area.

So take a spin on the National Pike—variously called Route 40, Alternate Route 40, Scenic Route 40, and State Highway 144. In addition to the pure pleasure of the drive, you'll have a chance to visit an artisans' community where mountain crafts such as quilting, ironwork, and wood carving are demonstrated in a small settlement of restored eighteenth-century cabins. You'll stay one night in a 150-year-old B&B, and another in a majestic old downtown hotel in historic Frostburg. There's a century-old country store to explore, and dinner in one of the mid-Atlantic's best Bavarian restaurants.

In short, driving the National Pike lets you explore and enjoy 200 years of American history. All this, and some of the prettiest countryside the state of Maryland has to offer. Gentlemen, start your engines!

DAY 1

Afternoon

Leave Washington by early afternoon on a Friday, if you can, to get a jump start on a terrific weekend. Take Interstate 270 to the outskirts of Frederick, then follow U.S. Highway 15 north a couple of miles to U.S. Highway 40 west. Follow U.S. Highway 40 west a half mile or so and turn left to get onto the National Pike (Alternate Route 40). You'll notice the difference almost immediately. The strip-mall commercialism of the western side of Frederick gives way to rolling countryside, and there's not a fast-food joint in sight!

About 2 miles up the Pike, there is a pullover at **Braddock Heights** with a beautiful view of the verdant valley below. A few miles farther is the little town of **Middletown**—which you would never even know about if you confined your driving to the expressway. Notice how the houses, with their low front porches, are built right up against the road. It's as if their owners didn't want to miss one minute of the traffic passing to and fro in front of them on the National Pike.

After another 10 or 12 miles, you'll drive through **Boonsboro,** and there you'll see your first franchise: a '50s-era Tastee-Freez. As you continue your drive, notice the bright red farmhouses and barns and stone fences in the area.

When you reach **Hagerstown,** about 35 miles from where you started on the Pike, abandon the Alternate Route 40 signs and take a driving tour through town in the square mile bounded by Potomac Street on the south, East Avenue on the east, Prospect Street on the north, and Memorial Boulevard on the west. It's a great way to see the European architecture, with Dutch- and German-influenced trimmings and roofs.

Don't miss the small, pretty **City Park** at 110 Key Street (at the intersection of Prospect Street and Memorial Boulevard), where you can visit the 1739 **Jonathan Hager House and Museum,** authentically restored with furnishings of the period, and the **Mansion House Art Center,** where local artists have studios. The Hager House (301–739–8393) is open Tuesday to Saturday 10:00 A.M. to 4:00 P.M., Sunday 2:00 to 5:00 P.M., April through December; closed Thanksgiving, Christmas, and the last week in November through the first Tuesday in December. Admission is $4.00 for adults and $2.00 for kids six to twelve; children under six are admitted free. The Mansion House Art Center (301–797–6813) is open Thursday to Saturday 10:00 A.M. to 4:00 P.M., Sunday 1:00 to 5:00 P.M., March through December.

DINNER: Take advantage of the city's German heritage with a Bavarian feast at **Schmankerl Stube,** 58 South Potomac Street (301–797–3354), thought by many to be the best German fare within a hundred miles of Washington.

The Schmankerl Stube is fragrant and homey, with wood beams and red-and-white-checked tablecloths. But the menu is elegant and varied. Salmon, frog legs, and baked Camembert are on the appetizer list, and Bavarian specialties include smoked pork loin, veal cutlets, sauerbraten, and red cabbage. There are even choices for vegetarians, a rare find in a German restaurant. Everything here is fresh and done to perfection, and there are numerous imported bottled beers, as well as a Munich brew on tap. Moderate.

After dinner, take U.S. Highway 40 west to seek out your lodgings, which are located about 12 miles west of Hagerstown in the small village of Clear Spring.

LODGING: Wildflowers Bed and Breakfast, 12739 Cohill Road, Clear Spring; (301) 842–1191. Although it's not a National Pike–era institution, Wildflowers is a beautiful place to bed down for the night. It's an organic farm (that grows produce and wildflowers) with a huge garden, a screened-in porch, a sunroom/greenhouse, solar heating, and a comforting woodstove. There are three guest rooms, which have shared baths. Rates: $60–$80 a night; you can rent all three rooms for a family for $150 a night.

DAY 2

Morning

BREAKFAST: Count on in-season organic fruit and homemade bread or rolls to be served at Wildflowers.

After breakfast, backtrack about 5 miles east on U.S. Highway 40. On the right-hand side of the road, at the top of a hill, you'll come to Wilson Village, the heart of which is **Wilson's General Store,** an absolutely terrific old emporium that has been in operation since 1852. Unlike kitschy country-store wanna-bes everywhere, Wilson's is a real treasure, without a false note in the place. All the beautiful old antique counters, shelves, cracker boxes, and containers are there, and ancient pots, pans, baskets, bridles, and farm equipment dangle from the ceiling.

It's not always clear what's for sale and what's not, because it seems more like a museum than a store. There are huge chunks of cheese in the antique cheese safe, crackers in the Sears Cracker box, dog collars, colored thread, bolts of cloth, seed packets, dozens of jars of penny candy on the counter, an antique tricycle on the ceiling, and lots of pretty blue-and-white reproduction crockery, and, yes, they're all for sale. There's even an old checkerboard set up, inviting you to sit down and play. Located just off Highway 40 at 14921 Rufus Wilson Road; (301) 582–4718. Open Monday to Saturday 7:30 A.M. to 6:00 P.M., Sunday 9:00 A.M. to 5:00 P.M.

Be sure your wanderings take you upstairs for an entirely different shopping experience, though it is owned by the same store. The **Upstairs Emporium** sells beautiful women's clothing, with everything from handwoven jackets to silk scarves. There are lots of unusual imports and original designs. Open Monday to Saturday 10:00 A.M. to 5:00 P.M., Sunday 1:00 to 5:00 P.M.

When you can pull yourself away from the country store, follow Alternate 40 west for 12 miles until it ends just past Indian Springs. Then you'll have to take Interstate 70 west for 9 miles along the upper Potomac River and State Highway 144 west for 2 miles to your next destination, **Hancock.**

Before lunch, take a half hour to study a little local history (and stretch your legs) with a walk along the **C&O Canal,** which runs right by Hancock. Pick up a map at the Visitor Information Center/Museum at 326 East Main Street, Hancock; (301) 678–5463, www.nps.gov/choh. This National Park Service facility also has a slide show and artifacts and photos of canal life.

For Washingtonians familiar with the pedestrian, bike, and dog congestion of the canal towpath north of Georgetown, this quiet section of the very same towpath will be a welcome contrast. You can walk for miles without running into anybody, with the Potomac by your side the whole way.

LUNCH: Make a beeline for **Weaver's Restaurant and Bakery,** which is right along the Pike at 77 West Main Street in Hancock; (301) 678–6346. Weaver's is clearly a beloved institution. The booths are full of locals, and lines form at the bakery counter for fancy decorated cakes, or baked specialties like "garlic pull-apart" rolls and potato fudge. (Try the potato fudge. It's like soft, smooth fondant swirled with peanut butter. Delicious!) The inexpensive lunch menu features sandwiches, salads, and blue-plate specials. The service is friendly, the coffee hot, and the food stick-to-the-ribs.

And, yes, Weaver's has doughnuts. In fact, the National Pike may be a doughnut fancier's version of heaven. For example, besides Weaver's, there's also Lorenzo's in Frostburg (301–689–6570) and Krumpe's in Hagerstown (301–733–6103). The latter is open only from 7:30 P.M. to 2:30 A.M.

Afternoon

Heading west from Hancock, the National Pike is State Highway 144 and it parallels Interstate 68. If you are interested in some of the geological history of the area, you might consider getting on I–68 at exit 77 and getting off at exit 74 in order to visit the **Sideling Hill Exhibit Center** located on the interstate. It shows some of the rock formations of the mountains in this area, as well as local flora and fauna; (301) 842–2155. Open daily; free.

Get back on the Pike for the approximately 40-mile drive from Hancock to Cumberland. Here the National Pike is variously labeled State Highway 144, Scenic Route 40, and Alternate Route 40. For the last 2 miles into Cumberland, you'll have to get on I–68 at exit 46. Get off again at exit 44 and take Alternate U.S. Highway 40 through town.

A highlight of your road trip will be winding through the **Cumberland Narrows.** The threadlike passage runs through a valley with mountains on either side of you. The layered rock is massively exposed and towers above you on both sides.

Be sure to stop at the **LaVale Toll Gate House,** about 5 miles west of Cumberland. This beautifully proportioned, seven-sided brick structure, with a tower, bright yellow door, and dark green shutters, was built in 1836 and was

LaVale Toll Gate House

one of the first toll-collecting facilities in America. You can see the posts on either side of the road, from which a chain was stretched to stop the horses, buggies, and carriages.

From LaVale, drive west on Alternate Route 40. Your late afternoon destination is Grantsville, just over 20 miles away.

As you continue your trip, keep your eyes peeled for the distinctive obelisk-shaped National Pike mile markers (looking like miniature Washington Monuments) that once marked every single mile on the Pike. Most are gone now, but every now and then you'll see one, standing about 3½ feet tall. Also notice the roadside parks, built by the Civilian Conservation Corps in the 1930s, which still serve as handy picnic stops for travelers.

When you arrive in **Grantsville,** look for the **Casselman Hotel.** It started out as a hostelry, serving Pike travelers in 1824. It is now showing its age, but it's still full of National Pike character. Its dining room serves Amish food, and downstairs is a bakery where Mennonite and Amish women whip up fresh rolls, pies, and bread, both to serve in the restaurant and to sell. Located on Main Street in Grantsville; (301) 895–5266.

Your final destination of the afternoon is the fascinating **Spruce Forest Artisans Village,** a small cluster of original eighteenth- and nineteenth-century log cabins that were moved to this secluded spot under tall pine trees. Located on Alternate Route 40, Grantsville; (301) 895–3332. Open Monday to Saturday 10:00 A.M. to 5:00 P.M.

The Artisans Village was the creation of an elderly Mennonite scholar, Dr. Alta Schrock. She started the nonprofit enterprise (which also includes a gift shop, a flourishing restaurant, and a museum) as a way to honor and save the ancient crafts of Appalachia.

Here, talented artisans in period dress work at their looms, forges, quilt frames, and potter's wheels just as they might have a hundred years ago. Each of the cabins is a working studio as well as a gift shop, and the artists are glad to answer questions about their work.

Take a moment to cross the grounds to the beautiful **Casselman River Bridge** just next door. It was the longest single-span stone bridge in the world when it was built about 150 years ago. Also nearby is Stanton's Mill, a restored 1797 grain mill operated by waterpower.

Be sure to leave yourself plenty of time to peek in at the **Penn Alps Craft Shop.** There are hundreds of crafts from Appalachia on display, including beautiful handmade baskets, textiles, carved birds, and dulcimers. The shop also cooperates with the Mennonite Ten Thousand Villages stores, so there are lots of Third World imports at low prices. Since the stores are nonprofit and usually run by volunteers, you can be sure that almost all of the modest price you pay for crafts goes directly to the overseas artisans for their labor. Open Monday through Saturday 9:00 A.M. to 7:00 P.M., Sunday 9:00 A.M. to 3:00 P.M.

DINNER: It's best to be hungry when you go to dinner at the **Penn Alps Restaurant,** located in the same building as the gift shop; (301) 895–5985, www.pennalps.com. The Penn Alps features a fairly standard middle-America menu, but with Mennonite and Pennsylvania Dutch dishes as well. Prices are moderate—a sausage, potato, coleslaw, and dried corn special with heaping portions costs about $10. There are also chicken, fish, and beef dishes on the menu. On Friday and Saturday nights, there's an all-you-can-eat smorgasbord; if you find there's a line, give the hostess your name, then wander in the gift shop until you're called.

After dinner, head back east on Alternate Route 40 about 14 miles to the historic town of Frostburg, where you'll stay overnight.

LODGING: Failingers Hotel Gunter, 11 West Main Street, Frostburg; (301) 689–6511. This once-grand seventeen-room hotel was partially restored in the 1960s, and the magnificent central staircase is Failingers' pride. Although the lobby and dining room are far from fancy, the Hotel Gunter captures the feel of what it was like to travel on the Pike a century ago. Rooms are $58 a night; a suite costs $80.

DAY 3

Morning

BREAKFAST: Failingers Hotel Gunter serves a continental breakfast for its guests.

After breakfast, you might want to take a stroll around **Frostburg,** a picturesque little town. Pick up a map at the hotel and explore Main Street and the adjoining cross streets, which are lined with historic buildings and homes. Notice the **Nelson Beall House,** built in 1876, at 49 West Main Street, **St. Michael's Church,** dating from 1870, at 28 East Main Street, and the **Frost Mansion** at 56 Frost Avenue, which was a renowned hotel retreat for Washington and Baltimore residents a hundred years ago.

Before you head home, stop at **Shops by the Depot,** where you can buy (or look at) antiques, pottery, Amish furniture, mountain crafts, and quilts. For kids, there are a handful of toy stores, including a Thomas the Tank Engine outlet. Located on Depot Street; (301) 689–3676. Open daily except Monday.

LUNCH: The Whistle Stop Cafe, located in the Shops by the Depot (301–689–3020), has sandwiches and ice-cream sodas. You can eat in, order lunch to go, or, if you're backtracking on the National Pike, stop at one of the spots you missed on your trip west.

Returning to Washington via the interstate system (I–68 east, I–70 east, and I–270 south) will take about three hours.

THERE'S MORE

Miller House. Hagerstown museum featuring an old-fashioned general store and a collection of antique dolls and clocks. Located at 135 West Washington Street; (301) 797–8782. Open Thursday to Saturday 1:00 to 4:00 P.M. Admission is $3.00 for adults, $2.00 for senior citizens, no charge for children under eighteen.

MARYLAND

Washington County Museum of Fine Arts. Hagerstown museum with a permanent art collection of old masters, portraits, and landscapes, as well as changing exhibits; also home to chamber music series. Located at City Park; (301) 739–5727, www.washcomuseum.org. Open Tuesday to Saturday 10:00 A.M. to 5:00 P.M., Sunday 1:00 to 5:00 P.M. Admission is free.

Western Maryland Scenic Railroad. Three-hour 1916 Baldwin steam locomotive ride along scenic railroad passes in the Allegheny Mountains; includes lunch stop in Frostburg. Located at 13 Canal Street, Cumberland; (301) 759–4400 or (800) 872–4650, www.wmsr.com. Open Tuesday to Sunday May through September, daily in October, and weekends in November and early December. Reservations are necessary; call for hours of departure. Summer ticket prices: $16.50 for adults, $14.50 for seniors, and $10.00 for children two to twelve. Children under two travel free.

Thrasher Carriage Museum. Collection of nineteenth- and twentieth-century horse-drawn conveyances, including sleighs, carriages, and dog carts. Located at the old railway depot in Frostburg; (301) 689–3380 or (800) 508–4748. Open Tuesday to Sunday 11:00 A.M. to 3:00 P.M. May through September; same days 11:00 A.M. to 6:00 P.M. in October; weekends 11:00 A.M. to 3:00 P.M. November and December; closed January through April. Admission is $2.00 for adults, $1.75 for senior citizens, and $1.00 for children twelve to eighteen; children under twelve are admitted free.

Deep Creek Lake. Maryland's largest freshwater lake, located south of the National Pike near Oakland; (301) 387–4386, www.deepcreeklake.org. Numerous attractions, including swimming, boating, fishing, hiking, and skiing in winter. Dozens of places to stay and eat.

SPECIAL EVENTS

June. Annual Heritage Days Festival. Food, music, crafts, children's rides in Cumberland. (301) 777–2787 or (800) 801–0004.

July. Summerfest and Quilt Show. Dozens of craft workers and quilters gather at Penn Alps in Grantsville; music and storytelling. (301) 895–3332.

August. Rocky Gap Country Music Festival. Cumberland event draws major country stars and an audience of thousands to Allegany College. (301) 724–2450 or (888) 762–5942.

August. Augustoberfest. Hagerstown celebrates its German heritage with food, music, and crafts. (301) 739–8577.

October. Springs Folk Festival just across the Pennsylvania state line from Grantsville on State Highway 669. Large event featuring arts, mountain crafts, continuous music, and Pennsylvania Dutch food. (814) 662–2051.

OTHER RECOMMENDED RESTAURANTS

Boonsboro

Old Pike Inn Grill and Draft Pub, 7700 Old National Pike; (301) 416–2444. Friendly pub in a very old cattle auction hall; good choice for fried catfish, chicken, steaks. Inexpensive to moderate.

Cumberland

Oxford House Restaurant, in the Inn at Walnut Bottom, 120 Greene Street; (301) 777–7101. Shrimp Pernod, salmon studded with poppy seeds, veal with sun-dried tomatoes, vegetarian tournedos, and traditional country food (beef, chicken, fish, stuffed pork chops) in a lovely dining room in downtown Cumberland. Moderate for lunch; moderate to expensive for dinner.

Fred Warner's Deutsches Restaurant, U.S. Highway 220, Cresaptown (just outside Cumberland); (301) 729–2361. Sausage, potato pancakes, homemade bread in charming old stone building. Moderate.

Inn at Folcks Mill, on U.S. Highway 40, 1 mile east of Cumberland; (301) 777–3553. Upstairs there's a fine restaurant serving new-American cuisine; downstairs in the pub you can get pizza baked in a wood-burning oven. Moderate.

When Pigs Fly, corner of Valley and Mechanic Streets; (301) 722–7447. Delicious barbecue and more. Inexpensive to moderate.

Hagerstown

Twilight's Ristorante, 43 South Potomac Street; (301) 791–9700. Northern Italian specialties, antipasto, salads, pasta; also deli on premises. Moderate.

Roccoco, 20 West Washington Street; (301) 790–3331. Jazzy brasserie serving adventuresome fusion cuisine such as spring rolls made with crispy duck, bamboo shoots, scallions, sweet peppers, zucchini, and goat cheese. The fancy pizzas are very good. Moderate to expensive.

Frostburg

Giuseppe's Italian Restaurant, 11 Bowery Street; (301) 689–2220. Pasta, veal, seafood, and vegetarian entrees in a casual setting. Moderate.

Au Petit Paris, 86 East Main Street; (301) 689–8946 or (800) 207–0956. French cuisine, good wine list, pleasant ambience. Moderate.

Cafe 101, 101 East Main Street; (301) 689–1243. Vegetarian restaurant with many vegan items, espresso. Open all day. Inexpensive.

Gandalf's, 16 West Main Street; (301) 689–2010. Eclectic selection of offerings, including organic and vegetarian meals as well as Mexican, African, and Thai dishes. Inexpensive.

For additional listings see Maryland Escape Five (page 117) and Pennsylvania Escape Six (page 260).

OTHER RECOMMENDED LODGINGS

Cumberland

Inn at Walnut Bottom, 120 Greene Street, Cumberland; (301) 777–0003 or (800) 286–9718, www.iwbinfo.com. Historic country inn with twelve air-conditioned rooms and suites, most with private baths. Phone and TV in every room; full breakfast included. Rates: $97–$119 for rooms, $186 for a two-bedroom suite.

Grantsville

Elliott House Victorian Inn, 146 Casselman Road; (301) 895–4250 or (800) 272–4090, www.elliotthouse.com. Elegant Victorian B&B on seven riverfront acres. Seven guest rooms, all with private baths, air-conditioning, cable TV and VCR, private telephones, antiques and quilts, hair dryers, complimentary coffee and soft drinks. The $75–$130 tariff includes dinner and breakfast for two at the adjacent Penn Alps Reastuarant. Two-day minimum on weekends. Children must be twelve or older.

Walnut Ridge Bed and Breakfast, 92 Main Street; (301) 895–4248 or (888) 419–2568, www.walnutridge.com. Two guest rooms and one suite in a farmhouse on the edge of town. Large porches, hot tubs, separate entrance, country breakfast. Rates: $75–$125.

Hagerstown

Beaver Creek House, 20432 Beaver Creek Road; (301) 797–4764 or (888) 942–9966, www.bbonline.com/md/beavercreek. Century-old Victorian country house with five guest rooms, all air-conditioned. Garden, screened porch, parlor fireplace; full country breakfast. Rates: $85–$95.

Wilson House B&B, 14921 Rufus Wilson Road, Clear Spring; (301) 582–4320. Lovely 1850s house with three guest rooms. Shared bath (claw-foot bathtubs), lots of antiques, full country breakfast. Rates: $50–$75.

For additional listings see Maryland Escape Five (page 117) and Pennsylvania Escape Six (page 260).

FOR MORE INFORMATION

Hagerstown/Washington County Convention and Visitors Bureau, 16 Public Square, Hagerstown, MD 21740; (301) 791–3246 or (800) 228–7829, www.marylandmemories.org.

Allegany County Visitors Bureau, Western Maryland Station, Mechanic and Harrison Streets, Cumberland, MD 21502; (301) 777–5138 or (800) 508–4748, www.marylandmountainside.com.

Garrett County Chamber of Commerce, 15 Visitors Center Drive, McHenry, MD 21541; (301) 387–4386, www.garrettchamber.com.

WEST VIRGINIA
ESCAPES

Berkeley Springs and Cacapon State Park

GEORGE WASHINGTON BATHED HERE

2 NIGHTS

Warm spring bathing • Hiking • Camping
Golf • Swimming • Shopping

Berkeley Springs State Park, in the far eastern neck of West Virginia, is the country's first state park and oldest health spa. Visitors and locals have been bathing here and drinking the famed mineral-rich water for centuries, and, happily, not much has changed over time.

The highlight of your weekend escape is a visit to Berkeley Springs to "take the waters" yourself. The handkerchief-size park in the center of town has two working bathhouses, a small museum, and a stone depression where sixteen-year-old George Washington is said to have bathed in 1748. The water allegedly cured him of rheumatic fever, inspiring Washington and his friends to plan the Town of Bath around the little spring. The official name of this small village of 2,500 permanent residents is still the Town of Bath, but everyone—including the Postal Service—calls it Berkeley Springs.

To this day, visitors float in the warm baths, children dabble in a riverlet running through the park, and visitors and locals freely collect gallons of the famed water in plastic jugs.

Cacapon Resort State Park, just 10 miles from Berkeley Springs, has several trails where you can walk for miles without seeing a soul. It also has an eighteen-hole golf course, horseback riding, tennis courts, volleyball nets, cabins to rent, and a pleasant lodge that has dining facilities and an indoor recreation area with Ping-Pong tables, shuffleboard, and a video game room.

DAY 1

Morning

Plan to be on the road by early morning so there's plenty of time for a full day's worth of activities. There are several routes to Berkeley Springs, but the one of choice is through Winchester, Virginia. Take I–66 west about 20 miles to exit 57 just beyond Fairfax, where you will pick up U.S. Highway 50 west. From then on, the drive is pure pleasure. The road winds its way through some of the prettiest countryside in the mid-Atlantic region, with honeysuckle-wreathed wood fences and banks of clover along the road, cows grazing in rolling meadows, and the thickly wooded mountains rising ahead of you.

Opting for U.S. Highway 50 offers another advantage. As you pass through Middleburg, the hunt-country capital of Virginia about an hour west of Washington, you can stop for a couple of fresh doughnuts at **The Upper Crust,** 2 North Pendleton Street; (540) 687–5666. If you leave without a bag full of cow puddles (butterscotch pecan cookies), you'll be making a mistake. If you're not planning a sit-down lunch on the way to Berkeley Springs, the Upper Crust also packs picnic baskets, which could contain English-style sausage rolls, tuna or egg salad sandwiches on just-baked bread, or pasta salad with chicken. Inexpensive.

Twenty miles past Middleburg on U.S. Highway 50, you'll come to the historic town of Winchester. Take a few minutes before lunch to stroll through **Old Town Winchester.** Like Berkeley Springs, Winchester was originally surveyed by George Washington for the family of Lord Fairfax, who owned much of northern Virginia. Washington enjoyed his stay at the spa, but he evidently fell in love with Winchester. He returned seven years later and, at the age of twenty-three, settled in and launched his political career with a successful run for the Virginia House of Burgesses. Many also credit Washington with promoting the planting of apple orchards in the area.

Winchester is home to more than a hundred original eighteenth-century buildings, dozens of lovely nineteenth-century Victorian homes, and a downtown outdoor walking and shopping mall, with several galleries, bookstores, shops, and restaurants.

LUNCH: Have lunch at the **Olde Towne Cafe,** 2 South Loudon Street (540–665–1805), which has a selection of soups, salads, sandwiches, and desserts, with nothing on the menu more than $5.00.

Berkeley Springs State Park

Afternoon

From Winchester, take Interstate 81 north about 25 miles, crossing the state line into West Virginia. Exit at State Highway 9 and follow it 20 miles west to Berkeley Springs.

The best thing of all about **Berkeley Springs** is the park with its bath-houses. For visitors accustomed to at-home Jacuzzis or health club steam rooms, a soak and massage at a state park may not seem like much. But don't miss it; you will be soaking in local history and lore as much as in mineral water! If you've made reservations for a late-afternoon or early-evening soak, you'll have plenty of time to explore the small town of Berkeley Springs first.

Start at **Berkeley Springs State Park,** in the center of town. The entire park covers only four square blocks and is the smallest state park in the country. It's worth stopping at **The Museum of the Berkeley Springs,** located on the second floor above the "old" Roman Bath House, built around 1820.

There you can get lots of information about the history and geology of the area and a brochure about how to use the bathhouses. The park is open during daylight hours; the museum is open Monday and Tuesday mornings, Thursday and Friday afternoons, Saturday 10:00 A.M. to 4:00 P.M., and Sunday noon to 4:00 P.M. Phone (304) 258–5860 for the park and (304) 258–2711 for the museum; www.berkeleyspringssp.com.

You'll find several interesting little shops during your stroll through town. **Mountain Laurel Crafts,** 101 North Washington Street (304–258–1919 or 888–809–2041), has pottery, woven items, and other crafts by more than fifty local artisans. The nearby **Berkeley Springs Antique Mall,** 100 Fairfax Street (304–258–5676), has thirty dealers selling mostly jewelry, old books, china, and trinkets. The collectibles are attractively displayed, and prices are great. Open daily, except Wednesday, from 10:00 A.M. to 5:00 P.M.

The healthful properties of Berkeley Springs are taken completely seriously by visitors and locals alike. When you arrive at the "new" (circa 1929) **Bath House,** you'll be ushered into the men's or women's side of the building, given towels, and told to strip by middle-aged attendants, who are all business. They'll then lead you to either a "relaxing bath" (an enormous raised bathtub) or a "Roman bath," where you step into a large, recessed pool. The water in both is kept at a constant 102 degrees, and there you soak, and muse, and relax while the stiffness eases from your muscles.

The bathhouses have the nostalgic feel of a high-school shower room, with the school gym teacher in attendance. But they don't need modern gimmicks to work their magic: Even the most suspicious cynic will emerge from a bath, shower, and massage feeling wonderful. The hour's bliss is worth every penny of the $22–$35 tab, which is considerably lower at the park than at most commercial spas around the country.

The bathhouses also offer steam baths and "infrared" heat treatments. Family bathing (up to four people) is permitted in the original 1820s Old Roman Bath House, which has nine private Roman baths, but no showers or massages. Rates at the Old Roman Bath House are $10.00 per adult, $5.00 for kids between six and twelve; the high temperature of the water makes it unsuitable for younger children.

You can cool off after your hot bath at the nation's oldest public outdoor swimming pool next door to the bathhouses.

The State Park Bath House is open daily 10:00 A.M. to 6:00 P.M., except Christmas, New Year's, and the second Monday in November; Friday hours are extended to 9:00 P.M. from April 1 through October 31. Reservations are strongly recommended and may be made up to fourteen days in advance. Call (304) 258–2711 or (800) 225–5982.

Before dinner, take a drive up to **Prospect Peak** for a fantastic view of the river valleys and town below. You can reach Prospect Peak from Berkeley Springs by heading west on State Highway 9. It's about a twenty-minute drive. *National Geographic* has called this three-state view one of "America's outstanding beauty spots."

DINNER: Backtrack on State Highway 9 to Cold Run Valley Road (you'll see the signs for Coolfont) and dine at the **Coolfont Resort's Treetop House Restaurant,** which offers a different buffet every night (from Italian to seafood to Tex-Mex), in addition to excellent steaks, Pacific Rim specialties, and creative vegetarian dishes. The Treetop has some of the best food in the area, at prices ranging from $12 to $28 for a full dinner. (304) 258–4500 or (800) 888–8768.

LODGING: The Manor, 415 Fairfax Street (304–258–1552), is a four-bedroom B&B located just a few blocks from Berkeley Springs State Park. The house and furnishings are exquisite, especially the quilts. The atmosphere is friendly, the breakfasts are bountiful, and the rates are reasonable: $85–$100 for a room. The Manor also has a three-room suite that rents for $130.

DAY 2

Morning

BREAKFAST: The Manor.

Before heading to Cacapon State Park for a day of outdoor fun, pick up a picnic lunch at **Inspiration Bakery and Cafe,** 312 North Washington Street; (304) 258–2292. Inspiration isn't hard to find; just follow your nose. You'll want to include a few pastries with your sandwiches and juice. Inexpensive.

Cacapon Resort State Park is located about 12 miles south of Berkeley Springs on U.S. Highway 522; (304) 258–1022 or (800) 225–5982, www. cacaponresort.com. Cacapon has enough activities to happily engage a visitor for weeks. A good way to start is with a hike in the park. Maps are available and paths nicely marked, and the mountain scenery, with streams, wildflowers, woods, and plenty of deer, is spectacular. The Ziler Loop Trail is a fairly rugged 5-mile hike that will take you three to four hours to traverse. Other trails or combinations of trails ranging in distance from a quarter mile to 10 miles are available.

LUNCH: Either picnic in the park or try the **Cacapon Restaurant** in the Main Lodge at Cacapon State Park, which serves pasta, chicken, beef, and seafood, as well as sandwiches. Phone (304) 258–1022. Inexpensive.

Afternoon

Cacapon Resort State Park has several miles of bridle paths, and you can rent horses at the park for only $15 an hour. It also has a clean beach for swimming and a lake for canoeing and fishing, as well as facilities for tennis, basketball, volleyball, Ping-Pong, and shuffleboard.

For a more leisurely afternoon, grab your novel and a lounge chair in the shade of the main lodge, and watch the golfers on the scenic course designed by Robert Trént Jones. (See There's More for rates.) All in all, Cacapon is a delightful family resort, and you'll be tempted back often.

DINNER: A favorite of locals and tourists alike is **Tari's Premier Cafe and Inn,** a festive restaurant featuring mountain-size sandwiches, Tex-Mex selections, pasta, and seafood at moderate prices. It is located at 123 North Washington Street, Berkeley Springs; (304) 258–1196.

After dinner, walk two doors down from Tari's and take in a movie at the **Star Theater,** 129 North Washington Street; (304) 258–1404. The Star is a 1940s movie house with a hand-lettered marquee, a fifty-year-old popcorn machine and cash register, and a $3.25 admission charge ($2.50 for children). For 50 cents extra, you can reserve an overstuffed sofa and pretend you're at home with an extra-large screen. The theater is open Friday, Saturday, and Sunday (plus Thursday in summer); the feature starts at 8:00 P.M.

LODGING: The Manor.

DAY 3

Morning

BREAKFAST: The Manor.

Walk off your breakfast with a climb up the hill immediately behind Berkeley Springs State Park for a look at another of the town's attractions, **Berkeley Castle.** (It's a steep quarter-mile walk uphill just behind the state park or, by car, a quarter-mile drive west of Berkeley Springs on State Route 9.) Berkeley Castle is a half-scale replica of an English castle, built by a doting older man, Colonel Samuel Taylor Suit, in 1885 for his twenty-two-year-old wife, Rosa, the daughter of an Alabama congressman. Sam met Rosa when she was "sweet seventeen" and courted her for five years, but she married him only after he agreed to build her a castle near Berkeley Springs. He died shortly thereafter, and she ran through his money in short order, living out her days in a one-room cabin up the hill. But the sad old castle is still there, and a climb to the roof gives you a good view of Berkeley Springs. Berkeley Castle is open daily except Christmas and New Year's Day from 8:00 A.M. to 8:00 P.M., but call ahead because special events sometimes preempt tours. Admission is $5.00 for adults and $2.50 for children age four to thirteen; children three and under are admitted free. Phone (304) 258–4000 or (800) 896–4001; www. berkeleysprings.com/bscastle.

LUNCH: The Country Inn, located adjacent to Berkeley Springs State Park at 207 South Washington Street (304–258–2210), has a hearty lunch menu, including turkey, ham, and roast beef as well as sandwiches, soups, and salads. Inexpensive to moderate.

Afternoon

You can return to Cacapon State Park and spend your afternoon on the golf course, at the lake, on the tennis court, or in the woods for one last hike before heading home. Or meander back to Washington through the Potomac River valley via State Highway 9, which takes you through Martinsburg, West Virginia—where there is lots of outlet shopping—and close by historic Harpers Ferry and the beautiful old village of Shepherdstown, both of which are worth a stop. You will pick up Virginia State Highway 7 just north of Leesburg, about 40 miles west of Washington. Take Virginia State Highway 7 east to I–66 or the Beltway to return home. If you're in a hurry, U.S. Highway 522 south from Berkeley Springs and Cacapon to Interstate 66 east is the fastest route.

THERE'S MORE

Golf. Cacapon State Park golf course is one of the most beautiful in the state without being overly difficult. Greens fees are $22 on weekdays and $26 on weekends. You can rent a cart for $20; (304) 258–1022.

The Ice House. An art and community center that also houses the Morgan County Arts Council; site for concerts, gallery shows, and community theater. Located at the corner of Independence and Mercer Streets; (304) 258–2300, www.macicehouse.org.

Concert Series. Free performances of blues, folk, jazz, and traditional music Saturdays at 5:30 P.M. in Berkeley Springs State Park during July and August, Friday evenings at the Ice House other months. (304) 258–2300.

Open Air Market. The Bath Street Open Air Market, located across the street from Berkeley Springs State Park, features local fruit, vegetables, flowers, and baked goods. Open Saturday 9:00 A.M. to noon, April through November; (304) 258–9147.

Old Factory Antique Mall. Located at 112 Williams Street, just off Washington Street at the north end of town (304–258–1788), the mall has fifty dealers selling antiques, crafts, and homemade fudge. Open 10:00 A.M. to 5:00 P.M. daily, except Wednesdays in January and February.

SPECIAL EVENTS

January–March. Festival of the Waters, Berkeley Springs. Held over the course of ten weekends, the festival includes Spa Feast, Toast of the Tap (a tasting of the waters that has been featured several times on national television), and other events. (304) 258–9147 or (800) 447–8797.

April. Uniquely West Virginia Wine and Food Festival. Arts and crafts, music, wine tasting, and food provided by local restaurants. Cacapon Resort State Park. (304) 258–9147 or (800) 447–8797.

April–May. Shenandoah Apple Blossom Festival in Winchester. Food, parades, circus rides, and what may be the largest band competition in the United States. (540) 662–3863.

October. Berkeley Springs Apple Butter Festival. Music, crafts, country cooking, apple butter making in the streets. (304) 258–3738 or (800) 447–8797.

OTHER RECOMMENDED RESTAURANTS

Panorama Steak House, 3 miles west of Berkeley Springs on West Virginia Highway 9; (304) 258–9370. Once a speakeasy, Panorama Steak House has kept the buzzer, but they'll let you in and you'll be happy about it. This is what West Virginians call a "supper club." Panorama is located at Prospect Peak; if you reserve early, you can get a window table with a view of West Virginia, Maryland, and Pennsylvania, as well as the Potomac and Great Cacapon River valleys. You can also get some of the best prime rib and steaks in the area. Moderate.

Fairfax Coffee House and Eatery, 116 Fairfax Street; (304) 258–8019. Unpretentious storefront restaurant with a splendid menu that changes monthly. Featured entrees one month included black bean tarts, pumpkin ravioli, and bratwurst with homemade sauerkraut. Moderate.

Lot 12 Public House, 302 Warren Street; (304) 258–6264. Contemporary cuisine (crispy roast duck with creamy polenta, spinach and Gorgonzola risotto cakes, spice-rubbed port tenderloins) served in a hundred-year-old house; nice wine list. Moderate to expensive.

Maria's Garden and Inn, located just 2 blocks north of Berkeley Springs State Park at 201 Independence Street; (304) 258–2021. Maria's specializes in Italian-American dishes, sandwiches, and down-home favorites such as chicken, turkey, ham, and roast beef. On display throughout the restaurant are statues, paintings, rosaries, and other religious articles honoring the Madonna. Inexpensive.

OTHER RECOMMENDED LODGINGS

Cacapon Resort State Park, located 10 miles south of Berkeley Springs on U.S. Highway 522 (304–258–1022 or 800–225–5982, www.cacaponresort.com), has three types of accommodations. Cacapon Lodge has forty-nine rooms with private baths ranging in price from $46 out of season to $62 in season. Cacapon Inn has eleven smaller rooms with shared baths; rates range from $35 to $39 a night. Cabins rent for $52 a night for an economy cabin to $115 a night for a modern cabin that sleeps eight people. All cabins have kitchens. On weekends, a two-day rental is required for all accommodations. During the summer, cabins must be reserved by the week. Reservations may be made twelve months in advance and, for peak weekends, reserving months in advance is necessary.

Coolfont Resort, just off State Route 9 west of Berkeley Springs on Cold Run Valley Road; (304) 258–4500 or (800) 888–8768, www.coolfont.com.

Coolfont offers something for everyone. Rooms in the Woodland House Lodge start at $95 per person per night with a two-day minimum; breakfast and dinner are included. Log cabins, chalets, and vacation homes are also available, starting at $114 a person. Coolfont is a complete spa with a modern health and fitness center, indoor pool, lake, horseback riding, tennis courts, and salon. Reserved campsites are available for tents and RVs at rates of $20–$36.

The Country Inn, 207 South Washington Street, Berkeley Springs; (304) 258–2210 or (800) 822–6630, www.countryinnwv.com. Located just next to Berkeley Springs State Park, this inn has seventy rooms, a delightful cottage garden, and a complete spa. Rates range from $39 a night for a double without bath to $160 for a spacious suite. Several economical packages are available that include meals at the restaurant and use of the spa.

Highlawn Inn, 304 Market Street; (304) 258–5700 or (888) 290–4163, www.berkleysprings.com/highlawninn. Really twelve guest rooms in four houses, some of them beautifully restored Victorians, one a comfortable cottage; full country breakfast served. Rates: $85–$185.

The Glens Country Estate, New Hope Road (3½ miles east of town on State Highway 9); (304) 258–4536, www.wvglens.com. Eight guest rooms in restored Victorian that caters to couples. Pool, decks, Jacuzzis, feather pillows, down comforters. Rates: $170–$230, which includes country breakfast and five-course dinner.

Aaron's Acre Bed and Breakfast, 501 Johnson Mill Road; (304) 258–4079, www.berkeleysprings.com/aarons. Cozy, restored farmhouse with wraparound porch and many antiques; full breakfast served. No children. Rates: $80–$100

The Woods Resort, on State Highway 9 west of Berkeley Springs; (304) 754–7972 or (800) 248–2222, www.thewoodsresort.com. Rooms in the two lodges have private phones, televisions, refrigerators, and whirlpool baths. Restaurant, pub, golf course, and other amenities. The $85–$130 tariff includes breakfast.

River House, Rock Ford Road, Great Cacapon (5 miles west of Berkeley Springs); (304) 258–4042. Country house with deck over river and three guest rooms. Swimming, canoeing, biking, fishing; kitchen privileges; kids and pets welcome. Rates: $45–$80.

FOR MORE INFORMATION

Travel Berkeley Springs, Inc. Convention and Visitors Bureau, 304 Fairfax Street, Berkeley Springs, WV 25411; (304) 258–9147 or (800) 447–8797.

For information about Berkeley Springs State Park, Cacapon Resort State Park, or any of the other West Virginia state parks, call the State Parks information service at (800) 225–5982 or check www.callwva.com.

Elkins and Canaan Valley

A FOUR-SEASON PARADISE

2 NIGHTS

*Appalachian arts and crafts • Hiking • Nature trails
Downhill and cross-country skiing • Scenic drives*

The Monongahela National Forest, a gigantic wilderness area in West Virginia's Allegheny Mountains, is home to some of the most magnificent parks in the United States. West Virginia is for people who love to hike, ski, take pictures, fish, and raft on white water. It's also for people who want to get away from cities and crowds and lose themselves in a place where the scenery is ravishing, the air is clean, and the surroundings remarkably noncommercial and unspoiled.

Among the best of West Virginia's many parks are Canaan Valley Resort Park and nearby Blackwater Falls State Park. They are your destination for this weekend escape, which also includes visits to Elkins, the home of an acclaimed monthlong summer folk-life festival, and a stop at Seneca Rocks to watch the rock climbers.

DAY 1

Morning

Your day begins with a leisurely drive into West Virginia. Take Interstate 66 west from Washington about 75 miles to Interstate 81 just past Front Royal, Virginia. Follow I–81 south for 4 miles to the second exit, marked Strasburg. There you'll be able to pick up State Highway 55 heading west into and through the Potomac Highlands section of West Virginia. Prepare to enjoy

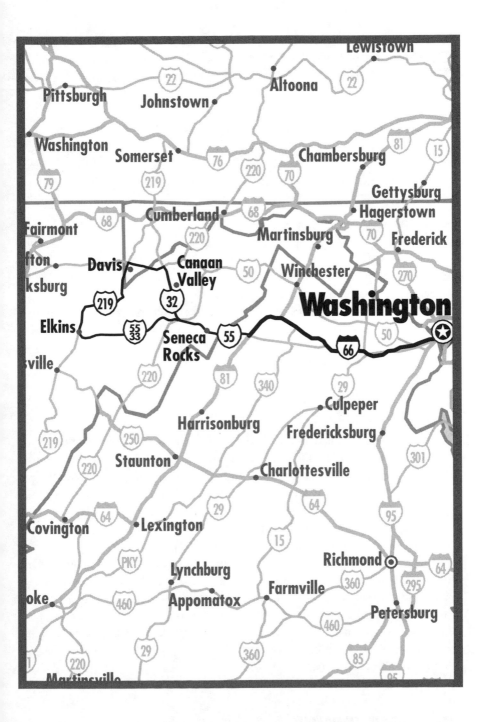

every minute of your drive on Route 55, which winds up and down mountain roads with 9 percent grades. As you go deeper into West Virginia, the sights along the way get more and more beautiful. The mountains loom ever closer, swathed in dense forest, and cattle graze in the meadows tucked in the gentle valleys between the slopes.

As you approach **Seneca Rocks** (about 80 miles and two hours after you pick up State Highway 55), the mountains become increasingly rugged until you can see the extraordinary thousand-foot-high outcropping of bare, sheer rock face that makes Seneca a destination of most serious local rock climbers. Phone (304) 567–2827 for the Seneca Rocks Visitors Center.

LUNCH: A great place to watch these athletes climb is from the front porch of a funky restaurant, called appropriately **The Front Porch,** located at the junction of State Highways 55 and 33; (304) 567–2555. The restaurant is the upstairs of Harper's Old Country Store, a mellow, old-time store that still sells groceries, hardware, hunting and fishing equipment, sheepskins, pottery, tourist stuff, and snacks. The Front Porch restaurant has a low-priced menu of whole-wheat pita sandwiches, salads, and spaghetti, with "fresh dough" pizza a specialty. Grab a table on the porch itself (they also serve indoors) and get out your binoculars. There's sure to be something interesting going on across the highway on the face of Seneca Rocks.

Afternoon

From Seneca Rocks, take State Highway 55 west about 12 miles, then head north on State Highway 32 about 10 miles to **Canaan Valley Resort State Park.** The park offers weeks' worth of things to do in gorgeous surroundings. Like all of West Virginia's state parks, it is immaculate, moderately priced, and unspoiled by commercial development. Check in at the Lodge, where you'll be staying the weekend, grab your skis, golf clubs, running shoes, hiking boots, swimsuit, tennis racket, or basketball, and get going!

Canaan Valley is popular year-round, and with good reason. If you visit in July or August to escape Washington's heat and humidity, it's likely to be a breezy 80 degrees at the park's 4,000-foot altitude and, at night, the temperature may even drop into the 60s. Summer visitors enjoy both an indoor and outdoor pool, tennis courts, golf links, and many miles of hiking trails. The scenery is truly lovely, as Canaan is in a valley surrounded by some of the highest peaks in West Virginia.

Canaan Valley Resort State Park

The best time to visit Canaan Valley, however, just might be the dead of winter. This "snow bowl" gets more snow than Vermont—averaging more than 150 inches per year—and, just in case the sky doesn't cooperate, the park has equipment to cover most of its slopes with machine-made snow. Canaan Valley is also a perfect ski resort for families; it offers baby-sitting as well as classes for kids.

The park has thirty-four slopes, with 30 percent of the ski terrain designated for beginners, 40 percent intermediate, and the remainder for experienced skiers. All-day adult lift tickets are $31 on weekdays and $42 on weekends. You can also buy cheaper half-day tickets or two- or three-day package plans. Fringe-season rates are significantly lower. Ski rental is $18 for adults, $15 for kids. Group and private lessons are also available.

In addition to the state park at Canaan Valley, there are numerous commercial resorts nearby. **Timberline Four Seasons Resort,** for example, offers competitively priced ski packages, and, when the snow is gone, it's a good place to rent mountain bikes and explore miles of rough trails. Phone (304) 866–4312 or (800) 766–9464; www.wvweb.com/trr.

For cross-country skiers, trails at Canaan Valley connect with nearby Dolly Sods Wilderness Area and White Grass Touring Center, making a 78-mile cross-country network. If you don't know yet if you're up to cross-country skiing and want to give it a try, rental equipment and lessons are available at Canaan Valley in the Nature Center Building.

DINNER: A good choice is the **Blackwater Brewing Company,** located a few miles north of the park on State Highway 32 (Williams Avenue) in Davis; (304) 259–4221. This brewpub and restaurant has a very good selection of German dishes, such as beer-batter fish, paprika chicken, and rouladen (rolled beef) with potato dumplings, an equally good selection of Italian entrees—mostly pasta, but a tasty pepper steak as well—plus the usual sandwiches you'd expect in a brewpub. Microbrews include a porter and a stout, which nicely complement the German food. Moderate.

LODGING: Canaan Valley Resort Park Lodge has 250 modern rooms and suites with remote-control TV, cable, and complimentary in-room coffee. Rates are $59–$99 for a room, $140 for a suite. Fifteen deluxe cabins start at $151 for a two-bedroom unit ($680 per week). There are also thirty-four campsites available in summer for an $18-per-day fee. On most weekends, a two-night minimum stay is required at the lodge. Midweek ski, golf, and family vacation packages are available. Phone (304) 866–4121 or (800) 622–4121; www.canaanresort.com.

DAY 2

Morning

BREAKFAST: At least one of your days in the area should be devoted to sightseeing in the area around Canaan Valley State Park. Begin by driving about 15 miles north on State Highway 32 to **Blackwater Falls State Park.** There, at the **Lodge Restaurant,** you can get a hearty and inexpensive breakfast with a fantastic view of Blackwater Canyon. Phone (304) 259–5216; www.blackwaterfalls.com.

The pride of the park is the falls itself. The park system has built a quarter-mile boardwalk so that it's an easy fifteen-minute walk to get down close to the falls; there's also a ramp to an overlook for visitors in wheelchairs. Bring lots of film, because you'll want to capture the breathtaking view of the lake and gorge, the 50-foot falls, and the rim of tall pines all around.

There's lots more to see and do at Blackwater Falls State Park. If you visit in summer, there's swimming and boating at Pendleton Lake, tennis courts, a volleyball court, and picnic facilities. Spring and summer are perfect for hiking or horseback riding; the park has horses and ponies for children, and usage fees are reasonable. Mountain biking is permitted on two of the eighteen trails.

In winter, Blackwater Falls offers sledding, and the extensive trail system is ideal for cross-country skiing. The trails are rated from beginner to advanced, and you can pick up a map at the lodge or recreation building that will show you how to combine trails to devise a loop at a distance and difficulty level to suit your tastes. A favorite trail in any season is the Balsam Fir Trail, a 1½-mile loop (beginning at the recreation building) that winds through beech and maple groves and then passes through a stand of balsam fir.

Just outside the park is **Davis,** a pleasant little town offering food, lodging, and services to the downhill and cross-country skiers, sledders, mountain bikers, climbers, kayakers, and yes, plain old tourists who have discovered the beauties of the Canaan Valley.

LUNCH: You can catch an early lunch at **Sirianni's Pizza Cafe** on Main Street in Davis; (304) 259–5454. Sirianni's offers pasta, hot and cold meat and vegetarian subs, and, of course, pizza (be warned: it's spicy!) in a friendly, generally crowded storefront restaurant.

Afternoon

Two miles north of the park entrance on State Highway 32, you'll connect with U.S. Highway 219. Follow it south for 34 miles and you'll be in **Elkins.**

Take some time to explore the town. You can pick up maps and brochures at the **Randolph County Convention and Visitors Bureau,** 200 Executive Plaza; (304) 636–2717 or (800) 422–3304, www. randolphcountywv.com. Elkins offers the opportunity to explore early Native American settlements in the area, take a historical tour of buildings erected by early European settlers, walk or drive through nearby Civil War battlefields, or enjoy the splendid Victorian architecture of **Davis and Elkins College;** (304) 637–1900**.**

The college, in particular, is worth a look. You'll see the Gate House, Albert Hall, the Boiler House Theatre, Graceland Mansion, and the fifty-six-room **Halliehurst Mansion.** College tour information is available from the visitors bureau, which can also supply a historic Elkins walking tour brochure with a map and information about twenty-six houses of particular interest. The walking tour will take you a little over an hour to complete.

For shoppers, there are lots of gift and craft shops in Elkins. Two particularly nice ones are the **Artists at Work Gallery,** 329 Davis Avenue (304–637–6309), where local artists work and sell their creations, and **Expressions,** 303 Davis Avenue (304–636–5087), a shop with handcrafted pottery, baskets, and toys, as well as local honey, syrup, and jams.

Plan your sight-seeing and shopping itinerary so that you'll have time for a doughnut break. Where U.S. Highway 33 meets U.S. Highway 219 north, you'll see **Ye Olde Doughnut Shop,** 400 South Randolph Avenue; (304) 636–0223. Open 4:00 A.M. to 3:30 P.M. It's where locals come to drink coffee, talk politics, and wrap themselves around blueberry turnovers and maple doughnuts. The shop doesn't appear to have changed in fifty years; grilled cheese sandwiches are only a dollar. Fast-food franchises are putting places like "Ye Olde" out of business, and it's a shame. Be a contrarian and buy an extra sack of fresh-made doughnuts for the road.

Elkins is also the site of the **Augusta Heritage Arts Workshops** at Davis and Elkins College. Here, for five weeks in July and August, musicians, folk dancers, artisans, and storytellers gather to share techniques, swap stories, and make music late into the night. There are dances, workshops for beginners, and jam sessions where teenagers and octogenarians play side by side.

The historic music and crafts of the Appalachian Mountains are the focus of the activities, so there's lots of country fiddling, zither playing, basket weaving, bread baking, quilting, and more. And for two weekends in August, the **Augusta Festival** spills out into the town itself, with a crafts fair and clogging, fiddling, and storytelling open to everybody. It's a wonderful occasion, and it draws a good-size crowd, so make your reservations early if you plan to attend. Phone (304) 636–2717 or (800) 422–3304; www.augustaheritage.com.

To find your final destination of the day, drive 3 miles east of Elkins on U.S. Highway 33. Just after Route 33 becomes a limited-access, four-lane road, you'll see a left turn exit for Stuarts Recreation Area. Take that exit and proceed just over a mile to a blue bridge that spans the Cheat River. Don't cross; the inn where you'll dine is located just short of the bridge.

DINNER: The Cheat River Inn, which looks from the outside like a private home, was operated as a tavern until 1988. Inside it still has the casual feel of a tavern, but this is one of the best restaurants in the state. The emphasis here is on fresh vegetables and fish, and many of the dishes have a hint of the Caribbean about them, a reflection of the owner's years of living in Key West.

When's the last time you've seen conch fritters and jerk ribs on a menu out-side a big city? Everything is delicious here, including the desserts, like choco-late amaretto brownies with ice cream, and key lime pie with raspberry sauce and whipped cream. Phone (304) 636–6265. Moderate.

After dinner, it's a thirty- to forty-minute drive back to Canaan Valley Resort Park via U.S. Highway 33 east (15 miles) and State Highway 32 north (10 miles).

LODGING: Canaan Valley Resort Park Lodge.

DAY 3

Morning

BREAKFAST: Enjoy a hearty pancake or waffle breakfast in the lodge's **Aspen Dining Room.** Inexpensive.

After breakfast, spend the rest of the day playing. If you want a break from skiing, rent a snowboard all day for $25, hone your ice skating skills at the out-door lighted rink for $5.00 ($2.50 for children), or relax in the lodge's health club, with its indoor pool, hot tub, sauna, and fitness center.

If you're visiting Canaan Valley in spring, summer, or fall, you can rent bikes at the Recreation Center, sign up for a guided tour at the Nature Center, or get in a couple of sets of tennis before lunch.

Golfers will enjoy the eighteen-hole, par-72, 6,982-yard championship course. Greens fees are $30–$33 for eighteen holes. You can rent clubs, carts, and even balls at the golf shop. For the kids, miniature golf is $2.50.

LUNCH: Aspen Dining Room at Canaan Valley Resort Park Lodge.

Afternoon

It's more than four hours back to Washington via State Highways 32 south and 55 east, linking up with I–81 north and then I–66 east, so plan your departure based on when you want to get home, and drive safely—especially if the roads are packed with snow.

THERE'S MORE

Dolly Sods Scenic Area and Wilderness Area. Sitting high atop the Allegheny plateau is the largest inland wetlands area in the United States.

You can spend hours exploring the scenic area by car on narrow gravel roads or discover the wilderness area on foot or horseback. The bogs, blueberries, and wildflowers will excite both photographers and painters. Located just east of Canaan Valley State Park; (304) 257–4488.

Climbing. Beginning, intermediate, and advanced lessons are available from Seneca Rocks Climbing School, (304) 567–2600 or (800) 548–0108; or from Seneca Rocks Mountain Guides, (304) 567–2115 or (800) 451–5108. Expect to pay about $80–$100 a day for a three-day lesson. Climbing shoes and technical equipment are provided. Both schools are located at the junction of State Highways 55 and 33.

Boating and White-water Rafting. You can canoe, fish, float in rubber canoes ("duckies"), or get shuttled to the white-water rafting section of the Cheat River (Class I to Class V rapids) from Blackwater Outdoor Center on State Highway 32 in Davis; (304) 478–4456 or (800) 328–4798.

Smoke Hole Caverns. Guided tour of 225-million-year-old cavern used by Seneca Indians to smoke game—and Union and Confederate soldiers to store ammunition—lasts forty-five minutes. Commercialized and sometimes crowded, but interesting. Open daily year-round from 9:00 A.M. to 5:00 P.M., later in summer months. The temperature is a constant 56 degrees in the caverns, so dress accordingly. Located on State Highway 55 about 13 miles north of Seneca Rocks; (304) 257–4442 or (800) 828–8478, www.smokehole.com. Admission is $8.00 for adults, $5.00 for children five to twelve; children under five are admitted free.

SPECIAL EVENTS

March. March Madness, a monthlong series of ski events, including the Governor's Cup Ski Race at Canaan Valley Resort Park. (304) 259–5315 or (800) 782–2775.

April. Annual Ramp Cookoff and Festival, Elkins. Ramps are wild leeks (members of the lily family) that grow in the forests of the Potomac Highland region of West Virginia in early spring. Ramps taste like green onions (times ten!), and, once you've eaten one, you'll remember what it tastes and smells like for days. So will your family and friends. The Elkins Festival gives a prize for the most potent concoction. A good introduction for the uninitiated is ramp jam, which makes for a pretty mean substitute topping for garlic bread. (304) 636–2717 or (800) 422–3304.

June. 24 Hours of Canaan. Longest bike race east of the Mississippi draws thousands to the Canaan Valley. (304) 259–5533.

July–August. Augusta Heritage Arts Workshops culminating in the Augusta Festival, Davis and Elkins College, Elkins. (304) 637–1209 or (800) 422–3304, www.augustaheritage.com.

September–October. The Mountain State Forest Festival, celebrated in Elkins and throughout the region, is the state's oldest and largest festival. It features exhibits and entertainment, arts and crafts, athletic contests, and spectator sports. (304) 636–1824, www.forestfestival.com.

OTHER RECOMMENDED RESTAURANTS

Canaan Valley

Golden Anchor and Portside Pub, State Highway 32 about 2 miles south of Canaan Valley State Park; (304) 866–2722. Fresh fish, crab, and other seafood specials near the slopes. Moderate.

Deerfield Restaurant, Deerfield Village Resort, State Highway 32 near the parks; (304) 866–4559. Steak, pasta, chicken in resort setting. Moderate.

Big John's Family Fixins, State Highway 32 between Canaan Valley and Blackwater Falls Parks; (304) 866–4418. Sandwiches, pizza, and video and board games. Inexpensive.

White Grass Cafe, Cross-Country Ski Resort, Freeland Road, Canaan Valley; (304) 866–4114. Ski hangout with gravel floor and potbellied stove. Good soup; vegetarian and fish dishes. Open daily in winter for lunch and, on weekends, for dinner as well. Inexpensive.

Elkins

The Mingo Room, Graceland Inn and Conference Center, Davis and Elkins College; (304) 637–1600 or (800) 624–3157. Continental and regional cuisine served in an elegant red-oak dining room; pleasant for Sunday brunch; reservations necessary. Moderate.

1863 Tavern, Elkins Motor Lodge, just west of town on U.S. Highway 33 (Harrison Avenue); (304) 636–1400. Everyone goes for the prime rib special; open for dinner only. Moderate.

OTHER RECOMMENDED LODGINGS

Canaan Valley

Blackwater Falls State Park Lodge has fifty-four air-conditioned rooms with private baths, color TV, and phones, and a common game room and sitting room. The park also has twenty-five deluxe year-round vacation cabins with stone fireplaces, and a sixty-five-unit tent and trailer campground that is open from May through October. For reservations, call (304) 259–5216 or (800) 225–5982; www.blackwaterfalls.com. Rates: lodge, $52–$85 for a double; cabins, $420–$540 a week in summer, $70–$90 a day (with a two-day minimum) in other seasons; campground, $11–$14 a night.

Black Bear Resort, Northside Cortland Road; (304) 866–4391 or (800) 553–2327, www.blackbearwv.com. Forty-four cottages and twelve inn suites with refrigerators, Jacuzzi tubs, and fireplaces; access to swimming pool and tennis courts. Rates: $90–$110.

Bright Morning Inn, William Avenue, Davis; (304) 259–5119. Former boardinghouse restored as a B&B with seven rooms and one suite, all with private baths. Rates: $55–$80, which includes full breakfast.

Hill House B&B, Fourth Street, Davis; (304) 259–5883, www.daviswv.com. Restored nineteenth-century Victorian with three rooms, shared bath, full breakfast; two-day minimum on weekends. Rates: $75.

Meyer House Bed and Breakfast, Thomas Avenue, Davis; (304) 259–5451, www.travelpick.com. An 1880s Victorian with five bedrooms, some with private baths; full breakfast. Rates: $55–$75.

Elkins

Cheat River Lodge, 3 miles east of Elkins on U.S. Highway 33; (304) 636–2301, wvweb.com/cheatriverlodge. Charming lodge with six guest rooms, all with two double beds, private baths, and a picture-window view of the Cheat River. Rates: $58–$73. Also available are six three- and four-bedroom cottages in the woods along the water. The cottages also have

kitchens and outdoor hot tubs. Rates: $136–$156 a night; weekly rental is $804.

Graceland Inn and Conference Center, Davis and Elkins College; (304) 637–1600 or (800) 624–3157. The inn has eleven rooms furnished with antiques and Victorian reproductions; all have private baths, many of which are marble-lined; many other amenities. Rates: $118–$180 for a double. The twenty-six rooms in the Conference Center have queen-size beds, private baths, TV, and private phones. Rates: $72.

The Retreat B&B, 214 Harpertown Road; (304) 636–2960 or (888) 636–2960. Four rooms with shared bath; one suite with private bath; continental breakfast. Rates: $65–$80.

Tunnel Mountain Inn, located east of Elkins near Stuarts Recreation Park, old Route 33; (304) 636–1684 or (888) 211–9173, www.wvonline.com/shareourbeds/tunnelmtn. Three guest rooms, all with private baths; large health-conscious country breakfasts. Rates: $65–$75.

FOR MORE INFORMATION

West Virginia Division of Tourism & Parks, State Capitol Complex, Charleston, WV 25305; (800) 225–5982, www.callwva.com.

Canaan Valley Resort State Park HC 70, Box 330, Davis, WV 26260; (304) 866–4121 or (800) 622–4121, www.canaanresort.com.

Tucker County Convention and Visitors Bureau, P.O. Box 565, Davis, WV 26260; (304) 259–5315 or (800) 782–2775, www.canaanvalley.org.

Randolph County Convention and Visitors Bureau, 200 Executive Plaza, Elkins, WV 26241; (304) 636–2717 or (800) 422–3304, www.randolph countywv.com.

WEST VIRGINIA

Lewisburg

WEST VIRGINIA HIGHLIGHTS

2 NIGHTS

Historic sites • Crafts and antiques shopping • Hiking
Beartown State Park • Scenic steam railroad ride

One of the best weekend escapes imaginable is a visit to the historic town of Lewisburg, which is about a five-hour drive from Washington, D.C. Lewisburg has all the advantages of other West Virginia destinations—clean air, cool temperatures, nearby mountains and forests, and abundant recreational facilities—but this little town is worth a visit in its own right because of its beauty and charm.

Your weekend escape to the area takes advantage of both town and country by including a ride up the mountainside on an ancient steam engine, a hike through a magical forest of tumbling cliffs and ferny glades, a stay at an antique-packed inn, and a walking tour through town that takes in historic buildings and interesting little shops. There's also time for a long hike and picnic lunch along the Greenbrier River, and a visit to a fancy resort near Lewisburg that once hid a secret bomb shelter for high government officials.

The Lewisburg area is a perfect weekend destination all four seasons of the year. Summer offers hiking, canoeing, fishing, swimming, and evenings of repertory theater and chamber music, or simply sitting in a rocking chair on the front porch of an inn and watching the fireflies come out. Spring brings out the wildflowers and swells the streams. Lewisburg is also a wonderful winter getaway: Cross-country skiing is readily available in the area, and local inns tend to have log fires blazing and hot cider handy for guests who breeze in from an afternoon trek.

But Lewisburg is best in the fall, when the trees turn red, yellow, brown, and orange and blanket the mountains like a patchwork quilt. It's a perfect time to visit roadside fruit stands for apples and take long walks through the woods or along the Greenbrier River. Make early hotel reservations for autumn visits—and don't forget your camera!

DAY 1

Morning

Start early in the day for the drive to Lewisburg. It's a smooth drive on the expressway, and you can make the trip in less than five hours by taking Interstate 66 west, Interstate 81 south, and Interstate 64 west. Take exit 169 (U.S. Highway 219 south), and Lewisburg is only a few miles from I–64.

However, if you save the easy driving for the return home and take the scenic route a portion of the way, the trip will be one of the best parts of the weekend. After taking I–66 west for 75 miles and I–81 south for about 50 miles, exit the freeway near Harrisonburg, Virginia, and take U.S. Highway 33 west. From the exit, it's 26 miles to West Virginia. There, the backcountry roads up, over, and down the Appalachian Mountains are like a roller coaster through paradise. The modest towns and farms are few and far between, and mostly it's just you and the mountains.

Once you reach West Virginia, continue west on U.S. Highway 33 for 33 miles to Judy Gap. As you turn south on State Highway 28, you will see **Spruce Knob,** the highest point in West Virginia—elevation 4,861 feet—just on your right. Follow State Highway 28 about 35 miles to a point just beyond Green Bank, then begin looking for the sign for Cass Scenic Railroad State Park, your first stopping point of the day.

LUNCH: You can get sandwiches, sodas, and ice cream at the building where you pick up your tickets for the train ride.

Afternoon

Cass Scenic Railroad State Park is one of the few places in the United States where an authentic steam engine locomotive still operates. Once a logging line that operated until 1911, the Cass Railroad uses old Shay locomotives that have been authentically restored. The logging cars have been converted into open-air passenger coaches. A train ride will take you up the

Cemetery in historic Lewisburg

mountain at an astonishingly steep incline of 11 percent, with several switch-backs and reverses along the way.

The ride takes about ninety minutes round-trip, including a short stop at Whittaker Station in a pretty meadow halfway up the mountain. There are, of course, wonderful vistas as the train climbs the mountain. If you're really an enthusiast, you can take the four-and-a-half-hour ride all the way to the top of Bald Knob (elevation 4,842 feet) for a stunning view of the surrounding mountains and valleys.

Reservations in advance are strongly recommended; (304) 456–4300 or (800) 225–5982, www.pocahontas.org/cass. The train to Whittaker Station departs Cass at 10:50 A.M., 1:00 P.M., and 3:00 P.M. daily from just before Memorial Day through Labor Day and for two weeks at the peak of the fall color season. For the rest of September and October, it runs Friday through Sunday. Closed November through May. Adult tickets are $10.00 on weekdays, $15.00 on weekends. Children five through twelve ride for $6.00 on weekdays and $11.00 weekends; children under five, free. The longer train ride to Bald Knob departs Cass at noon and costs $3.00 to $4.00 more than the short ride.

Your next stop en route to Lewisburg is tiny **Beartown State Park,** a forest wonderland on Droop Mountain, approximately an hour-and-a-half drive from Cass. To get there, follow State Highway 28 south for 22 miles to Huntersville, State Highway 39 west for 6 miles to Marlinton, and U.S. Highway 219 south about 15 miles. Watch for the small sign on your left after you pass through the town of Droop.

Beartown State Park is an area of gigantic rock outcroppings that have been exposed, eroded, and forested over the eons. So named because bears found natural homes in the caves, Beartown has an eerie, fantastic beauty that surpasses description, and is an absolute must-see when you are in West Virginia. There is a half-mile boardwalk that goes up, under, and around the geological formations. If you're lucky, you'll be the only one on the walkway, so that you can hear the wind sighing in the stratospherically tall pines overhead and the water dripping from the rocks. Beartown, like all the West Virginia state parks, is free of charge. Open 8:00 A.M. to 6:00 P.M. daily except in winter. Phone (304) 653–4254; www.wvparks.com/beartown.

By late afternoon or early evening, you'll arrive at the town of **Lewisburg,** about 23 miles south of Beartown State Park on U.S. Highway 219. There are several places to stay in the area, but the best is the **General Lewis Inn,** 301 East Washington Street; (304) 645–2600 or (800) 628–4454, www.generallewisinn.com. The General Lewis Inn started out as a home, built in 1834. It has had numerous additions since then and now has twenty-six guest rooms. It's as inviting a place to stay as you'll ever find.

Although it is packed with antiques, there's nothing "ye olde," fussy, or precious about the General Lewis. Rooms are eccentrically furnished with a jumble of old stuff, including century-old prints on the walls and high four-poster beds, all of which are more than a hundred years old. The dining room has cheerfully mismatched cotton tablecloths and napkins, and an old quilt is flung over the hall railing.

The downstairs lobby area is as warm and cozy as your grandmother's house; there's likely to be a fire in the grate on chilly days (with rockers surrounding it), and board games and jigsaw puzzles are set on tables. Be sure to take a look at the side hallway on the ground floor. The walls are covered, higgledy-piggledy, with antiques, from ancient horse bridles to kitchen tools to helmets and guns. Outside, huge rocking chairs line the front porch.

Rates for this jewel of an inn are low. Rooms with double beds, private baths, air-conditioning, telephones, and cable television are $75–$91. A suite with two large rooms (and three separate beds) is a modest $106–$116.

DINNER: For your first night in Lewisburg, stay for dinner at the **General Lewis Inn.** Service is friendly and leisurely and the menu is traditional. The buttermilk biscuits are perfect, and you will get a good steak or chop in pleasant surroundings. Moderate.

LODGING: The General Lewis Inn.

DAY 2

Morning

After you scramble into your clothes, grab a wake-up cup of coffee in the living room of the inn, then take an early-morning walk through town.

BREAKFAST: About 6 blocks down Washington Street is the **Del Sol Cafe and Market,** where you can get cappuccino, espresso, pastries, and, best of all, the *Washington Post* and *New York Times.* It opens at 8:00 A.M. Located at 206 West Washington Street; (304) 645–5515. Inexpensive.

Spend the rest of the morning exploring Lewisburg. You can pick up a free pamphlet and a map to Lewisburg at the General Lewis Inn or at the **Lewisburg Visitors Center,** Carnegie Hall, 105 Church Street; (304) 645–7917 or (800) 833–2068. The pamphlet also includes a listing of most of the antique and specialty stores in Lewisburg, as well as the restaurants and lodging establishments. At the visitors center, you can also get materials for a one-hour, thirty-nine-site self-guided walking tour or a two-and-a-half-hour, seventy-two-site tour.

Of particular historic interest in one of the state's oldest cities are Carnegie Hall itself (see There's More), built in 1902 as an auditorium for Lewisburg Female Institute, later Greenbrier College; the Old Stone Church, across the street from Carnegie Hall, which is the oldest church in continuous use west of the Allegheny Mountains; North House Museum, just north of Carnegie Hall, where the attractions are the woodwork, period furniture, and china; and the Greenbrier County Library, across the street from the museum, which served as a hospital during the Civil War. If you're a Civil War buff, the visitors center has literature, maps, and a self-guided tour of the major sites of the May 1862 battle.

But save some time for shopping. Among Lewisburg's attractions are several pleasant little stores. There are a number of nice gift shops, including **J. Fenton Gallery/Quilts Unlimited,** 113 East Washington Street (304–647–4208), which has quilts, jewelry, and other handcrafted items; and the

Old Hardware Gallery, 118 West Washington Street (304–645–2236), a huge old hardware store that now sells decorative glass, Christmas items, wooden crafts, pottery, and more. At 203 East Washington is **Clayworks,** a pottery studio and showroom open to the public; (304) 647–5800. There are also bookstores, clothing stores, and three very nice antiques stores in the 100 block of East Washington Street. Most of the stores are open Monday through Saturday from 9:00 A.M. to 5:00 P.M.

LUNCH: For lunch, stop back at the Del Sol Cafe and Market and have them bag up some drinks and sandwiches for a picnic, then head off for a lengthy hike along the beautiful Greenbrier River Trail. If you prefer to sit for a while before hitting the trail, consider **Food and Friends,** 213 West Washington Street; (304) 645–4548. The menu is eclectic, including Tex-Mex, which is your best bet. Inexpensive.

Afternoon

To get to the base of a very scenic trail near Lewisburg, drive about 2 miles east of Lewisburg on U.S. Highway 60, turning left immediately before you get to the bridge over the Greenbrier River. Drive 1½ miles north to a parking lot (on the left-hand side of the road) where there is a small sign announcing parking for the **Greenbrier River Trail;** (304) 799–4087.

The Greenbrier River Trail is one of those walks that draw you farther and farther, because each bend in the river brings some freshly beautiful sight. The trail has hills on either side and the river sparkles down the middle, broken up with large boulders that create eddies and tiny rapids. In the fall (when the leaves are absolutely gorgeous), the river is often low enough to hop across in rocky areas.

The river trail extends 76 miles north from the outskirts of Lewisburg nearly all the way to Cass, crossing thirty-five bridges and passing through two tunnels. You might consider renting mountain bikes and seeing some of it that way. The path is loosely graveled and relatively flat, making it an easy ride. (See There's More for information on renting bicycles in Lewisburg.)

After a shower and a rest back at the General Lewis Inn, dinner is a short ten-minute drive away.

DINNER: "Supper clubs" are popular in West Virginia, and there's a very nice one about 5 miles east of Lewisburg: **The Cabin Club,** U.S. Highway 60; (304) 536–2202. Try the spinach salad topped with hot and sour bacon dressing, follow up with veal pappiette and portobello mushrooms, finish with bread pudding for dessert, and you'll go home happy. Moderate to expensive.

On summer evenings, you might scope out the **Greenbrier Valley Theatre,** a local repertory group that gives regular summer Thursday, Friday, and Saturday evening performances of plays and musicals, beginning at 8:00 P.M., at the Greenbrier Valley Airport, north of town on U.S. Highway 219. During the nonsummer months, there are occasional performances at the Theatre quarters at 113 East Washington Street. For information and tickets, call (304) 645–3838 or (800) 833–2068; www.gvtheatre.org.

LODGING: The General Lewis Inn.

DAY 3

Morning

BREAKFAST: The General Lewis Inn serves full country breakfasts, including wonderful biscuits with sausage gravy, as well as cereal and muffins.

Before you leave the General Lewis Inn, be sure to stroll through the backyard. There are several quiet areas where you can peruse the morning paper. There is also a croquet set freely available to guests; you might want to set it up and knock around a few balls.

Your final destination in the area is the famous **Greenbrier** resort, located in White Sulphur Springs just 7 miles east of Lewisburg on U.S. Highway 60. This lavish edifice is thought by some to be the finest resort east of the Mississippi. It has some 700 rooms, and is set on 6,500 beautiful acres. But one of the most interesting things about the Greenbrier was, until recently, one of the best-kept secrets in America.

In the 1950s, during the height of the Cold War "bomb scare," the U.S. government built an enormous bomb shelter underneath the resort. This wasn't a shelter for local West Virginia residents; rather it was intended to be a postnuclear hideaway for the U.S. Congress. According to the *Washington Post,* the three-story, 150-room bunker included meeting rooms for the Congress and could provide food, shelter, and filtered air for up to 1,000 government decision-makers for a month or two. The lawmakers were to enter through elaborate decontamination chambers and were to be issued "survival bags" containing toothpaste, hair tonic, and deodorant. The accommodations consisted of bunk beds, and the provisions included such delicacies as freeze-dried chicken a la king. Now that the secret of the bunker is out, the Greenbrier is offering ninety-minute public tours of the underground facility for $25. Try to arrange one before you visit; on Sundays, the 9:30 A.M. tour is for Greenbrier guests only, but the 1:15 P.M. tour is open to the general public. Phone (304) 536–1110 or (800) 624–6070; www.greenbrier.com..

You'll note that the Greenbrier folks take better care of their guests above-ground. The resort has velvet-turfed golf courses, a spa, horseback riding, beautiful indoor and outdoor swimming pools, tennis courts, a private bowling alley, and gorgeous rooms. The upper lobby is so fancy that there's a sign on the stairs leading to it that warns guests that men must wear jackets "or attractive golf sweaters" to even walk through it. After 6:00 P.M., golf sweaters are out and jackets are required.

The price for staying at the resort is predictably high ($410–$798 a night for a party of two), although the tariff includes dinner and breakfast. But you can take a turn through the beautiful grounds for free. On a ridge across from the lodge, there is a line of small, upscale gift shops that are fun to prowl.

LUNCH: Draper's Cafe at the Greenbrier has reuben sandwiches and chili with scallions and blue corn chips that are fantastic. Forget about your diet and heap on the sour cream, but leave room for one of the cafe's famous desserts.

Afternoon

After lunch seek out the Greenbrier Resort's **Gourmet Shop**, set smack in the middle of another row of shops in the main lodge. The Gourmet Shop sells doughnuts, but only if you've placed an order twenty-four hours in advance (304–536–1110, ext. 7291). You may have to order a minimum of a dozen doughnuts, but it is nearly a five-hour drive back home via Interstates 64 east, 81 north, and 66 east.

THERE'S MORE

Carnegie Hall. Carnegie Hall, 105 Church Street, has a museum and gift shop, a foreign and art film series, the free Ivy Terrace Concert Series on the lawn, a children's film series, a classical music series, and numerous changing art exhibits. To find out what's happening there during your visit to Lewisburg, phone (304) 645–7917; www.carnegie-hall.com.

Biking. Woods, Water, and Wheels, 200 West Washington Street; (304) 645–5200 or (888) 306–5539, www.xplorewv.com. It costs $40 to rent a mountain bike all day. For a fee they will transport you and your bike up the Greenbrier River Trail, and you can bike back to town. Reservations are necessary.

Canoeing. The folks at Greenbrier River Campgrounds rent canoes for $25–$40 for an afternoon. They also rent inner tubes, fishing gear, and mountain bikes. Located on State Highway 63 south of Lewisburg near Ronceverte; (304) 645–2760 or (800) 775–2203. Open April through October.

Golf. The Greenbrier, where for years Sam Snead was the club pro, has three championship eighteen-hole golf courses. Greens fees and cart rental cost $135 for guests staying at the resort and $245 for guests of guests, April through October; off-season rates are about $60 cheaper. Phone (304) 536–1110 or (800) 624–6070.

Pearl S. Buck Museum. If you're not a train fan and want a stopping point midway to Lewisburg, consider a visit to this small museum in Hillsboro on U.S. Highway 219 just north of Beartown State Park; (304) 653–4430. Buck is the only American woman to win both the Nobel Prize for Literature and the Pulitzer Prize. The tour of the museum emphasizes the house rather than her writings, and it's kid-friendly. Open 9:00 A.M. to 5:00 P.M. Monday through Saturday, 1:00 to 5:00 P.M. on Sunday. Closed November through March. Admission is $4.00 for adults and $1.00 for students; children under six are admitted free.

SPECIAL EVENTS

January. Shanghai Parade. For more than 150 years, the citizens of Lewisburg have held a community parade on New Year's Day afternoon. If you're there, you might see fire trucks, horses, scout troops, the high school band, a toddler dance class, and a bunch of people in costumes banging on pots and pans; all are having fun. There are no rules and no committee to screen entrants. (304) 645–1000 or (800) 833–2068.

March–April. Quilt National. The nation's oldest juried quilt show is held every other year (odd-numbered years) in Lewisburg. Thousands of quilters from around the world vie to enter. (304) 645–7917.

June. Lewisburg Antique Show and Sale, West Virginia State Fairgrounds, on the southern edge of Lewisburg. (304) 645–1000 or (800) 833–2068.

August. West Virginia State Fair. Nine-day event featuring agricultural exhibits, livestock and horse shows, a midway, a circus, and nationally known entertainers. (304) 645–1090; www.wvstatefair.com.

October. Taste of Our Towns. A festival of food and entertainment to benefit Carnegie Hall. (304) 645–7917.

OTHER RECOMMENDED RESTAURANTS

Washington Street Inn, 208 West Washington; (304) 645–1744. New restaurant in the second oldest house in Lewisburg offers classical continental cuisine (venison, New Zealand lamb, lobster) in a relaxed setting. Extensive wine list; piano bar and patio dining. Moderate to expensive.

Miss Ellie's, 110 South Jefferson Street; (304) 645–5085. Freshly prepared soups, sandwiches, desserts; good vegetarian selection. Inexpensive to moderate.

Julian's Restaurant and Coffee Bar, 102 South Lafayette; (304) 645–4145. New-American and northern Italian cuisine; its fans call it one of the best restaurants in the state. Open for dinner only, Wednesday through Sunday. Moderate.

Blake's Restaurant and Lounge, 705 East Main Street; (304) 536–1221. Hearty German and American food and beer. Moderate.

Lewis Theatre and Silver Screen Cafe, 113 North Court Street; (304) 645–6038. Enjoy soup, sandwiches, and desserts on the balcony while you watch first-run movies on the big screen; $3.00 for adults, $2.00 for children. Call for current feature and show times.

Clingman's Market, 102 East Washington Street; (304) 645–1990. Delightful carryout with first-rate vegetarian specials; limited seating on premises. Open for breakfast and lunch. Inexpensive.

Ol' Victorian River House Restaurant, 301 Railroad Avenue, Alderson (8 miles south of Lewisburg on State Highway 12); (304) 445–2955. Continental and American cuisine served in several small rooms in an old Victorian house; large menu selection. Moderate.

OTHER RECOMMENDED LODGINGS

Lynn's Inn, 3 miles north of Lewisburg just off U.S. Highway 219; (304) 645–2003 or (800) 304–2003. Pleasant four-bedroom B&B with private baths, antiques and local craft items. Farm setting with a large front porch and rockers; continental breakfast. Rates: $60–$75.

White Oaks Bed and Breakfast, Big Draft Road, White Sulphur Springs; (304) 536–3402 or (800) 536–3402, www.whiteoaksbb.com. Pleasant four-bedroom B&B in the country. Shared baths; full breakfast. Rates; $120.

Lillian's Bed and Breakfast, 204 North Main Street, White Sulphur Springs; (304) 536–1048 or (877) 536–1048, www.wvonline.net/lillians. Century-old Victorian with three guest rooms, all with private baths. Full country breakfast; antiques for sale on the premises. Rates; $90.

Swift Level, 3 miles west of Lewisburg on U.S. Highway 60; (304) 645–1155. Beautiful 1827 mansion on rolling farmland. The two bedrooms in the main house rent for $165 a night, four bunkhouse rooms (with shared bath and no breakfast) rent for $100. There is also a log cabin that rents for $175 a night.

Brier Inn Motel, 540 North Jefferson, on U.S. Highway 219 just north of Lewisburg; (304) 645–7722. More than 150 rooms and suites; conference rooms; restaurants on premises; in-room phones and TV; game room; swimming pool. Rates: $43–$80.

The James Wylie House, 7 miles east of Lewisburg at 208 East Main Street, White Sulphur Springs; (304) 536–9444 or (800) 870–1613. B&B with Flemish-bond brickwork. Three nicely furnished rooms with private baths, TV, full breakfast. Behind the B&B is an eighteenth-century log cabin guest house with the original stone fireplace. Rates: $90 for a double, $120 for the log cabin.

FOR MORE INFORMATION

Lewisburg Visitors Center, Carnegie Hall, 105 Church Street, Lewisburg, WV 24901; (304) 645–1000 or (800) 833–2068, www.greenbrierwv.com/lewisburg/lewisburg.html.

Pipestem State Park
and the New River Gorge

WEST VIRGINIA JEWELS

3 NIGHTS

Pipestem State Park • Bluestone State Park • New River Gorge
Hiking • Boating • White-water rafting • Coal mine tour

Once synonymous with coal mining, steel manufacturing, and gaping ecological destruction, West Virginia today is deservedly famous for the beauty of the Appalachian Mountains chain that runs its length and the great variety of outdoor activities in its magnificent state park system.

The transformation is nothing short of astonishing. The New River Gorge, the canyon that cuts through the lushly forested Appalachian Mountains, is called by some the Grand Canyon of the East. Once it was the site of intensive coal mining, logging, and railroad operations; at the New River Gorge Canyon Rim Visitors Center, you can see photographs and films of that era. Today, it's hard to believe that the stripped, gouged, ruined hills in the photographs are the same ones you see before your very eyes.

During this four-day escape, you will have a chance to explore both old and new West Virginia. Your itinerary starts with a long drive from the city to Pipestem Resort State Park, a mountainous park that is sometimes called the Jewel of the West Virginia Park System. Minutes away from Pipestem is Bluestone State Park for those more interested in water sports. About an hour's drive from Pipestem is the New River Gorge, one of the premier recreational areas in the eastern United States. You can't leave West Virginia without getting into a raft to ride the white water, and rafting outfitters in the area offer trips varying from the gentle to the wild and woolly.

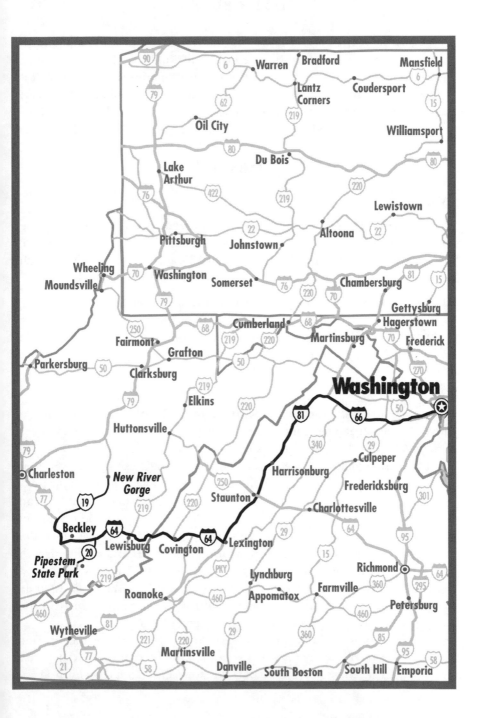

Finally, on your way back to Washington, you'll visit the old mining town of Beckley and explore what life used to be like in West Virginia during an underground tour of a real mine with a former coal miner as your guide. It is quite a contrast to West Virginia's natural beauties, but one that will enhance your respect for the strength and courage of the state's coal miners, whose labor "by the ton" played such a vital role in the industrialization of America.

DAY 1

Morning

The quickest route to Pipestem is via the interstate system. Take Interstate 66 west about 78 miles to Interstate 81, I–81 south 107 miles to Lexington, Virginia, Interstate 64 west 105 miles to exit 139, and State Highway 20 south about 30 miles to the park. Allow five to six hours for the 330-mile drive.

LUNCH: A good place to stop for lunch on the way is the **Southern Inn,** 37 South Main Street, in Lexington, Virginia, about three hours into your trip; (540) 463–3612. You can get sandwiches or regional dishes there at reasonable prices, and it's only a mile or so off the interstate.

Afternoon

When you arrive at **Pipestem Resort State Park,** take a few moments to drive through the huge park to acclimate yourself; then make **McKeever Lodge** (also called the Main Lodge) your first stop.

There, park guides will spend as much time as you'd like helping you plan your stay. Make sure you pick up a trail guide as well as a general map of the park.

No matter how tired you might be when you arrive, stretch your legs and refresh your spirits with a two-hour hike, which may be the most beautiful walk you've ever taken. Begin by walking from the Main Lodge down the mountain on the River Trail. It is approximately 2½ miles to the bottom, with just the right amount of scrambling over rocks to make it interesting. After a mile or so, the River Trail intersects with the Canyon Rim Trail. Take a 1-mile detour on the Canyon Rim Trail and you'll have a breathtaking view of the canyon and Bluestone River a thousand feet below you.

The Canyon Rim Trail rejoins the River Trail close to where it left it. One of the best parts of the hike is when you reach the bottom of the canyon on the River Trail. There you'll ford the Bluestone River (there is no bridge),

where the water probably won't be higher than your knees unless there has been flooding. The River Trail continues along the Bluestone for another mile or so of level walking on a service road.

As you walk along the river, keep your eyes open for *Spiraea alba,* the 6-foot-tall shrub whose woody, hollow stems were used by Native Americans and early European settlers as pipe stems, giving the nearby town and the park their name. The shrub blooms all summer, and the small white flowers are very fragrant.

At the end of the service road is the park's second lodge, **Mountain Creek Lodge.** When you reach it, reward yourself with a tram ride up the hill, which takes about ten minutes and costs $3.00 for adults and $2.00 for children under twelve. (Note: The tram is open full-time during the summer only. Inquire at the Main Lodge before you start your hike; you may have to retrace your steps.) The tram is really fun: It sways just enough to be pleasantly scary, and the views of the mountain and gorge below are fantastic.

At the top of the tram ride, at **Canyon Rim Center,** there are several gift shops, including one that sells the beautiful crafts of Appalachia. Look for carved wooden boxes and "collapsible" baskets, tooled leather goods, woven baskets, and pots of honey and jam.

You can return to McKeever Lodge where you started your hike on the main park road. The 4-mile hike with tram ride takes about two hours. Double that if you're walking back up the hill.

DINNER: The Bluestone Dining Room on the seventh floor of McKeever Lodge (304–466–1800, ext. 360) serves regional beef, chicken, and fish dishes, and there will be at least one pasta dish for vegetarians. There is also a large salad bar. The view from the dining room is spectacular; try to schedule dinner so you can watch the sun go down behind the mountains. Moderate.

LODGING: You have many choices of accommodations at Pipestem, including camping, two-, three-, and four-bedroom luxury cabins, and spacious rooms and suites at the resort's two lodges. Be sure to call ahead for reservations, especially during autumn, which is a particularly popular time at Pipestem; (304) 466–1800 or (800) 225–5982, www.pipestemresort.com. Lodge rooms are $57–$74 a night; suites are $90–$163; cottages are $80 and up a night. Cottages must be rented by the week in the summer. Rates start at $700. Pipestem also has eighty-two campsites, which rent for $16–$18 a night.

Evening

After dinner, stroll over to the **Outdoor Amphitheater.** There are educational programs and slide shows on weeknights and theatrical and musical performances on weekends.

DAY 2

Morning

BREAKFAST: For breakfast, the Bluestone Dining Room leans toward bacon, eggs, pancakes, fruit, and cereal.

After breakfast, you have plenty of options at Pipestem. There are horses and miles of bridle trails, an eighteen-hole golf course, a par-3 golf course, a driving range, lighted tennis courts, and indoor and outdoor swimming pools. At Long Branch Lake in the park, you can fish for largemouth bass, bluegill, crappie, and channel catfish. You can also rent a canoe or a paddleboat.

The park also offers archery, shuffleboard, Ping-Pong, a game room, a reading room, miniature golf, a nature center, an arboretum, and, of course, lots more trails to hike, as well as some trails marked for mountain bikes. During the winter, there is a sled run, and several of the trails are open for cross-country skiing.

LUNCH: Depending on where you are in the park, grab a quick lunch at the **Black Bear Snack Bar** in McKeever Lodge or at the **Mountain Creek Dining Room** in the lodge at the bottom of the canyon. Both offer a wide range of moderately priced, family-friendly sandwiches, soups, and salads.

Afternoon

After lunch, take a short 9-mile drive north on State Highway 20 and check out another wonderful park, **Bluestone State Park;** (304) 466–2805, www.bluestonesp.com. Because the park sits adjacent to Bluestone Lake, West Virginia's second largest body of water, water-related activities are the primary recreational choices. You can enjoy boating and fishing and a large swimming pool. But there are also hiking trails, shuffleboard, croquet, badminton, volleyball, Ping-Pong, horseshoes, and a softball field. If you forgot to bring your Frisbee, you can rent one at Bluestone for 50 cents an hour.

DINNER: Oak Supper Club, Indian Ridge Road just off State Highway 20 near Pipestem (look for the signs); (304) 466–4800. It's known for its steaks, prime rib, chicken, trout, generous servings, and casual farmhouse setting; open for dinner only. Moderate.

The **Pipestem Drive-in Theater** on State Highway 20 a few miles south of the park shows first-run family movies. Adult admission is $4.00; children get in for $1.00; Sunday is $8.00-a-car night. Call (304) 384–7382 to see what's playing.

LODGING: Pipestem Resort State Park.

DAY 3

Morning and Afternoon

Get up very early and drive directly to the Fayetteville-Lansing area on the **New River,** where you'll meet your guides, change into river gear, and prepare for a **white-water rafting** trip. Don't worry about breakfast; they'll almost certainly give you a continental breakfast and lunch as part of your rafting adventure. To get to the New River recreational area, take State Highway 20 south about 7 miles to Interstate 77 (West Virginia Turnpike). Then take I–77 north 34 miles to exit 48 and U.S. Highway 19 north another 14 miles to Fayetteville, the hub of white-water rafting activity on the New River. Lansing, where several of the outfitters have their shops, is another couple of miles up the road.

There are numerous rafting companies that provide equipment and guides for a trip down the New River. The guides travel with you, so even children and first-timers can safely have a wonderful time on the river. All you need is advance reservations (see There's More for a listing of companies and phone numbers) and proper attire: in warm weather, swimsuits or shorts, T-shirts, sunglasses, sunblock, visor hat, and a windbreaker. If you go in the spring or fall, a wet suit is advised, as well as a waterproof jacket and wool clothing. (Wet suits can be rented at most rafting facilities.)

Beginners and families should consider a trip on the Upper New River, which has gentle rapids that don't require much maneuvering. Most of the larger outfitters in the area offer a four- to six-hour beginning rafting trip, which includes breakfast and a picnic lunch. Expect to pay $60–$90 per adult (half that for children) for the trip.

If you're looking for more adventure, try a full-day trip on the Lower New River. After your outfitter buses you to the river and provides you with a flotation vest and safety helmet, you'll jump into an oversize inflatable "boat" and

Rafting on the New River

begin your wild and wet four- to six-hour roller-coaster ride over Class III to Class V rapids.

With the help of your guide, you learn to surf the waves, maneuver around partially submerged boulders, soar over ledges, and shoot rapids with names like "Surprise," "Double Z," and "Miller's Folly." At the end of the run, you'll be soaking wet, tired to the bone, and totally exhilarated. You might even want to add an extra day to your trip and sample the nearby Gauley River, ranked among the top ten rivers in the world (and among the top two in the United States) for rafting. Lower New River trips cost $80–$140 per person.

A number of outfitters also offer half-day trips, special trips for bird-watchers, or trips with your own private guide. In fact, the best way to plan a day of white-water rafting is to talk with several of the outfitters and, if their package trips don't suit your wishes, work with them to design an individual tour for your family or group.

DINNER: After your rafting adventure, refresh yourself with dinner at **Sedona Grille,** 106 East Maple Street, Fayetteville; (304) 574–3411. Sedona attracts rafters, hikers, and just plain tourists who all seem to enjoy the inexpensive

Southwestern specials. (The most expensive item on the menu is less than $9.00.) Kids can get spaghetti, a grilled cheese, or hamburger with fries for $2.29.

Be sure to stop at the **Canyon Rim Visitors Center** on U.S. Highway 19 on the north side of the river as you're driving back to Pipestem. The center includes a boardwalk through the woods to give you the best look at the magnificent New River Gorge below. The bridge, the world's largest single steel-arch bridge, is pretty impressive as well.

At Canyon Rim Visitors Center, there is also a very nice small museum with pictures, films, text, and artifacts depicting the history of the New River and the Gorge. There you can see the extraordinary transformation of the area from a wilderness paradise to an industrial center back to the forested recreational area that it is today. Open 9:00 A.M. to 5:00 P.M., until nightfall in summer. Phone (304) 574–2115; www.nps.gov/neri.

LODGING: Pipestem Resort State Park.

DAY 4

Morning

BREAKFAST: Bluestone Dining Room, McKeever Lodge.

After breakfast, pack your car and begin the trip back to Washington. At Hinton, just north of Pipestem, turn west on State Highway 3 and follow it north and west to **Beckley,** a detour that will take you only a half hour or so.

Beckley is an old coal mining town. Although it's been years since the big mines were active in the area, the history of the mines and the brave men who worked in them has been preserved at the **Beckley Exhibition Coal Mine,** located in New River Park on Ewart Avenue in Beckley; (304) 256–1747, wvweb.com/www/exhibition_coal_mine. Open daily 10:00 A.M. to 5:30 P.M., early April through November 1. Admission is $8.00 for adults, $7.00 for seniors, $5.00 for children four to twelve; children under four are admitted free.

At the Exhibition Mine, there is a museum with photographs, mining tools, and memorabilia from the great days of mining.

But it is the forty-minute mine tour that makes the trip to Beckley special. Once a working mine, the exhibition mine is now open for visitors to tour on slowly moving railcars along the old track laid through the tunnels. You'll be accompanied by a real miner who is as knowledgeable as he is entertaining. He makes several stops along the way to demonstrate where the mules would have pulled the coal cars, and how a miner would use dynamite to expose a seam of coal. For one breathless moment, he switches off the lights, to show visitors what it was like before the days of electricity in the mines. Blinding black descends instantly, until, with a welcome hiss, your guide lights up the old-fashioned gas lantern attached to his hat, and the tour continues. Note: Wear warm clothing—the temperature is a constant 58 degrees in the mine.

After the tour, you can visit the Coal Company House, a tiny three-room house that was home to a mining family as recently as the 1940s, and the imposing Superintendent House, a ninety-year-old, three-story mansion. Also located at New River Park is the Youth Museum of Southern West Virginia and the Mountain Homestead, if you decide to make a day of it in Beckley.

Return home from Beckley via I–77 north, I–64 east, I–81 north, and I–66 east. Allow five to six hours.

Your best bets for a lunch stop on the way are an hour east of Beckley in Lewisburg (see West Virginia Escape Three, page 166), or you can wait another couple of hours and return to the Southern Inn in Lexington, Virginia, a popular lunch spot.

THERE'S MORE

White-water Rafting. There are a score of rafting outfitters in the area. Among them are Class VI River Runners in Lansing, (304) 574–0704 or (800) 252–7784, www.raftwv.com; Rivers Whitewater Rafting Resort in Lansing, (304) 574–3834 or (800) 879–7483, www.riversresort.com; and New River Scenic Whitewater Tours in Hinton, (304) 466–2288 or (800) 292–0880, www.newriverscenic.com. For more information about white-water rafting, contact the Southern West Virginia Convention and Visitors Bureau at (304) 252–2244 or (800) 847–4898, www.visitwv.org.

Canoeing. If you're looking for a gentler water adventure, several companies rent canoes for paddling around on rivers closer to Pipestem. Try Cantrell Canoes and Rafts, State Highway 20 below Bluestone Dam, Hinton; (304) 466–0595 or (800) 470–7238.

Shopping. Tamarack, at exit 45 of West Virginia Turnpike (I–77) near Beckley, has lots of West Virginia–made crafts and products in a 60,000-square-foot shopping, food court, and entertainment complex. Open daily 9:00 A.M. to 7:00 P.M., later in the summer. (304) 256–6843 or (888) 262–7225; www.tamarackwv.com.

Golf. Glade Springs Resort has a challenging eighteen-hole course that many consider one of the best courses in the state. Located at 200 Lake Drive, Daniels; (304) 763–2000 or (800) 634–5233. Eighteen holes of golf at Glade Springs will cost you $50–$70 if you are a guest, more if you are not. A round of golf at Pipestem Resort State Park will cost you $37–$46 with cart rental; Pipestem's par-3 course costs $29. (304) 466–1800.

Theater West Virginia. Broadway musicals and other entertainment at an outdoor amphitheater north of Beckley at Grandview State Park; (304) 256–6800 or (800) 666–9142, wvweb.com/www/twv.

Historic Fayette Theatre. Bluegrass bands, traditional Irish folk songs, country and western, rock, storytelling, plays, and other post-rafting entertainment. Located at 115 South Court Street, Fayetteville; (304) 574–4655.

SPECIAL EVENTS

March. Appalachian Heritage Weekend. Arts, crafts, and music at Pipestem State Park. (304) 466–1800 or (800) 225–5982.

May–September. Pipestem State Park Outdoor Amphitheater play and music series with performances on Saturday nights. (304) 466–1800 or (800) 225–5982.

July–August. West Virginia State Water Festival. Parades, pageants, events, and activities throughout the area. (304) 466–5155.

August. Annual Appalachian Arts and Crafts Festival in Beckley. (304) 252–7328.

October. New River Gorge Bridge Day Festival. West Virginia's largest single-day festival; rafting, chili cook-off, music, and more. (304) 465–5617 or (800) 927–0263.

OTHER RECOMMENDED RESTAURANTS

Pipestem Area

Riverside Room, about 20 miles east of Pipestem on State Highway 3 in the Pence Springs Hotel; (304) 445–2600 or (800) 826–1829. Gourmet English country and Colonial meals (venison, game pie, beef, trout) served by wait staff in period dress. Moderate to expensive.

Kirk's Restaurant, State Highway 20 about 12 miles north of Pipestem; (304) 466–4600. Casual restaurant overlooking the New River. Kirk's serves family-style meals at dinner; also open for breakfast and lunch. Inexpensive to moderate.

New River Gorge Area

Smokey's Charcoal Grille, Ames Heights Road, Lansing; (304) 574–4905. Always crowded eatery specializing in sandwiches, chicken, and ribs. Moderate.

Dirty Ernie's Rib Pit, 310 Keller Avenue, Fayetteville; (304) 574–4822. Hot wings, cheese sticks, soup, salad, chicken, pasta, and, of course, baby back ribs. Moderate.

Fat Tire Deli, 103 Keller Avenue, Fayetteville; (304) 574–0599. Traditional and vegetarian subs, salads, bagels, and muffins. Inexpensive.

Beckley

Ryan's Family Steak House, 1320 Eisenhower Drive; (304) 252–0522. Hand-cut steaks, hundred-item salad bar. Moderate.

Glade Springs Clubhouse Dining Room, Glade Springs Resort (U.S. Highway 19, 6 miles south of Beckley in Daniels); (304) 763–2900. Casual fine dining with a spectacular view of the golf course; open to the public. Moderate.

Best place for doughnuts: Confection Connection, 249 Eisenhower Drive; (304) 252–3274.

OTHER RECOMMENDED LODGINGS

Pipestem Area

Bluestone State Park, State Highway 20 south of Hinton; (304) 466–2805 or (800) 225–5982, www.bluestonesp.com. Bluestone has twenty-five deluxe cabins and eighty-seven campsites. Cabin rates are $71–$83; weekly rates are $450–$503. Campsites are $12–$16.

Pence Springs Hotel, about 20 miles east of Pipestem on State Highway 3 near Pence Springs; (304) 445–2606 or (800) 826–1829. Once a mineral spa, then a Roaring Twenties resort, then a girls' school, then the West Virginia State Prison for Women, it is now a country bed-and-breakfast inn. The restoration isn't complete, but the fourteen rooms that are done and furnished in the style of the 1920s are homey and comfortable. The large, complimentary country breakfasts are a crowd favorite, and there is a restaurant on the premises for lunches and dinner. On Sundays in the summer and fall, a very large flea market is held on the hotel grounds. Rates: $70 –$99.

Walnut Grove Inn, Broadway Road just off State Highway 20, 1½ miles north of Pipestem State Park; (304) 466–6119 or (800) 701–1237. Conveniently located hundred-year-old farmhouse with five guest rooms, swimming pool for guest use. Biscuits and gravy or similar hearty fare for breakfast. Rates: $50–$75.

Beckley Area

Glade Springs Resort, 200 Lake Drive, Daniels (on U.S. Highway 19 about 6 miles south of Beckley); (304) 763–2000 or (800) 634–5233, www.gladesprings.com. Full-scale resort with suites, villas, and cottages; tennis, horseback riding, indoor and outdoor pools, golf course. Rates: $109–$165.

Country Inn and Suites, 2120 Harper Road, Beckley; (304) 252–5100 or (800) 456–4000. New chain motel with 157 rooms. Indoor and outdoor swimming pools and whirlpools, game room, fitness center; continental breakfast. Rates: $69–$135.

New River Gorge Area

Historic Morris Harvey House Bed and Breakfast, 201 West Maple Avenue, Fayetteville; (304) 574–1902. Three-story Victorian located 1 mile south of New River Bridge. Four guest rooms, two share a shower; full breakfast of fruit, muffins, and eggs. Open April through October. Rates: $85 and up.

Historic White Horse Bed and Breakfast, 120 Fayette Avenue, Fayetteville; (304) 574–1400, wvweb.com/www/white_horse_bb. Large town home on several wooded acres has six guest rooms and a detached cottage; breakfast always includes fruit and pastry. Rooms are $80–$100; the cottage is $110.

The Bunk House, first driveway on the left on Lansing Road, Lansing; (304) 574–0265. Rafters favorite: For $15 a night, you get a bunk bed and access to a kitchen and washer and dryer.

FOR MORE INFORMATION

West Virginia Division of Tourism and Parks, State Capitol Complex, P.O. Box 50312, Charleston, WV 25305–0312; (800) 225–5982, www.callwva.com.

Southern West Virginia Convention and Visitors Bureau, 511 Ewart Avenue, Beckley, WV 25801; (304) 252–2244 or (800) 847–4898, www.visitwv. org.

New River Convention and Visitors Bureau, 310 Oyler Avenue, Oak Hill, WV 25901; (304) 465–5617 or (800) 927–0263, www.newrivercvb.com.

PENNSYLVANIA
ESCAPES

Philadelphia

BIRTHPLACE OF INDEPENDENCE

2 NIGHTS

*Historic sites • Old markets • Walking tour of neighborhoods
Museums • Night life • Spectator sports • Ethnic dining*

Philadelphia is a delicious mélange of contrasts, from the joyful frenzy of the Italian market to the solemn dignity of Independence Hall, from the Mummers Parade to fine jazz—with a huge city park, hundreds of museums and galleries, the Liberty Bell, and Philly's famous cheesesteaks thrown in for good measure. Couple that with Philadelphia's well-deserved reputation as one of America's friendliest cities, and the charm of 200-year-old brick streets and horse-drawn carriages, and you begin to appreciate what the City of Brotherly Love has to offer.

Although Philadelphia's precious landmarks of American independence (Independence Hall and the Liberty Bell) are reason enough to visit, your quick escape to the city also includes a walking tour of the historic area and adds the Philadelphia Museum of Art and the Rodin Museum, shopping and gawking in funky South Street, a pasta feast in Little Italy, and late-night jazz. It's almost an insult to Philadelphia to pack it all into three too-short days.

DAY 1

Morning

It is about a three-hour drive to Philadelphia from Washington on Interstate 95. Continue on I–95 until you reach Interstate 676 just north of the down-

town area and take I–676 to the North Fifteenth Street exit. Drive a few blocks south and you're in the heart of downtown Philadelphia.

Given that most people consider Philadelphia a food-lover's mecca, it's a must to get on the road in time to make it for lunch. Philadelphia offers a world of choices, but the best way to meet the city is to eat your way through the **Reading Terminal Market.** Home to dozens of small grocery and food stalls, with plenty of places to sit and eat, the market offers such Pennsylvania Dutch exotica as "chicken and waffles," scrapple, and homemade soft pretzels (sold by shy Mennonite girls in sober dress and net caps). You'll also find Greek and Italian specialties, Southern fried catfish and barbecued ribs, hoagies of all sizes and flavors, and Asian takeout. In between are butcher shops, espresso bars, fish stands, flower sellers, and African import stalls. Located at Twelfth and Arch Streets; (215) 922–2317. Open Monday to Saturday 8:00 A.M. to 6:00 P.M.

LUNCH: For a real Philadelphia lunch, try a cheesesteak sandwich with provolone, onions, and peppers at **Rick's Steaks** (formerly called Olivieri's Prince of Steaks) in Reading Terminal Market; (215) 925–4320. Open Monday to Saturday 10:00 A.M. to 4:00 P.M.; inexpensive. Top it off with a butterscotch vanilla ice-cream cone from **Bassetts Ice Cream** (215–922–1771) or a cup of coffee and a cream cheese and chocolate chip cannoli at **Termini Brothers Bakery**; (215) 629–1790.

Afternoon

Before leaving the downtown area, be sure to drive by the ornate **City Hall,** topped by a bronze statue of city father William Penn, the Quaker humanist and libertarian. Guided tours of the interior are available weekdays at 12:30 P.M., and the Observation Deck is open weekdays 10:00 A.M. to 3:00 P.M. for a splendid view of the city. Located at Philadelphia City Hall, Broad and Market Streets; (215) 686–9074.

Then it's on to the historic district, where you'll drop your bags and your car at **Thomas Bond House,** a restored eighteenth-century bed-and-breakfast inn located in Independence National Historical Park at 129 South Second Street between Chestnut and Walnut Streets; (215) 923–8523 or (800) 845–2663, www.winstonsaleminn.com/philadelphia. The twelve guest rooms in the 225-year-old house have all been carefully restored in the Colonial style, and all have four-poster beds, fireplaces, and private baths. Room rates vary from $95 to $160 and include breakfast, afternoon wine and cheese, an evening brandy in winter, and complimentary coffee, tea, and soda all day long.

After you've checked in, embark on a walking tour of old Philadelphia. Start your trek at **Independence National Historical Park**'s visitors center, South Third and Chestnut (215) 597–8974, www.nps.gov/inde), open daily from 9:00 A.M. to 5:00 P.M. Park rangers are extremely helpful and not only will give you maps, but, once they know your particular interests, will note appropriate stops on the route. A gift shop on the premises is loaded with books and souvenirs, and a half-hour film provides an excellent introduction to Philadelphia's role in the birth of the United States of America.

Independence National Historical Park is 17 blocks of arguably the most important historic buildings in the United States. The attractions are all free of charge, authentic, noncommercial, and interesting. The park itself is leafy, green, and quiet, with plenty of benches under big shade trees when you need a rest on your walking tour.

As you emerge from the visitors center, be sure to notice the grassy sites marking the location of the original Quaker meetinghouse and school room, and Carpenters' Hall, where the First Continental Congress met in 1774. Then peek in at the **Second Bank of the United States,** 420 Chestnut Street, and admire the main banking room's salmon and green barrel-vaulted ceiling and black and white marble floors. The bank also contains the **Second Bank Portrait Gallery,** which features several portraits of the nation's founders by Charles Wilson Peale and others. Open daily 10:00 A.M. to 5:00 P.M.; (215) 597–8974. On summer afternoons, local theater groups often perform free musical one-act plays on the bank's Greek Revival steps. Admission is $2.00 for everyone over seventeen, free for youngsters.

Long lines may look daunting, but be sure to make **Independence Hall** a priority. Here, in the "cradle of liberty," the Declaration of Independence was debated and eventually approved on July 4, 1776. Eleven years later, the Constitutional Convention met in the Assembly Room, argued, compromised, and drafted the Constitution of the United States of America. A thirty-minute tour starts every fifteen minutes or so and it's worth the wait. Located on Chestnut Street between South Fifth and South Sixth Streets; (215) 597–8974. Open daily 9:00 A.M. to 5:00 P.M., sometimes later in summer months.

Flanking Independence Hall are **Congress Hall,** where the U.S. Congress met from 1790 to 1800 when Philadelphia was the capital of the United States, and **Old City Hall,** the original meeting place of the U.S. Supreme Court. Both are must-sees.

A block north of Independence Hall is the modern glass and marble pavilion housing the **Liberty Bell,** which can be seen from the outside even when the building is closed. The fact that the bell is mobbed with tourists (many from abroad) testifies to its enduring attraction as the preeminent symbol of American independence. Located on Market Street between Fifth and Sixth Streets. Open daily 9:00 A.M. to 5:00 P.M., sometimes later in summer months. Phone (215) 597–8974.

Other places of interest within a couple of blocks of the park are **Declaration House,** where Thomas Jefferson wrote the first draft of the Declaration of Independence (open daily 9:00 A.M. to 5:00 P.M.; Seventh and Market Streets; 215–597–8974); **Christ Church,** where Washington and Franklin often worshiped (open Monday to Saturday 9:00 A.M. to 5:00 P.M., Sunday 1:00 to 5:00 P.M.; Second Street, just north of Market Street; 215–922–1695); and **Betsy Ross House,** where the famed seamstress may or may not have lived and may or may not have sewn the first American flag—neither debate keeps the tourists away (open Tuesday to Sunday 10:00 A.M. to 5:00 P.M.; 239 Arch Street; 215–627–5343). Also nearby is the **United States Mint,** the largest mint in the world (open daily 9:00 A.M. to 4:30 P.M., closed weekends from September to April and on Sundays in May and June; Fifth and Arch Streets; 215–597–7350).

When you are walked out, return to the Thomas Bond House for a glass of sherry and a biscuit, compliments of the inn. On cooler days there might be a fire in the parlor, which is a great place to put your feet up before going out for the evening.

If you are lucky enough to be in Philadelphia on the first Friday of the month, you must do as chic Philadelphians do and stroll 3 blocks north of the inn to tiny, picturesque Elfreth's Alley, the oldest continuously inhabited residential street in America. It's a 1-block row of eighteenth-century houses, many of which are still private residences. On "First Friday," the shops and galleries on the street treat visitors to free hors d'oeuvres, while they shop, look, and are looked at.

DINNER: Head downtown for one of the best Chinese meals of your life at **Susanna Foo,** 1512 Walnut Street; (215) 545–2666. Start with the dim sum appetizers, then sample one of the French/Chinese/California fusion specialties like tea-smoked squab with corn and taro pudding. Expensive.

After dinner, head over to **Zanzibar Blue,** for coffee and dessert or a drink and, not incidentally, some of the best jazz in Philadelphia. Located at 200 South Broad Street; (215) 735–5200.

LODGING: Thomas Bond House.

DAY 2

Morning

BREAKFAST: The Thomas Bond House serves freshly squeezed orange juice, muffins, and coffee on weekdays and a full breakfast on weekends.

After breakfast at the inn, you're set for the second short walking tour of the weekend. This time, you'll scour Society Hill, Antiques Row, and Center City.

Two historic houses on the southern edge of Independence National Historical Park are worth a visit. The **Bishop White House,** home of the first Episcopal bishop of Philadelphia, is an excellent example of an upper-class Colonial home. The **Todd House,** once home to Dolley Payne Todd (who later married James Madison), is considerably more modest. Both houses are on Walnut Street between Third and Fourth Streets. They're open to the public and, for $2.00, you can arrange a National Park Service tour of the houses at the Independence National Historical Park Visitors Center.

Two blocks south at 321 South Fourth Street is the twenty-two-room **Physick House** where Philip Syng Physick, the "Father of American Surgery," lived. It's the only freestanding house remaining in Society Hill. Open Thursday to Saturday 11:00 A.M. to 2:00 P.M., Sunday 1:00 to 4:00 P.M. Tours are available, call for times; (215) 925–7866. Admission is $3.00 for adults, $2.00 for children six to twelve; children under six are admitted free.

As you wander through **Society Hill,** a pleasant neighborhood only recently gentrified, keep an eye out for some of the short, charming side streets such as Delancey Street, between Second and Sixth Streets, and St. Peter's Way, between Third and Fourth Streets.

Several churches in the Society Hill neighborhood also deserve a visit: Old St. Mary's Church at 252 South Fourth Street was the city's main Roman Catholic church in Colonial times; St. Peter's Church and Graveyard at 313 Pine Street is a delightful 200-year-old Episcopal church; and the Old Pine Street Church at 412 Pine Street is the city's oldest Presbyterian church.

As you walk west on Pine Street, you leave Society Hill and enter the Washington Square West neighborhood. Allow plenty of time for browsing along **Antique Row** on Pine Street between South Ninth and South Seventeenth Streets. Some of the stores are open by appointment only, but most are open between 11:00 A.M. and 3:00 P.M.

Before stopping for lunch, walk a few blocks north on South Seventh Street to **Washington Square,** a serene park where you'll see the Tomb of the Unknown Soldier of the Revolutionary War. One block north of the park on Sansom Street between South Seventh and South Eighth Streets is **Jewelers' Row,** a brick-paved block with millions of dollars worth of precious stones. At South Sixth and Sansom Streets as you head back toward the park is the **Curtis Center of Norman Rockwell Art,** which has on display all of Rockwell's 324 *Saturday Evening Post* cover illustrations. Open Monday to Saturday 10:00 A.M. to 4:00 P.M., Sunday 11:00 A.M. to 4:00 P.M. Admission is $2.00 for adults and $1.50 for senior citizens and students; children under twelve are admitted free. Phone (215) 922–4345.

LUNCH: A fun lunch stop is **City Tavern,** 138 South Second Street (215–413–1443), a five-story historic tavern frequented by Washington, Adams, Jefferson, and Franklin. Its ten dining rooms have been restored with period furniture, and the menu offers authentic Colonial-era dishes, including turkey potpie, salmon and corn cakes, braised rabbit, duck sausage, and mushroom bisque. And don't neglect the Thomas Jefferson dark ale, brewed extra strong especially for the tavern. Moderate to expensive.

Afternoon

After lunch, stroll about a half mile south on Second Street and you'll be introduced to a completely different side of Philadelphia. Hip, bustling, witty **South Street** is approximately 9 blocks of shops, restaurants, galleries, and coffee bars. With its vintage clothing shops, bookstores, street musicians, and gorgeous men on skates, South Street is the place to find stores with such names as Condom Kingdom and Three Hairy Sisters. It's not all counterculture, either. South Street has antiques stores, jewelry stores, bookshops, and much more.

No pilgrimage to Philadelphia would be complete without a tribute to the Mummers. So collect your car, and head for the **Mummers Museum** in South Philly, 1100 South Second Street; (215) 336–3050, www. riverfrontmummers.com/mummersmuseum.html. Open Tuesday to Saturday 9:30 A.M. to 5:00 P.M., Sunday noon to 5:00 P.M. Admission is $2.50 for adults and $2.00 for senior citizens and children under twelve.

Mumming is an ancient Christmas ritual in England. In Philadelphia it's a 200-year-old tradition that culminates every year in the famous New Year's Day Mummers Parade. It's a sort of Italian-German-Caribbean Philadelphia Mardi Gras in which 25,000 men dress up in extraordinary creations of feath-

Italian Market

ers and glitter (some weighing more than 100 pounds) and parade through town picking banjos to the delight of thousands of locals and visitors alike.

If you aren't lucky enough to catch their act on New Year's Day (or at several concerts given later in the year), the Mummers Museum has loads of information and Mummer paraphernalia.

Finish your afternoon at the city's famous **Italian Market,** five pungent, noisy, wonderful blocks of outdoor grocery stalls in the heart of Little Italy. Philadelphians go there to shop for fresh fish, homemade pasta, and freshly butchered meat. With its sidewalks crammed with vendors shouting back and forth, customers haggling, children dodging and racing, and tourists admiring, it's another slice of Philadelphia life. It's located on South Ninth Street between Christian and Dickenson Streets. Vendor hours vary, but most are open Monday to Saturday from 9:00 A.M. to 5:00 P.M. Phone (215) 592–1295.

DINNER: Little Italy is home to lots of great restaurants. For a real treat, opt for a longtime local favorite, **Dante's and Luigi's,** 762 South Tenth Street; (215) 922–9501. It's a no-frills Italian restaurant with Formica tabletops, glass-block windows, and pink painted walls. The extensive menu includes classic Italian-American favorites and much more. The veal and seafood dishes are particularly good, but be sure to get a side of pasta with "tomato gravy," as they call marinara sauce in South Philly. Open for lunch Sunday through Tuesday, lunch and dinner Wednesday through Saturday. Moderate.

You might end your evening at the theater or concert hall. Philadelphia is truly a cultural center, with a world-class orchestra, three opera companies, several dance companies, and nearly a dozen theaters presenting musicals, comedy, and drama. You can get information on what's happening and times of performances by consulting the "Guide to the Lively Arts" section in the daily *Philadelphia Inquirer* or by picking up a copy of *Philadelphia Spotlite* (available at the downtown visitors center and at most hotels). From September to May, the **Philadelphia Orchestra** performs at the Academy of Music, Broad and Locust Streets; (215) 893–1900. During the summer, performances are held at the Mann Music Center in West Fairmount Park; (215) 567–0707.

LODGING: Thomas Bond House.

DAY 3

Morning

BREAKFAST: Thomas Bond House.

After breakfast, head for the Fairmount Park area of town, where many of the art museums are located.

A good place to start your tour is at the wonderful **Rodin Museum,** Twenty-second Street and Benjamin Franklin Parkway; (215) 763–8100, www.rodinmuseum.org. This shrine to the great sculptor features the largest collection of his works outside of France. There's *The Thinker* as you enter the grounds, and the horrifying *Gates of Hell* at the doorway to the building. The *Burghers of Calais* dominates the main gallery, and other Rodin studies are arranged along the walls. Open Tuesday to Sunday 10:00 A.M. to 5:00 P.M.; a $3.00 donation is requested.

Next stop is a climb up the stairs made famous in the movie *Rocky,* to the gigantic **Philadelphia Museum of Art,** Twenty-sixth Street and Benjamin Franklin Parkway; (215) 763–8100, www.philamuseum.org. On weekends, the terrace area is aswarm with helmeted in-line skaters working out, hanging out, or climbing perilously up and down the crumbling stone steps. Inside, the museum has well over a hundred galleries with a fabulous collection, featuring medieval and early Renaissance art, Near Eastern and Asian art, four wings of European art, and magnificent collections of American, early twentieth-century, and contemporary art.

Rather than try to take in the whole place at one gulp, you might hone in on a particular period. A good choice would be the collection of Impressionists, with dozens of paintings by Manet, Degas, Cézanne, Cassatt, and Renoir. Enjoy the exquisite privilege of seeing the original of van Gogh's *Sunflowers*. Note also the pink and blue Matisse mural above the entrance in the lobby. Open Tuesday to Sunday 10:00 A.M. to 5:00 P.M. and Wednesday evenings until 8:00 P.M. Admission is $8.00 for adults; $5.00 for senior citizens, full-time students, and children five to seventeen; children under five are admitted free.

LUNCH: For a spectacular brunch or lunch, drive a couple of miles to the **White Dog Cafe**, 3420 Sansom Street; (215) 386–9224, www.whitedog. com. At weekend brunch, your choices will range from brioche French toast with sun-dried apricots to stir-fried free-range beef and tofu in ginger-peanut sauce. For weekday lunch, try the broccoli Parmesan bisque followed by a roasted eggplant/provolone/sautéed spinach sandwich or a salmon burger on potato dill bread. Moderate to expensive.

Afternoon

During your last few hours in town, you have several options. You can sit and admire the wonderful bronze Swann Memorial Fountain with its spouting turtles and joyfully writhing nudes at **Logan Circle** at Nineteenth Street and Benjamin Franklin Parkway. The fountain was designed by Alexander Stirling Calder.

You can also visit **Rittenhouse Square,** Walnut Street between Eighteenth and Nineteenth Streets. The neighborhood around the square is Philadelphia's classiest, and there are several shops and restaurants where you can get a cup of coffee or a cool drink.

Best of all, take a stroll or a drive through **Fairmount Park,** located west and north of downtown; (215) 685–0000. A gigantic swath of green running along the Schuylkill River, Fairmount Park is the nation's largest landscaped city-owned park. The park includes more than 4,000 acres of natural beauty, with a forested gorge, a Japanese garden, a covered bridge, tennis courts, ball fields and playgrounds, several early-American homes, and more than 200 pieces of outdoor sculpture. Kelly Drive is a particularly pleasant place to stroll or bike.

Your drive home to Washington on Interstate 95 will take about three hours, just enough time to plan your next quick escape to Philadelphia.

THERE'S MORE

Benjamin Franklin Bridge. At night, the Ben Franklin Bridge is not just a route to South Jersey; it's a pulsating light show stretching across the Delaware River and a favorite strolling place for Philadelphians of all ages.

The Franklin Institute Science Museum. North Twentieth Street and Benjamin Franklin Parkway; (215) 448–1200. The Franklin Institute is really several museums in one building. In the Science Center, there are four floors of hands-on exhibits including a Baldwin locomotive, a 20-foot-high walk-through human heart, and exhibits on aviation, electricity, and mechanics. The Tuttleman Omniverse Theater presents short Omnimax action movies on its four-story-high 180-degree screen with fifty-six loudspeakers. The Fels Planetarium is one of America's oldest, but it has been updated with the latest in projection equipment, and there are laser presentations on Friday and Saturday evenings. The Mandell Cybercenter has interactive exhibits on future technology. The museum is open daily from 9:30 A.M. to 5:00 P.M. The Mandell Cybercenter, the Fels Planetarium, and the Tuttleman Omniverse Theater stay open until 9:00 P.M. on Friday and Saturday. Call (215) 448–1254 for features, show times, and advance ticket purchases. The basic all-day museum admission charge is $9.75 for adults and $8.50 for senior citizens and children four to twelve; children under four are admitted free. (Evening prices are slightly lower.) Add $3.00 (adults) or $2.00 (children) for Omni, and the same for the planetarium.

Afro-American Historical and Cultural Museum. 701 Arch Street; (215) 574–0380, www.aampmuseum.org. Built in 1976 for the Bicentennial, the museum offers exhibits on black history, art, literature, and culture. It also has an excellent bookstore and gift shop. Open Tuesday to Saturday 10:00 A.M. to 5:00 P.M., Sunday noon to 5:00 P.M. Admission is $6.00 for adults and $4.00 for seniors and students five to eleven; children under five are admitted free.

Philadelphia Zoological Gardens. Thirty-fourth Street and Girard Avenue; (215) 243–1100, www.phillyzoo.org. America's first zoo. Catch the polar bears diving off 12-foot cliffs and stand in line to see Jezebel and Vinkel, the first white lions ever exhibited in North America. Open daily 10:00 A.M. to 4:00 P.M., later in summer. Admission is $8.50 for adults, $6.00 for senior citizens and children two to eleven; children under two are admitted free.

New Jersey State Aquarium. One Riverside Drive, Camden, New Jersey; (609) 365–3300, njaquarium.org. Board the Riverbus at Walnut Street and South Delaware (also called South Christopher Columbus Boulevard) in downtown Philadelphia and take a ten-minute, four-dollar ferry ride to one of America's best aquariums. It's worth the admission to watch the kids (and adults) squeal as they pet the sharks and rays! Open daily 10:00 A.M. to 5:00 P.M., extended hours in summer. Admission is $11.95 for adults, $8.95 for children under twelve.

Please Touch Museum. 210 North Twenty-first Street; (215) 963–0667, www.pleasetouchmuseum.org. One of the first museums designed especially for children under age seven. It's still a huge hit with the younger set, especially the full-size bus, functioning television station, kitchen, and circus ring. Open daily 9:00 A.M. to 4:30 P.M., extended hours in summer. Admission is $6.95.

Eastern State Penitentiary. This was the model penal structure 160 years ago; more than 300 prisons around the world were built to its specifications. It's huge—at the time it was built, it was the largest construction project in U.S. history—and it's ghastly. But it's definitely worth seeing. Open Wednesday to Sunday 10:00 A.M. to 5:00 P.M. in summer, Saturday and Sunday only during May and October. Admission is $7.00 for adults, $5.00 for senior citizens, and $3.00 for children seven through eighteen. No tours for children under seven. Located at 2125 Fairmount Avenue; (215) 236–3300, www.easternstate.org.

Rosenbach Museum and Library. This magnificent collection of rare books and manuscripts includes the manuscript of James Joyce's *Ulysses* and a major original collection of art by Maurice Sendak. The museum also has a fine collection of decorative arts. Open Tuesday to Sunday 11:00 A.M to 4:00 P.M. Admission is $5.00 for adults, $3.50 for seniors and children six to seventeen; children under six are admitted free. Located at 200 Delancy Street; (215) 732–1600.

The Barnes Foundation Gallery. Located at 300 North Latch's Lane, Merion (just off U.S. Highway 1 a few miles outside the Philadelphia city limits); (610) 667–0290, www.thebarnes.org. Amazing collection of French modern and Postimpressionist paintings, including 180 works by Renoir and 69 by Cézanne; also fine collections of ceramics, Native American jewelry, and antique furniture. Open Friday and Saturday 9:30 A.M. to 5:00 P.M., Sunday 12:30 to 5:00 P.M. Admission is $5.00 per person.

Einstein Books and Toys that Matter. Delightful, impossible-to-describe shop with books, puppets, chess sets, puzzles, Philadelphia souvenirs, and much, much more. Open Monday to Saturday 9:00 A.M. to 7:00 P.M., Sunday 10:00 A.M. to 6:00 P.M. Located at 1627 Walnut Street; (215) 665–3622.

Professional Sports. The Sports Complex is located in South Philadelphia, at South Broad Street and Pattison Avenue. You can catch Phillies baseball games or Eagles football games at Veterans Stadium. The Spectrum is home to the NBA's Philadelphia 76ers and the NHL's Philadelphia Flyers. For Phillies tickets, call (215) 463–1000. For Eagles tickets, call (215) 463–5500. For 76ers tickets, call (215) 339–7676. For hockey tickets, or tickets to any of the other special events at the Spectrum (including the circus), call (215) 336–3600.

SPECIAL EVENTS

January 1. Mummers Parade, an all-day event centering on a parade of costumed string bands from Broad Street in South Philadelphia to City Hall. (215) 336–3050.

March. St. Patrick's Day Parade, Benjamin Franklin Parkway. (215) 636-1666.

March. Philadelphia Flower Show, the nation's largest indoor flower show. Philadelphia Civic Center, Thirty-fourth Street and Civic Center Boulevard. (215) 988–8800.

May. Dad Vail Regatta. More than a hundred colleges compete in the largest rowing event in the nation on the Schuylkill River in Fairmount Park. (215) 636–1666.

June. Rittenhouse Square Fine Arts Annual. America's oldest and largest outdoor juried art show, featuring paintings and sculpture by more than one hundred Delaware Valley artists. Rittenhouse Square, Eighteenth and Walnut Streets. (215) 636–1666.

July. The Freedom Festival includes several days of events culminating in fireworks on the Fourth of July. (215) 636–1666.

August. Philadelphia's Folk Festival is the nation's largest folk music event. Music, food, crafts, and lots of folk dancing at Old Poole Farm in Schwenksville, northwest of Philadelphia. (215) 242–0150.

OTHER RECOMMENDED RESTAURANTS

Old Original Bookbinders, 125 Walnut Street; (215) 925–7027. An enormous restaurant serving enormous meals; it's where the elite have been meeting to eat since 1865. There's nothing nouvelle about the menu; it's red meat, seafood, and first-rate shellfish. Reservations required. Expensive.

Striped Bass, 1500 Walnut Street; (215) 732–4444. Glamorous, all-seafood restaurant that may be the critics' choice as Philadelphia's top restaurant. Try the marinated sea bass served with garlicky spinach and jasmine rice. Expensive.

Friday, Saturday, Sunday, located just off Rittenhouse Square in a tiny town house at 261 South Twenty-first Street; (215) 546–4232. For more than twenty years, this has been one of Philadelphia's most romantic restaurants, serving excellent salads, seafood, lamb, beef, poultry, and desserts. Moderate to expensive.

Jack's Firehouse, 2130 Fairmount Avenue; (215) 232–9000. Really located in an old firehouse, Jack's specializes in "back of the stove" Southern cooking such as black-eyed pea and ham hock soup, buffalo stew, and fried chicken. There's light jazz or live piano music. Moderate to expensive.

Le Bec Fin, 1523 Walnut Street; (215) 567–1000. One of America's premier restaurants. Everything about it—the dining room, the service, the exquisitely prepared food—is elegant. The menu is prix fixe: $36 for lunch, $118 for dinner. Expect the likes of thinly sliced tuna perfumed with lime and herbs, followed by jumbo New Jersey quail filled with leeks, mushrooms, foie gras, and bread stuffing. Or perhaps you might get vichyssoise garnished with lobster and caviar, followed by scallops wrapped in sole fillet and smothered in sea urchin butter sauce. And, of course, salad and dessert.

Cedars Restaurant, 616 South Second Street; (215) 925–4950. Casual, family-owned and -run Middle Eastern favorite with excellent food and moderate prices.

Overture's Restaurant, 609 East Passyunk Avenue; (215) 627–3455. Classy continental restaurant consistently rated one of the top twenty eating spots in the city. Moderate to expensive.

Rembrandt's, Twenty-third and Aspen Streets; (215) 763–2228. New-American cuisine, romantic setting. Good choice for Sunday brunch in the museum area—you can enjoy classical piano and viola music with your Belgian waffles. Moderate.

Ray's Cafe and Tea House, 141 North Ninth Street; (215) 922–5122. Small, inexpensive Chinese restaurant where everything is prepared by hand to order. Worth a visit in the summer for its delicious iced coffee (cold water drips slowly through fine-ground coffee and ends up tasting like coffee ice cream). Inexpensive.

Best doughnuts in the area: Beiler's Bakery, Reading Terminal Market; (215) 351–0735.

OTHER RECOMMENDED LODGINGS

La Reserve, also called Center City Bed & Breakfast, 1804 Pine Street; (215) 735–1137. A very well-preserved and well-maintained town house with rooms and suites ranging in price from $45 to $99. Breakfasts are bountiful, and you can amuse yourself by playing the grand piano or borrowing a book from the library.

Penn's View Inn, 14 North Front Street; (215) 922–7600 or (800) 331–7634. Near Independence National Historical Park, this twenty-seven room inn is nicely furnished with Colonial reproductions. All rooms have a view of the Delaware River and many have fireplaces and Jacuzzis. Rates: $99–$180.

Shippen Way Inn, 416–418 Bainbridge Street; (215) 627–7266 or (800) 245–4873. Restored inn with nine rooms, all with private baths, phones, and air-conditioning. Continental breakfast; afternoon wine and cheese or tea. Rates: $70–$105.

Ten Eleven Clinton Bed and Breakfast, 1011 Clinton Street; (215) 923–8144, www.teneleven.com. Center city B&B with seven suites; all have bedrooms, living rooms, and kitchens stocked with breakfast items. Rates: $125–$200, two-night minimum.

Best Western Independence Park Hotel, 235 Chestnut Street; (215) 922–4443 or (800) 624–2988. Small (36 rooms), pleasantly decorated Victorian hotel near Independence Park. Rates: $105–$155, including continental breakfast.

The Gables, 4520 Chester Avenue; (215) 662–1918. Pleasant bed-and-breakfast near the University of Pennsylvania has ten guest rooms, most with private baths. Wraparound porch, gardens, fireplaces; full breakfast served. Rates: $60–$100.

Clarion Suites Convention Center, 1010 Race Street; (215) 922–1730 or (800) 252–7466. Gracious, old all-suites hotel. Ninety-six units with full kitchen and dining area; continental breakfast. Parking, fitness room, bar and cafe on the premises. Rates: $99–$169.

The Omni Hotel at Independence Park, 401 Chestnut Street; (215) 925–0000 or (800) 843–6664. Deluxe hotel (150 rooms) just blocks from the park and South Street shopping. Fitness center, pool, gourmet restaurant, and twenty-four-hour room service. Rates: $99–$195.

FOR MORE INFORMATION

Philadelphia Convention and Visitors Bureau, 1515 Market Street, Philadelphia, PA 19102; (215) 636–1666 or (800) 537–7676, www.pcvb.org.

Once you are in Philadelphia visit the Independence National Historical Park Visitors Center, South Third and Chestnut Streets; (215) 597–8974. The center has an extensive array of maps, guidebooks, and information about Philadelphia and the surrounding areas, as well as information about the park itself.

For more information see www.libertynet.com, www.philly.com, and www.gophila.com.

Lancaster County

PENNSYLVANIA DUTCH COUNTRY

2 NIGHTS

Amish farm and museum • Back-roads driving and sight-seeing
Quilt shopping • Watch and clock museum • Pretzel factory

Lancaster County, Pennsylvania, is home to some of America's largest Amish and Mennonite communities. A trip to beautiful southeastern Pennsylvania permits the visitor a glimpse into the lives of these quiet, unworldly families, who live today much the same as their ancestors did when they fled Europe in the eighteenth century to escape persecution for their religious beliefs.

Don't be in a hurry; the best part of your visit to Lancaster County may well be the drive along backcountry roads, where you will see bearded Amish men at work in their lush fields with horse-drawn plows and reapers. Amish and Mennonite women and girls, with their hair always covered by a net cap or cotton bonnet, sell produce from their gardens at roadside stands; little boys glide by on old-fashioned, foot-powered scooters; and horses pulling buggies and carriages trot along the road, seemingly oblivious to the roar of the modern world all around them. And you won't have any trouble identifying Amish farms: They are absolutely plain—no shutters, no decorations, no trim, and no power lines.

Unfortunately, there is a great deal of commercialism in the heart of Pennsylvania Dutch country, and many of the towns tend to be jammed with tourists. Your itinerary keeps you off the kitschy strip along U.S. Highway 30 as much as possible and includes some of the nicest ways to experience Mennonite and Amish culture, food, and crafts.

You'll have an opportunity to tour a typical Amish farm (now run commercially by others), to visit a farmers' market, to conduct a treasure hunt for the perfect quilt, and to sample authentic Pennsylvania Dutch cooking at its best.

You'll also tour the historic Cloister in Ephrata, shop at the Mennonite-run Ten Thousand Villages store and a very modern complex of upscale art boutiques, and still have time for stops at a pretzel factory, a bakery, and a fascinating watch and clock museum.

DAY 1

Morning

Although Lancaster County is only about 110 miles from Washington, traffic and back-roads driving can make it a three-hour trip. Get an early-morning start so you can arrive by lunchtime. The best route is to take Interstate 95 to the Baltimore Beltway (Interstate 695), follow the beltway west and north to Interstate 83 (exit 24), take I–83 north 40 miles to York, Pennsylvania, and take traffic-laden U.S. Highway 30 east 14 miles to the Susquehanna River. Once you cross the long bridge, you're in Lancaster County and it's time to take to the back roads and enjoy the scenery.

Take the first exit at the east edge of the bridge and head north on State Highway 441 for 2 miles. Turn right on State Highway 23 and go east almost 2 miles to Kinderhook Road. Turn left and drive 1 mile north to Pinkerton Road. Turn left on Pinkerton Road and within a mile you'll see the sign for Groff's Farm Restaurant.

LUNCH: Groff's Farm Restaurant, 650 Pinkerton Road in Mount Joy (717–653–2048), is smack in the middle of the countryside, set in a big, restored farmhouse. Groff's is roundly praised for its fabulous home-style cooking (with rave reviews by the likes of James Beard and Craig Claiborne), yet it still manages to be unpretentious; in the evening, meals are served family style.

A favorite on the menu is Chicken Stoltzfus, chunks of chicken in cream sauce served on buttery pastry squares. Entrees (including fish, steaks, and ham) are served with fresh vegetables, homemade bread, and farm relishes. And Groff's famous cracker pudding comes without ordering! Prices are moderate, with lunch entrees averaging $7.00. Groff's gives away all its secrets in a pair of cookbooks you can buy while you're there. Lunch is served from

11:30 A.M. to 1:30 P.M., family-style dinner from 5:00 to 7:30 P.M.; closed Sunday and Monday. Reservations are required.

Afternoon

To get to the town of **Lancaster** from Groff's, retrace your route 1 mile on Pinkerton Road and 1 mile on Kinderhook Road to State Highway 23 and follow it east about 8 miles to King Street, the main eastbound street through Lancaster. If possible, park near the center of town (Penn Square, where King Street and Queen Street intersect). At the **Central Market,** the nation's oldest publicly owned farmers' market, you can buy Amish baked goods and fresh meat and produce. It's located just west of the square on King Street. Open Tuesday and Friday 6:00 A.M. to 4:00 P.M., Saturday 6:00 A.M. to 2:00 P.M.; (717) 291–4723.

The **Lancaster Visitors Information Center** is 2 blocks south on Queen Street. If you're interested in a walking tour of Lancaster, you can obtain a brochure at the Information Center. Do pick up a map of the general area; it's essential for navigating the back roads of Lancaster County, and the friendly guides will help you plan your trip in detail.

Don't dally in Lancaster; the real beauty of Pennsylvania Dutch country is in the countryside. After you pick up your map and brochures, drive east on King Street (State Highway 462) until you reach State Highway 340, the Old Philadelphia Pike. Follow State Highway 340 east a few miles to the heart of Lancaster County, the neighboring towns of **Intercourse** and **Bird-in-Hand,** located about 5 miles apart on State Highway 340.

There you'll find lots of commercialism, but you will also get to see something of authentic Amish life. Horses and buggies are plentiful in these towns, and Amish men and women do their shopping at the local stores, just like everybody else. Mennonite women and girls in sober dresses, aprons, and head coverings work in many of the establishments, and their clothes aren't some kind of tourist gimmick. If you listen quietly, you can hear some Mennonite and Amish speaking Pennsylvania Dutch, a dialect of German.

A good place to start your inquiry about Amish and Mennonite life is **The People's Place** in Intercourse, the more eastern of the two towns. It has a beautiful display of Amish quilts on the walls, and a slide show that offers a respectful description of Amish and Mennonite life. Located at 3513 Old Philadelphia Pike, Intercourse; (717) 768–7171. Open Monday to Saturday 9:30 A.M. to 5:00 P.M. The affiliated **People's Place Country Store** just across the street has a very large selection of quilts, quilted pillows and place mats, wooden toys, Amish dolls, and other gifts. It stays open to 8:00 P.M. Wednesday to Friday, April through October. The **People's Place Quilt Museum,** locted upstairs, is also worth a visit.

Diagonally across the street from the Country Store is **Nancy's Corner,** 3503 Old Philadelphia Pike, Intercourse; (717) 768–8790. It also has a large selection of Amish and Mennonite quilts, wall hangings, and other area crafts. Open Monday to Saturday 9:00 A.M. to 5:00 P.M., often later in summer months.

When you've had a chance to look to your heart's content, drive back west a few miles on State Highway 340 to Bird-in-Hand, where you'll find another fine quilt shop. **Fisher's,** 2713A Old Philadelphia Pike, Bird-in-Hand (717–392–5440), has some unusually interesting quilts and wall hangings in the dark and vivid colors and plain block patterns that are the hallmark of Amish design, as well as the pastel-colored pieced and appliquéd quilts that are more popular with tourists. Open Monday to Saturday 9:00 A.M. to 5:00 P.M.

A word about quilt prices: All of the quilts at the stores mentioned here are handmade. Considering the hundreds of hours that went into making them, their prices—in the $500–$1,000 range, depending on the size—are a real bargain, but to customers more used to factory-made goods, they may seem high. Just remember that when you buy a handmade quilt, you are buying an original work of art!

As you leave Fisher's, stop downstairs at the **Bird-in-Hand Bakery** (717–768–8273) and pick up some local treats, like sticky buns, cream-filled "whoopie pies," and sticky molasses "shoo-fly" pies.

To get to your final destination of the day, where you'll dine and spend the night, you can take State Highway 340 and U.S. Highway 30 west back to Lancaster and then State Highway 501 north 10 miles to Lititz. But also consider consulting the area map you picked up at the information center and devising your own circuitous back-roads drive to Lititz. Prosperous farms, plump cattle, flower and vegetable gardens, and rolling hills and valleys are all around. Keep your eyes open for more horse-drawn buggies and Amish stands by the roadside selling fresh fruit and baked goods.

DINNER AND LODGING: The **General Sutter Inn,** located at the intersection of Routes 501 and 772 in downtown Lititz, is a beautiful old inn, in operation since 1764, when it was founded by the Moravian Church. Its lobby is furnished like a Victorian parlor, complete with a large ornate birdcage, with noisy inhabitants inside. The inn's **1764 House** dining room specializes in steaks, pasta, chicken, and veal dishes. Prices are moderate to expensive.

The General Sutter Inn's sixteen guest rooms and suites are all furnished with antiques, and there is a coffeeshop for lunch and dinner, in addition to the formal dining room. Located at 14 East Main Street, Lititz; (717) 626–2115, www.generalsutterinn.com. Rates: $65–$140.

DAY 2

Morning

BREAKFAST: Glassmeyers Restaurant, 23 North Broad Street, Lititz; (717) 626–2345. One of the best bargains in town: For $2.50 you will get scrambled eggs, hash browns, and toast in a pleasant environment with friendly service. Closed Sundays.

Follow breakfast with a walking tour of **Lititz.** It's small enough to see in an hour or two, and you'll enjoy the historic buildings, pretty tree-lined streets, and attractive shops. Don't miss **Sturgis Pretzel House,** 219 East Main Street, Lititz (717–626–4354, www.sturgispretzel.com.), where you can tour the oldest commercial pretzel bakery in America and watch pretzels being baked in 200-year-old ovens. The soft pretzels are baked to order and are divine. Open Monday to Saturday 9:00 A.M. to 5:00 P.M. The **Wilbur Chocolate Company's Candy Americana Museum and Store,** 46 North Broad Street, Lititz (717–626–3249, www.wilburbuds.com), does not have as much hoopla as Hershey, but the displays from the old chocolate factory are fun. Open Monday to Saturday 9:00 A.M. to 5:00 P.M. And right across the street is **The Kowerski Gallery,** a showplace for local artists who do photography, watercolors, and folk art (49 North Broad Street; 717–626–0424).

Other points of interest in Lititz are the 200-year-old **Moravian Church** at 8 Church Square (717–626–8515); the exteriors of the beautiful 250-year-old houses that line Main Street; and the **Mueller House and Museum,** 137 East Main Street (717–626–7958), which is nicely furnished and has local memorabilia. Mueller House is open Monday to Saturday 10:00 A.M. to 4:00 P.M. Admission is $3.00 for adults and $1.50 for students; children under six are admitted free.

After your walking tour, hit the road again for another back-roads drive through Lancaster County's lovely countryside. You will be looking for the little town of New Holland, where some of the area's finest Amish quilts are to be found. To get there, take State Highway 772 (East Main Street) east and south about 6 or 7 miles to State Highway 23, turn left, and follow State Highway 23 through Leola to New Holland. As you approach the town on West Main Street, keep your eyes open for quilts tossing in the breeze over a clothesline. That will be **Witmer's Quilts,** 1070 West Main Street, New Holland; (717) 656–9526. The "shop" opens at 8:00 A.M. Monday through Saturday and closes at 6:00 P.M. except on Monday and Friday, when it stays open until 8:00 P.M.

Emma Witmer not only has scores of spectacular quilts, she also gives you a tour of them, which will turn you into as big a quilt fan as she is. The quilts are housed in the upstairs of a little brick house on the Witmer farm, where the family also runs a large buggy wheel shop. You just walk in and head upstairs, where two small rooms are stuffed to the ceiling with ravishing quilts. Mrs. Witmer doesn't make all the quilts herself. She commissions them from Amish women in the area and sells them in her small shop. She also has some Laotian refugee women needling for her, and some of their unique pleated and appliquéd handicraft are incorporated into the quilts that Emma designs.

For customers to view the quilts, Mrs. Witmer needs a helper to stand on the opposite side of a big double bed to help her throw back each one and reveal the next. When a new quilt comes into view, Emma calls out its name—which in some cases she made up herself. There are dozens of variations on traditional patched designs, and even more beautiful appliquéd quilts in astonishingly lovely patterns.

Mrs. Witmer also has old and used quilts, and some genuine antiques. A gorgeous silk "crazy quilt" made from old neckties in the late 1800s recently sold for $800. Prices on the modern quilts are among the best in the area. Appliqués in queen and king size are in the $600–$1,200 price range, and pieced quilts significantly less. But even if you don't intend to buy, Mrs. Witmer's is a wonderful stop. Her love for the quilts is infectious, and you just might end up taking one home after all.

Your lunch stop and afternoon adventures are in the town of **Ephrata,** north of New Holland. From the quilt shop, drive east into New Holland on State Highway 23. In the center of town, take a left on Railroad Avenue and drive 2 miles north to State Highway 322; then turn left and follow State Highway 322 into Ephrata. In Ephrata, turn right on State Highway 272 and drive a few blocks to your lunch stop on the left.

LUNCH: Nav Jiwan International Tea Room, located within Ten Thousand Villages Gift Shop, has an attractive, low-cost menu featuring different foods of the world every week. One day, when Native American food was featured, the menu included stuffed pumpkin, oyster-potato cakes, fry bread, and suc-cotash. Another week you might find the cuisine of Mexico, Indonesia, or Nigeria served here. No matter what your tastes, the International Tea Room is a quiet place to get off your feet and have a cup of tea or coffee with a dessert. Located at 240 North Reading Road (State Highway 272), Ephrata; (717) 721–8400. Open Monday to Saturday 10:00 A.M. to 3:00 P.M., Friday 10:00 A.M. to 8:00 P.M. Inexpensive.

Afternoon

After lunch, stick around for some shopping. Established by the Mennonite Central Committee as a nonprofit shop, **Ten Thousand Villages** (formerly Selfhelp Crafts of the World) sells high-quality handicrafts from dozens of countries in Asia, Latin America, Africa, and the Middle East. Most of the store's help is volunteer, and the shop has made a commitment to paying the craftsmen and -women good wages for their products. When you purchase brass items, textiles, baskets, rugs, carved boxes, jewelry, and Christmas orna-ments here, you can be sure no child labor was used in their production, and that the purchase helps generate income in poor countries. Open Monday to Saturday 9:00 A.M. to 5:00 P.M., Friday until 9:00 P.M. Phone (717) 721–8400.

If you can tear yourself away from Ten Thousand Villages, the town of Ephrata has much more to offer. Plan to spend at least an hour at the **Ephrata Cloister,** one of America's earliest communal societies. There, an eighteenth-century community of religious celibates lived in complete austerity, with nar-row benches for beds and wooden blocks for pillows. Yet, for all their asceticism, the cloister residents created original music and engaged in signif-icant printing and publishing operations. Today, some ten of the original build-ings have been restored on the grounds. Even though no one lives there now, the serenity and spiritualism of the cloister's residents pervade the entire restoration. It is a fascinating encounter with the past, and not to be missed on your visit to the area. Located at 632 West Main Street, Ephrata; (717) 733–6600, www.phmc.state.pa.us. Open Monday to Saturday 9:00 A.M. to 5:00 P.M., Sunday noon to 5:00 P.M. Closed most holidays. Admission is $5.00 for adults, $4.50 for senior citizens, and $3.00 for children six to twelve; chil-dren under six are admitted free. Family tickets are $14.

End your afternoon with a stop at **The Artworks at Doneckers.** This four-story marketplace is stuffed full of artists' studios selling everything from antiques to jewelry to original paintings to handmade wooden crafts. There are more than fifty galleries in all, and some of the best are on the top floors. Attached to the galleries is an old-fashioned food court and farmers' market selling traditional Lancaster sweets, which you can wash down with a cup of gourmet coffee. Located at 100 North State Street, Ephrata; (717) 738–9503. Open Monday to Saturday 10:00 A.M. to 5:00 P.M., Sunday noon to 4:00 P.M.

DINNER: Splurge at the handsome **Log Cabin Restaurant,** 11 Lehoy Forest Drive, Leola; (717) 626–1181, www.logcabinrestaurant.com. Open for dinner only. Reservations necessary. You have to look for the Log Cabin, as it is tucked away in a residential neighborhood on the outskirts of Leola. Follow State Highway 272 south 5 miles from Ephrata and turn right on Rosehill Road. From there, it's a matter of following the signs through the woods, over a covered bridge, and through more woods. But don't give up—it's worth it.

You'll know you've arrived when you see an interesting and attractive group of low buildings hung on the outside with dozens of paintings. Is that a Picasso? A Miró? Could it possibly be? No, it's not, just the owner having a good time. An artist himself, he playfully made reproductions of some well-known works and hung them outside his restaurant.

Inside, the decor is casual and pretty at the same time, with lots of original eighteenth- and nineteenth-century art on the walls of the seven distinct dining rooms. Menu, service, and prices are distinctly classy, so this is a meal for a special occasion. Entrees are in the $20–$35 range and include steaks, lamb chops, veal, lobster, and duckling. The desserts are baked on the premises.

Ask at the Log Cabin for directions back to Lititz, which is only 5 miles away via the shortcut. Or drive back down Rosehill Road, take State Highway 272 north 1 mile, turn left, and take State Highway 772 about 7 miles to Lititz.

LODGING: The General Sutter Inn.

DAY 3

Morning

BREAKFAST: The General Sutter Inn's coffeeshop offers generous breakfasts at moderate prices.

It's your last day in Lancaster County, but there's much more to see and do. After breakfast, drive south on State Highway 501 about 6 miles to U.S. Highway 30. Follow the motel- and outlet-laden strip east about 3 miles to the **Amish Farm and House,** 2395 Route 30 East, Lancaster; (717) 394–6185, amishfarmandhouse.com. Open daily from 8:30 A.M. to 5:00 P.M. Admission is $5.95 for adults and $3.50 for children five to eleven; children under five are admitted free.

If you are really interested in learning about the Amish, the best way to do so would be to stay with an Amish or Mennonite family for a while. (If you're interested, see There's More for suggestions.) But if you only have a few days, the Amish Farm and House may be the best alternative. It is a commercial enterprise, and you won't see any conservative Amish on the premises. But it was once the home of an old-order Amish family, and both the house and farm have a certain authenticity about them.

Try to arrive in time for the first tour of the house, at 9:00 A.M., because crowds get large, particularly in the summer, and can be distracting from the peaceful and simple surroundings. On the tour, you'll get to see the very plain furniture, clothing, and furnishings of the old-order Amish; these items have changed very little over the last 300 years. There is no electricity, and newly bought appliances like electric sewing machines have been modified so that they can be run by foot treadle. You'll also learn something of the group's culture and values. Religious services are in family homes and last for three and a half hours, with worshipers sitting on hard benches. Singing, which lasts for thirty-five minutes without interruption, is in German, as is Bible reading.

The life of the old-order Amish seems austere when you see the bare walls and severe clothing (women's aprons are pinned on with straight pins—buttons are thought to be decorative and are avoided). At the same time, one senses the commitment to community and family that is the source of Amish strength and joy.

If you managed to get to the Amish Farm and House early, you might also manage to beat the lunch crowds at noon. Sundays present even more of a problem because many of the restaurants in the area are closed. But if you're willing to brave the crowds for a real Pennsylvania Dutch smorgasbord, opt for Miller's, about 1 mile east of the Amish Farm on U.S. Highway 30.

LUNCH: Miller's Smorgasbord Dinner, U.S. Highway 30, 2 miles east of Route 896 (717–687–6621 or 800–669–3568), is open daily for "dinner" from noon to 8:00 P.M. If your idea of a great dinner includes ham, chicken, roast beef, turkey, and going back for seconds, you've come to the right place; Miller's has been dishing up all-you-can-eat meals for more than sixty years.

If you're not in a buffet mood, Miller's "signature" dish is chicken and waffles. Moderate.

Afternoon

Your final destination on the road home is the **National Watch and Clock Museum** in Columbia. You can reach it by backtracking on U.S. Highway 30 west for 3 or 4 miles to State Highway 462 and then proceeding west through Lancaster and on another twenty minutes to Columbia. Located at 514 Poplar Street; (717) 684–8261, www.nawcc.org. Open Tuesday to Saturday 10:00 A.M. to 5:00 P.M., Sunday (May through September only) noon to 4:00 P.M. Admission is $6.00 for adults, $5.00 for senior citizens, $4.00 for children six to twelve, and free for children under six. A family admission is $16.

This little-known gem of a museum, established about twenty years ago, contains a collection of some 8,000 timepieces, from beautifully intricate gold pocket watches to a whole roomful of stately old grandfather clocks. There are cuckoos, chimes, and a water clock, as well as ancient sundials and other timekeepers. The museum's adjoining rooms are quiet and cool, and all around you are clocks, ticking like heartbeats.

A highlight is the Stephen Engle Monumental Clock. Built in 1878, this enormous, room-size clock includes a procession of apostles (which occurs at 9:55, 11:55, 1:55, and 3:55), two barrel organs, and pirouetting Revolutionary War soldiers. The apostolic procession is stunning; stick around for it if you can.

Your return trip from Lancaster County via U.S. Highway 30 to York, I–83 to the Baltimore Beltway (I–695), and I–95 from Baltimore to Washington should take you less than two and a half hours.

THERE'S MORE

A Day on a Farm. The Mennonite Information Center (717–299–0954, www.mennoniteinfoctr.com) can provide you with a list of farm bed-and-breakfasts and a list of Amish families who accept guests for dinner. For other options consult www.pafarmstay.com and www.padutchcountry.com/workfarm.htm.

Hans Herr House. Tours of the oldest house in Lancaster County, which has been restored in the Colonial Mennonite fashion, are available Monday through Saturday 9:00 A.M. to 4:00 P.M. April through November. Located on Hans Herr Drive (off U.S. Highway 222) about 6 miles south of Lancaster; (717) 464–4438. Admission is $3.50 for everyone over age twelve, $1.00 for children seven to twelve; children under seven are admitted free.

Buggy Rides. Several enterprises offer buggy rides through the country in authentic Amish and Mennonite carriages. Aaron and Jessica's Buggy Rides (717–768–8828) is located on State Route 340 between Intercourse and Bird-in-Hand. Abe's Buggy Rides (717–392–1794) is just west of Bird-in-Hand on State Highway 340. Expect to pay about $10.00 per adult and $5.00 per child for a forty-five-minute ride.

Outlet Shopping. Most of the outlet stores in the area are located on U.S. Highway 30 on a 5-mile strip just east of Lancaster, although several are on State Highway 896 south of Route 30. You can shop for just about anything from rugs and china to shoes and name-brand clothes.

Railroad Museum of Pennsylvania. The Railroad Museum in downtown Strasburg has about thirty-five locomotives and more than fifty railcars on display; (717) 687–8628, www.rrmuseumpa.org. Open Monday to Saturday (closed Mondays from November through March) 9:00 A.M. to 5:00 P.M., Sunday noon to 5:00 P.M. Admission is $6.00 for adults, $5.50 for senior citizens, $4.00 for children six to twelve; children under six are admitted free. Family tickets are $16.

Strasburg Rail Road. This "short line" railroad offers a forty-five-minute steam train ride from Strasburg to Paradise in a fancy parlor car, an open-air observation car, an old-fashioned wooden coach, or a century-old dining car. Located on State Route 741 just east of Strasburg; (717) 687–7522, www.strasburgrailroad.com. Open daily May through October, weekends November through April. Call for schedule and reservations; there are three to twelve trips a day depending on the season. Tickets cost $8.25 for everyone twelve and older and $4.00 for children three to eleven; children under three ride free.

The National Toy Train Museum. Paradise Lane, just east of Strasburg; (717) 687–8976, www.traincollectors.org/toytrain.html. First-rate toy train display with five operating layouts. Open daily May through October, weekends November through April, 10:00 A.M. to 5:00 P.M. Admission is $3.00 for adults, $1.50 for children five to twelve; children under five get in free.

Pottery. A large selection of beautiful old-fashioned salt-glazed stoneware and redware is available from Eldreth Pottery, 246 North Decatur Street, Strasburg; (717) 687–8445, www/eldrethpottery.com. Open Monday to Saturday 9:00 A.M. to 5:00 P.M., Sunday 1:00 to 5:00 P.M.; open until 8:00 P.M. on Fridays, July through December.

SPECIAL EVENTS

April. Quilter's Heritage Celebration. Annual Lancaster event at which quilts are displayed and sold. (800) 233–0121.

June. Lititz Outdoor Crafts Show. Craft artists display and sell their work; food, music. (717) 626–1510.

July. Lititz Independence Day celebration, featuring candles in the park rather than fireworks.

August–September. Pennsylvania Dutch Balloon and Craft Festival. Annual event in Strasburg includes hot air balloon and helicopter rides, food, music, craft show. (717) 687–7691.

August–October. Pennsylvania Rennaissance Faire. Re-creation of sixteenth-century English country fair on the grounds of the Mt. Hope Estate and Winery, 15 miles north of Lancaster on State Highway 72. Food, crafts, minstrels, jousting matches. Open weekends only. Admission. (717) 665–7021.

OTHER RECOMMENDED RESTAURANTS

The Stockyard Inn, 1147 Lititz Pike (on State Highway 501 just south of U.S. Highway 30), Lancaster; (717) 394–7975. Former home of President Buchanan, converted into an inn in 1900. Steak, prime rib, seafood in a historic setting. Moderate to expensive.

Stoltzfus Farm Restaurant, 1 block east of Intercourse on State Highway 772 East; (717) 768–8156. Excellent homemade sausage, farm setting, family-style meals. Moderate.

Good'n Plenty Restaurant, Route 896, Smoketown; (717) 394–7111. Family-style dining with pork and sauerkraut guaranteed to be on the table, large crowds. Moderate.

Akron Restaurant, Route 272, Akron; (717) 859–1181. Extensive sandwich selection, but try the chicken potpie if you're there on Thursday, or the baked oyster pie if you visit on Friday. Inexpensive to moderate.

The Restaurant at Doneckers, 333 North State Street, Ephrata; (717) 738–9501. Upscale ambience, French-American menu. Expensive.

Isaac's Deli, the Shops at Traintown, Strasburg; (717) 687–7699. Small local chain with made-from-scratch soups and super sandwiches. Inexpensive.

Best place for doughnuts: Achenbach's, 325 East Main Street, Leola; (717) 656–6671. More than twenty choices, including blueberry jelly doughnuts, sticky buns, whoopie pies, and other Pennsylvania Dutch treats.

See other restaurant listings under Other Recommended Lodgings.

OTHER RECOMMENDED LODGINGS

Alden House Bed and Breakfast, 62 East Main Street, Lititz; (717) 627–3363 or (800) 584–0753, www.aldenhouse.com. Five nicely furnished guest rooms with private baths in 1850s house located near center of town; large country breakfasts. Rates: $90–$120.

Swiss Woods B&B, 500 Blantz Road, Lititz; (717) 627–3358 or (800) 594–8018, swisswoods.com. Swiss chalet; seven rooms with private baths, some with Jacuzzis. Large garden; full breakfasts. Rates: $99–$175.

Alice's Manheim Manor, 140 South Charlotte Street, Manheim; (717) 664–4168 or (888) 224–4346, www.manheimmanor.com. An 1856 Victorian with six guest rooms, all with air-conditioning, cable TV, and private baths; full-course breakfast served. Rates: $100–$159.

Red Caboose Motel and Restaurant, Paradise Lane just east of Strasburg; (717) 687–5000. Sleep in one of a dozen real cabooses made into modern motel rooms and efficiencies. Rates: $43–$85 depending on season. Family units with bunk beds are $53–$105. Family-oriented restaurant on the premises.

The Railroad House Restaurant and B&B, West Front and South Perry Streets, Marietta; (717) 426–4141. Twelve-room inn with exposed-brick walls, antique furnishings, Oriental rugs, gardens; full breakfast included. Restaurant on premises. Rates: $79–$119.

Limestone Inn, 33 East Main Street, Strasburg; (717) 687–8392 or (800) 278–8392. Pleasant Georgian B&B in downtown Strasburg. Six guest rooms, three with private baths; full breakfast served. Rates: $85–$110.

Historic Strasburg Inn, One Historic Drive, Strasburg; (717) 687–7691 or (800) 872–0201, www.historicstrasburginn.com Beautiful country inn on fifty-eight acres with 101 guest rooms, Colonial furnishings. Three restaurants on the premises; buffet breakfast. Rates: $119–$159.

Willow Valley Family Resort, 2416 Willow Street Pike, Lancaster; (717) 464–2711 or (800) 444–1714, www.willowvalley.com. Family-oriented resort, 3 miles south of downtown Lancaster on U.S. Highway 222, with more than 350 guest rooms. Two restaurants, three pools, golf course, tennis, playground, animals to pet, wagon rides. Rates: $89–$159.

1725 Historic Witmers Tavern and Inn, 2014 Old Philadelphia Pike, Lancaster; (717) 299–5305. The area's oldest continuously operating inn has seven guest rooms, two with private baths. Antiques in the rooms and for sale on the premises. Wood-burning stoves; continental breakfast. Rates: $60–$90.

All Seasons Bed and Breakfast Association of Lancaster County, P.O. Box 435, Paradise, PA 17562; (717) 687–0333, www.amishcountrybb.com. The association will help you find a room in one of its member establishments.

FOR MORE INFORMATION

Pennsylvania Dutch Convention and Visitors Bureau, 501 Greenfield Road (Greenfield Road exit off U.S. Highway 30), Lancaster, PA 17601; (717) 299–8901 or (800) 723–8824, www.padutchcountry.com.

Downtown Lancaster Visitors Information Center, South Queen and Vine Streets, Lancaster, PA 17601; (717) 397–3531, www.lcci.com.

PENNSYLVANIA

Gettysburg and Hershey

A TALE OF TWO PARKS

2 NIGHTS

Civil War battlefield • Chocolate factory
Amusement park • Garden • Zoo

Fourscore and seven years ago our fathers brought forth on this continent a new nation, conceived in liberty, and dedicated to the proposition that all men are created equal.

Now we are engaged in a great civil war, testing whether that nation, or any nation so conceived and so dedicated, can long endure. We are met on a great battlefield of that war. . . .

Thus began one of the greatest speeches in American history: Abraham Lincoln's address at Gettysburg, Pennsylvania, on November 19, 1863. As the U.S. Park Service brochure notes, Lincoln's eloquence four and a half months after the battle "transformed Gettysburg from a scene of carnage into a symbol, giving meaning to the sacrifice of the dead and inspiration to the living."

Gettysburg National Military Park is the centerpiece of a weekend escape to south-central Pennsylvania. The battle of Gettysburg holds a particular fascination for many, not only because it is considered to be the decisive battle of the Civil War, but because the carnage there was so extensive. In the first three days of July 1863, some 51,000 soldiers were killed, wounded, or captured. Gettysburg was the war's costliest battle for both sides, and the bloodiest event on American soil in history.

After the somber nature of Gettysburg, you'll enjoy extending your trip to Hershey to visit the amusement park and Chocolate World just an hour away,

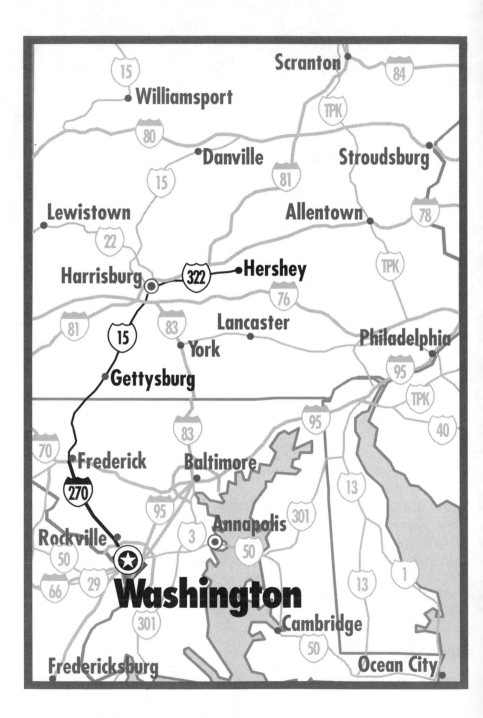

especially if you have children along. The spirit of Hershey is as frivolous as Gettysburg's is serious, but both are wonderful places that can be enjoyed, with or without children.

DAY 1

Morning

Your first day's destination is Gettysburg, Pennsylvania, approximately two hours from Washington. To get there, take Interstate 270 north 45 miles to Frederick, Maryland, then U.S. Highway 15 north 38 miles to Gettysburg. Once you cross the state line into Pennsylvania, look for the Business Route 15 signs and follow them.

When you arrive in Gettysburg, make the visitors center at the **Gettysburg National Military Park** your first stop. It's located on Taneytown Road (State Highway 134, just off Business Route 15); (717) 334–1124, www.nps.gov/gett. Gettysburg National Military Park is open daily 6:00 A.M. to 10:00 P.M.; the park's visitors center is open 8:00 A.M. to 5:00 P.M. Admission to the park itself is free, but a fee is charged for some of the attractions.

The visitors center has orientation displays, Civil War exhibits, and a **Museum of the Civil War.** It also has a fascinating "Electric Map," which uses different-colored lights to show the troop movements and tactics during the course of the three-day battle. Admission to the half-hour Electric Map show is $3.00 for adults, $2.50 for seniors, and $1.50 for children six to fifteen; children under six are admitted free.

Among the wealth of sights at the visitors center, there is a free film about the battle, *Gettysburg 1863,* and an interesting program at the nearby **Cyclorama Center.** In the program, park rangers offer a narrated light-and-sound tour of an enormous 360-degree painting that spans the rounded theater. Completed in 1884, this work by Paul Philloteaux depicts the entire battle of Gettysburg. Cycloramas were common in nineteenth-century America. Today, the Gettysburg Cyclorama is one of only twenty left in the world, two of which are in the United States. Open daily 9:00 A.M. to 5:00 P.M. Admission is $3.00 for adults, $2.50 for seniors, and $1.50 for children six to fifteen; children under six are admitted free.

LUNCH: After your orientation to the battle of Gettysburg at the visitors center and the Cyclorama, take a break for lunch at **KrackerJack's Cafe and Spirits,** 619 Baltimore Street (just up the road from the park); (717) 334–5648.

There you can get fresh pasta, Georgia barbecue, a charbroiled hamburger, or a deli sandwich in a relaxed indoor or outdoor setting. Moderate.

Afternoon

After lunch, return to the park for a walking or driving tour of the battlefield sights. Rangers conduct free tours at regular intervals or can provide you with the names of Civil War experts who will give you a private tour for a fee. The Park Service also arranges numerous walking tours with a special emphasis on particular military maneuvers, and offers special programs for children.

The driving loop through Gettysburg National Military Park is 18 miles long and is well marked by the Park Service with informative signs about the intricate military maneuvers of the three-day campaign. You'll see such landmarks as the High Water Mark, where—on the second day of the battle—the Confederates were said to have reached their highest military achievement of the Civil War with the capture of much of the land near General Meade's headquarters on Cemetery Ridge. Hours later, the Union forces repulsed Pickett's Charge, turning the war to the North's advantage and eventually forcing the Confederates to fall back.

Don't leave the park without walking through the National Cemetery, where thousands of the Union and Confederate soldiers who died during the battle of Gettysburg are buried. It was here that Lincoln delivered his two-minute speech four and a half months later, dedicating the cemetery to the proposition that "government of the people, by the people, for the people, shall not perish from the earth." A walk through the cemetery at dusk is a fitting way to end your day at Gettysburg.

DINNER: Dobbin House, 89 Steinwehr Avenue in Gettysburg; (717) 334–2100, dobbinhouse.com. Built in 1776, this inn is the oldest building in Gettysburg and has a long and honorable history. It was used as a hospital during the Civil War for wounded soldiers from both sides and, in the 1850s, was a way station on the Underground Railway for runaway slaves. As part of the house's meticulous restoration, life-size models have been placed in the ceiling crawl space where the real slaves hid.

These days, Dobbin House is a fine restaurant with Colonial-era food served by waitstaff in period dress. Lunch is served in the Springhouse Tavern, in the basement of the house. Moderately priced sandwiches, salads, and soups are available, as well as such homey desserts as hot apple pie and warm gingerbread. For dinner, head for the **Alexander Dobbin Dining Rooms,** a set of six different candlelit rooms, and enjoy either the "Colonial fare of the day" or your choice of roast duck, lamb chops, imperial crab, or any of a number of examples of traditional American cuisine. Dinner at Dobbin House is moderate to expensive.

LODGING: Gettystown Inn, the bed-and-breakfast half of the Dobbin House, has five comfortable guest rooms and suites decorated with period furniture and Oriental rugs. All rooms have private baths and air-conditioning. Rates: $85–$105.

DAY 2

Morning

BREAKFAST: Enjoy a full breakfast of pancakes and eggs in the parlor of Dobbin House.

After breakfast, drive to **Hershey,** a little more than an hour away. Take U.S. Highway 15 north 36 miles to Harrisburg, State Highway 581 east across the J. Harris Bridge and through town (about 8 miles), and U.S. Highway 322 (follow the signs) east about 13 miles to Hershey.

At Hershey you'll find an entirely different kind of scene than at Gettysburg. Hershey is an exuberant, merry celebration of a great American commercial success story.

Although there are numerous treats at Hershey, start at the **Chocolate World** visitors center, where you get a free tour of the chocolate factory. Alas, it's not the real chocolate factory, but rather a Disney-like mock-up. But it does provide a twelve-minute electric tram ride that shows the various stages of chocolate making. Best of all are the machines that squeeze out the billions of Hershey kisses, give each of them a paper topknot, and coat them in foil.

At one point on the tour, a sign says SMILE, and you'd better do so because within a few seconds a camera will take your picture as your automated cart rounds the corner. Then, as if by magic, at the end of the tour you'll be presented with the opportunity to buy the photo for $10, and it's all so ridiculous that it's almost impossible to resist. (You get a free chocolate bar at the end of the ride no matter what.)

There are—needless to say—thousands of chocolate-related things to buy, from tiny Hershey espresso mugs to homemade cookies to chocolate in every conceivable shape and form. And if you don't like Hershey bars, don't worry—Hershey makes Reese's Peanut Butter Cups too!

Chocolate World is located just off Hersheypark Drive; (717) 534–4900, www.hersheys.com/chocworld. Monday to Saturday, it opens at 9:00 A.M., Sunday at noon; closing time varies depending on the season and day of the week.

After you've had your tour, head for **Hersheypark,** just yards away. The park was built by Hershey founder Milton Hershey for his employees and their children. The thing grew and grew, and today it's a full-fledged tourist attraction. Like Chocolate World, Hersheypark is located on Hersheypark Drive; (717) 534–3900 or (800) 437–7439. Open daily in the summer and some weekends in May and September at 10:00 A.M.; rides open at 10:30 A.M. The park closes between 6:00 P.M. and 11:00 P.M. depending on season and day of the week. Admission is $30.95 for everyone between the ages of nine and fifty-four. Seniors and juniors get in for $16.95. Children under three get in free. The admission charge covers the cost of all rides.

LUNCH: Finding a place for lunch won't be a problem at Hersheypark, if you have room after all the chocolate you've eaten. Choices include fast-food stands selling ice cream, chili dogs, funnel cakes, and French fries, as well as sit-down restaurants specializing in Italian food, Mexican food, or chicken and burgers. Prices are moderate.

Afternoon

Once you're in Hersheypark, it's pretty hard to leave. Plan to spend the entire afternoon there. The rides are labeled by candy name to designate what age group may ride them. The Hershey Kiss rides (labeled with a K) are for the littlest children, and those labeled with a B (for the Bar None candy bar) are for older kids. Rides range from gentle carousels for toddlers to the gut-flinging Sidewinder roller coaster for adolescents and adults. Four of the rides go through water, so bring swimsuits. (The park offers changing rooms with lockers for your clothes and belongings.)

DINNER: The **Union Canal House** is a small country inn and restaurant about a mile from Hersheypark. It's located at 107 South Hanover Street in the village of Union Deposit; (717) 566–0054. Don't let the inn's modest exterior fool you; there has been a tavern on the site for hundreds of years, and the interior is filled with Pennsylvania Colonial furniture. The downstairs is a fine restaurant that specializes in prime rib and seafood but it also has a selection of daily specials ranging from seared yellowfin tuna served rare with pepper sauce, to angel-hair pasta Gorgonzola, to grilled baby rack of lamb. Moderate to expensive.

LODGING: The Union Canal House has nine rooms and one suite. All have private baths and color TVs, and all sleep up to four people. Rates: $55–$85 for the rooms and $165 for the suite.

DAY 3

Morning

BREAKFAST: The Union Canal House serves a full country breakfast between 9:00 and 10:00 A.M. in the restaurant downstairs.

After breakfast, take some time to explore the other attractions in the Hershey area. Start with **Hershey Gardens,** Hotel Road across from the Hotel Hershey; (717) 534–3492. Open daily 9:00 A.M. to 6:00 P.M. April through September, 9:00 A.M. to 5:00 P.M. in October; closed in winter. Admission is $5.00 for adults, $4.50 for seniors, and $2.50 for children over two; children under two are admitted free.

The gardens are enormous. There are two rose gardens (one contains transplants from varieties that Mrs. Hershey grew more than ninety years ago, the other is a newly planted garden with more than three acres of roses); rhododendrons and azaleas; vegetables, shrubs, and ornamental grasses; a rock garden with seventy varieties of holly; a tiny Japanese garden complete with bridge, island, and viewing stones; and a large seasonal display garden that features summer annuals and autumn chrysanthemums.

Follow your walk among the plants with a walk among the animals at **ZooAmerica,** run by the Hershey folks. At this eleven-acre walk-through zoo, you can see more than seventy-five species of animals from five different regions of North America. Crowd favorites include the free-roaming bison and the playful prairie dogs. The zoo is located on Park Avenue across the road from Hersheypark. Open daily 10:00 A.M. to 5:00 P.M. from September through mid-June, 10:00 A.M. to 8:00 P.M. mid-June through August. Admission is $5.75 for adults, $5.25 for seniors, $4.50 for children ages three to twelve; children under three are admitted free. Phone (717) 534–3860 or (800) 437–7439.

LUNCH: End your stay in Hershey with brunch in the **Circular Dining Room at the Hotel Hershey;** (717) 534–8800. There you can feast on eggs, waffles, ham, roast beef, fruit, and desserts as you admire the stained glass windows. The room was designed by Milton Hershey so as to ensure that no one got stuck sitting in a corner. Expensive.

To return to Washington, take U.S. Highway 422, then U.S. Highway 322 west to Harrisburg, Interstate 83 south to the Baltimore Beltway, Interstate 695 around Baltimore, and Interstate 95 south to Washington. The trip will take you about three hours.

THERE'S MORE

Eisenhower National Historic Site. Video, house and grounds tour, and special exhibits at the Eisenhower Farm, a national historic site maintained by the Park Service. The tour leaves from the visitors center at Gettysburg National Military Park; (717) 338–9114, www.nps.gov/eise. Open daily 9:00 A.M. to 4:00 P.M. April through October, closed on Monday and Tuesday other months. Admission is $5.25 for adults, $3.25 for students, and $2.25 for children age six to twelve; children under six are admitted free.

Gettysburg Railroad. Ninety-minute, 16-mile steam engine ride through the countryside near Gettysburg. Departs from 106 North Washington Street, Gettysburg; (717) 334–6932 or (888) 948–7246, www. gettysburgrailroad.com. Open weekends in spring and fall, daily in July and August; two or three departures daily. Admission is $9.00 for adults, $8.00 for seniors, and $5.00 for children ages three to twelve. Fifty-mile dinner trips also available.

Golf. The Hershey Resorts offer guests at the Hotel and Lodge the opportunity to play at three championship-level, eighteen-hole courses and two nine-hole courses. Best is the par-73 West Course where Ben Hogan served as club pro for ten years. Greens fees and cart rental are $110. The beautiful South Course is a bargain at $39–$47. Phone (717) 533–2464.

Hershey Museum. Unpretentious museum that tells the story of Milton Hershey's life and displays some of his Pennsylvania German collection of furniture, textiles, and folk art and his outstanding collection of Native American pottery. Located at 170 West Hersheypark Drive; (717) 534–3439. Open daily 10:00 A.M. to 5:00 P.M., until 6:00 P.M. in summer. Admission is $5.00 for adults, $4.50 for seniors, $2.50 for children three to fifteen; children under three are admitted free.

SPECIAL EVENTS

May. Spring Bluegrass Festival. Bands and crowds in Gettysburg. (717) 642–8749.

June–July. Civil War Heritage Days. During the last weekend in June and the first week of July, there are parades, concerts, and lectures in Gettysburg, and a reenactment of the 1863 battle at Gettysburg National Military Park, complete with artillery fire and thousands of marching "soldiers." (717) 334–6274.

October. The National Apple. Harvest Festival. Large gathering in Arendtsville, 10 miles northwest of Gettysburg, featuring hundreds of arts-and-crafts displays, games and contests, orchard tours, and apples in all their manifestations. (717) 334–6274.

November. Remembrance Day. Parade and wreath-laying ceremony held in observance of anniversary of Lincoln's Gettysburg Address. (717) 334–6274.

November–December. Christmas in Hershey. Six-week-long Hershey promotional event featuring, among other things, an annual preholiday German Christmas with food, music, and crafts and a postholiday Teddy Bear Jubilee with parades and other child-centered activities. (717) 534–3439 or (800) 533–3131.

OTHER RECOMMENDED RESTAURANTS

Gettysburg

Farnsworth House Inn, 401 Baltimore Street; (717) 334–8838. Civil War–era menu features peanut soup, game pie, spoonbread; candlelight and garden dining. Located in a historic house converted to a B&B inn; not open for lunch. Moderate.

The Herr Tavern and Public House, 900 Chambersburg Road (U.S. Highway 30 west); (717) 334–4332 or (800) 362–9849. American and continental cuisine in a charming old inn. Moderate to expensive.

The Altland House, U.S. Highway 30 east, Abbottstown (twenty minutes from Gettysburg); (717) 259–9535. A 1790s tavern converted to casual country restaurant serving first-rate traditional American fare; said to be a favorite of President Eisenhower after he retired to his nearby farm. Moderate.

General Pickett's Buffet Restaurant, 571 Steinwehr Avenue; (717) 334–7580. All-you-can-eat beef, chicken, ham, salad, dessert; a family favorite. Inexpensive to moderate.

Centuries on the Square (at the Gettysburg Hotel), One Lincoln Square; (717) 337–2000. Large hotel-based restaurant in the heart of downtown. Continental cuisine; dining room and outdoor cafe. Moderate to expensive.

Best place for doughnuts: Festival Foods, 1275 York Road; (717) 337–3334. Small local chain produces very good doughnuts.

Hershey

Fenicci's, 102 West Chocolate Avenue; (717) 533–7159. Traditional Italian restaurant with pasta, veal, and sandwiches. Inexpensive to moderate.

Catherine's, 845 East Chocolate Avenue; (717) 533–9050. Continental cuisine served in a restaurant started nearly fifty years ago by Milton Hershey's Swiss chef but now under new management. Beef, pasta, and seafood specials. Moderate.

OTHER RECOMMENDED LODGINGS

Gettysburg

Baladerry Inn, 40 Hospital Road; (717) 337–1342, www.baladerryinn.com. Quiet eight-bedroom B&B in the country just outside Gettysburg; served as a field hospital during the Civil War. Tennis court and gardens; large rooms with queen-size or twin beds and private baths; full country breakfast. Rates: $94–$135.

Keystone Inn Bed and Breakfast, 231 Hanover Street; (717) 337–3888. Large Victorian with beautiful woodwork, antiques, lace trim, and lots of flowers inside and out. Five guest rooms and one suite, all with private bath; full breakfast. Rates: $69–$109.

Brafferton Inn, 44 York Street; (717) 337–3423. Recently restored 1780s home in historic district with twelve guest rooms, all with private bath. Spacious common areas include atrium, deck, garden, and sitting rooms; full break-fast. Rates: $90–$160.

Gaslight Inn, 33 East Middle Street; (717) 337–9100. Downtown B&B with eight guest rooms, all with private baths. Fireplaces, gardens; dinners served by reservation. Rates: $100–$170.

Appleford Inn, 218 Carlisle Street; (717) 337–1711 or (800) 275–3373. Elegant Victorian with nine guest rooms. Fireplaces, period furniture, classical music; candlelight breakfast. Rates: $85–$165.

James Gettys Hotel, 27 Chambersburg Street; (717) 337–1334, www.james gettyshotel.com. Renovated 195-year-old historic hotel with eleven guest suites; each has a bedroom, sitting room, kitchenette, and private bath. Rates: $115–$135.

Hershey

Hotel Hershey, Hotel Road; (717) 533–3311 or (800) 533–3131. Huge luxury resort hotel built in the 1930s, but modernized several times since. More than 240 large rooms; restaurants on premises. Rates: $160–$250.

Hershey Lodge and Convention Center, West Chocolate Avenue and University Drive; (717) 533–3311 or (800) 533–3131. Family-friendly lodge with 457 rooms and suites, three restaurants, a first-run movie theater, two swimming pools, and a nightclub on the premises. Rates: $109–$169.

Hershey Highmeadow Campground, 1200 Matlack Road; (717) 566–0902. Part of the Hershey Resorts complex, the campground has more than 290 sites. Campers have access to swimming and wading pools and free shuttle bus service to Hershey attractions. Rates: $20–$37.

Addey's Inn of Hershey, 150 East Governor Road; (717) 533–2593, www.addeysinn.com. Inn with twelve rooms and one suite; many amenities, including playground and tennis courts. Rates: rooms $47–$97, suite $114–$199.

Pinehurst Inn Bed and Breakfast, 50 Northeast Drive; (717) 533–2603. Former Milton Hershey–sponsored home for orphan boys is now a B&B with fifteen guest rooms and large common areas; full breakfast served. Rates: $55–$75.

Spinner's Inn, 645 East Chocolate Avenue; (717) 533–9157, www.
spinnersinn.com. Family-run motel with fifty-two rooms, all with air-
conditioning and cable TV; swimming pool and game room. Rates:
$49–$129.

White Rose Motel, 1060 East Chocolate Avenue, Hershey; (717) 533–9876,
www.whiterosemotelcom. Motel close to Hersheypark with cable TV and
refrigerators in rooms, heated pool, nearby restaurants. Rates: $44–$112.

FOR MORE INFORMATION

Gettysburg Visitors Bureau, 35 Carlisle Street, Gettysburg, PA 17325; (717)
334–6274, www.gettysburg.com.

Harrisburg/Hershey/Carlisle Tourism and Convention Bureau, 114 Walnut
Street, P.O. Box 969, Harrisburg, PA 17108; (717) 975–8161, www.
visithhc.com.

Hershey, Information and Reservations, 300 Park Boulevard, Hershey, PA
17033; (800) 437–7439, www.hersheys.com.

For more information see www.hersheypa.com.

Laurel Highlands

MOUNTAIN RETREAT

2 NIGHTS

Family resort • Outdoor activities
Children's amusement park • Shopping

When Washington's streets are slushy and one drab winter day blends into the next, it's time to break out of the weather-imposed claustrophobia and head for the hills. The hills of choice are Pennsylvania's lovely Laurel Highlands, where you can ski and hike, work out at a fitness center, and swim in a heated indoor swimming pool.

Winter isn't the only time to enjoy a weekend escape to the Laurel Highlands. Hiking, bicycling, swimming, and fishing are also available in this beautiful, secluded area of Pennsylvania.

The weekend also includes a sight-seeing trip to tiny Ligonier, a nearby town that has two interesting museums, lots of shops and restaurants, and an amusement park built with tiny children in mind. Oh, and there's a place on the route where you can buy doughnuts.

DAY 1

Morning

Drive to Somerset, Pennsylvania, via Interstate 270 north to Interstate 70, I–70 west to the Pennsylvania Turnpike (Interstate 76), and the turnpike west to exit 10. The 180-mile drive will take about three and a half hours, so when you get to Somerset, you'll probably be ready for lunch.

LUNCH: Stop at the **Summit Diner,** a genuine, open-twenty-four-hours-a-day, old-time classic, with a menu to match. If a grilled cheese sandwich and a slice of pie—or scrambled eggs, hash browns, and toast any time of the day or night—are your idea of a good thing, you've come to the right place. The diner is located at 791 North Center Avenue (State Highway 985) in Somerset; (814) 445–7154. Inexpensive.

Afternoon

After lunch, drive to **Hidden Valley Four Seasons Resort** on State Highway 31, approximately 10 miles northwest of Somerset; (814) 443–8000 or (800) 458–0175, www.hiddenvalleyresort.com. The resort's address is 1 Craighead Drive, Hidden Valley, but just look for the signs on State Highway 31.

Once you're checked in at the resort, head for the great outdoors. If you go in winter, there are twenty-five ski slopes and eight lifts that operate daily from 9:00 A.M. to 10:00 P.M. There's a ski school with more than a hundred instructors who give individual and group lessons at all skill levels. There are also 30 miles of groomed cross-country ski trails that link up with another 20 miles in adjacent state parks and forests.

On weekends you can ski for nine hours (choose the daylight package that lasts from 9:00 A.M. to 6:00 P.M. or the twilight package that lasts from 1:00 to 10:00 P.M.) for $40 per adult. Children under twelve and senior citizens ski for $32. Weekday rates are $30 and $24. If you're a night owl or you arrive really late, you get a $5.00–$10.00 price break if you wait until 4:00 P.M. to hit the trails. For general ski information, phone (814) 443–2600. For the ski report hotline, phone (800) 443–7544.

You can rent skis, boots, and poles for $20. Snowboards rent for $30 a day. Private lessons will cost you about $45 an hour; group lessons, about $18 an hour. If your kids aren't old enough for the slopes, there's a child-care service for kids under age eight that charges $5.00 an hour per child. The kids get stories, movies, and snacks. There's also a special ski orientation school for three- to five-year-olds, which has half-day and full-day classes for $30–$50.

Hidden Valley is also great fun in summer. There's a modern playground for kids, plus four heated swimming pools, three of them outdoors. There's also a small freshwater lake for fishing, sailing, kayaking, canoeing, or taking a leisurely paddleboat ride. At the Lake House equipment room, you can rent or borrow fishing poles, basketballs, volleyballs, and a croquet set. The lake is available for use from 11:00 A.M. to 7:00 P.M.; the swimming pools are open 10:00 A.M. to 8:00 P.M.

Next door, at **Kooser State Park,** there's an even larger lake with a small beach for swimming and picnicking; (814) 445–8673.

In spring, summer, or fall, you'll enjoy the 30 miles of well-marked hiking trails inside the resort, which connect with many more miles of trails in nearby state parks and forests. Resort guests get complimentary use of mountain bikes and helmets.

Hidden Valley's golf course sits on top of a mountain with a 3,000-foot peak and 30-mile vistas. It's considered one of the top courses in Pennsylvania, and it's certainly one of the most beautiful. Greens fees on the eighteen-hole, par-72 course are $59–$69 a day; cart rental is included.

DINNER: Have dinner at Hidden Valley's **Hearthside Restaurant,** a casual place with a crackling fire and a contemporary menu. Clearly catering to a health-conscious clientele, the Hearthside offers lots of vegetarian choices, homemade soups, and salads; it also has inventive meat and seafood entrees like Pennsylvania Dutch–style duck, peach and pecan chicken, and blackened scallops. Friday night features a seafood buffet. Sunday's brunch buffet is also popular. Moderate.

LODGING: There are dozens of accommodation possibilities at Hidden Valley resort. There are studios and suites at the inn; one- to three-bedroom condominiums and town houses that you can rent; and casual "dormitory style" lodging (read: many bunk beds in a large room) for individuals and groups at the Lake House. There are also a half dozen packages. In summer you can get a family package that includes lodging at the inn, breakfast and dinner at the Hearthside Restaurant, and use of the health and fitness facility, mountain bikes, and all other resort amenities for $189 a night. During ski season, expect to pay 25 to 50 percent more. The range for lodging rates is $89–$350 a night.

DAY 2

Morning

BREAKFAST: The Hearthside Restaurant offers fruit and granola or eggs Florentine, as well as a dozen other breakfast choices. Or you can buy coffee, doughnuts, juice, milk, cereal, and other groceries at the deli grocery store at the main lodge, and fix your own in your suite or room. (All rooms and suites, including the dormitory-style rooms, have kitchen facilities.)

Spend the morning at the **Sports Club,** Hidden Valley's health and fitness facility, complete with racquetball courts, indoor pool, weight room, modern exercise room, sauna, whirlpool, suntan bed, and massage room. There's also a video game room and a hair salon. The Sports Club is open daily from 8:00 A.M. to 10:00 P.M.

Or, weather permitting, head for the **Tennis Club,** which has six clay courts and four hard-surface courts. All of the courts are open dawn to dusk April through October; some are lighted for night play.

When you're ready for a break, take a thirty- to forty-minute drive into Ligonier (5 miles west on State Highway 31, about 12 hilly, scenic miles north on State Highway 381, and 3 miles west on U.S. Highway 30).

LUNCH: Have lunch at the **Ligonier Tavern,** a fun and funky old pink and turquoise Victorian home that was converted to a restaurant in 1935. Today, the redecorated interior with several adjoining dining rooms is very pretty, and the menu is eclectic. You can start with fresh fruit, escargot, or fried cheese sticks and proceed to broccoli, carrot, and spinach lasagna; roast duckling Montmorency; or homemade meat loaf with gravy. Be sure to save room for dessert. In warm months, you can eat outside on the screened front porch or on the upstairs balcony. The Ligonier Tavern is located at 137 West Main Street; (724) 238–4831. Moderate.

Afternoon

After lunch, wander around **Ligonier,** which has several gift, toy, clothing, and antiques shops clustered around the diamond in the center of town, where a gazebo sits on a patch of green. The Finishing Touch, 210 West Main Street, has Christmas collectibles. The Toy Box, 108 South Market Street, has puppets, puzzles, and educational toys. And Main Exhibit, 301 West Main Street, has contemporary art, jewelry, pottery, and sculpture.

Consider also a visit to **Fort Ligonier,** a full-scale, on-site reconstruction of the 1758 fort where the young George Washington fought with the British against the French. At the fort, there is a museum with period rooms, exhibits, dioramas, and a slide show. You might also catch a battle encampment or reenactment or an archaeological dig while you're there. Located at the intersection of U.S. Highway 30 and State Highway 711; (724) 238–9701, www. ligonier.com/fortligonier.html. Open Monday to Saturday 10:00 A.M. to 4:30 P.M., Sunday noon to 4:30 P.M., April through October. Admission is $5.50 for adults, $2.75 for seniors, and $1.50 for children age six to fourteen; children under six are admitted free.

If it's summer and you have young children, don't miss **Idlewild Park,** a child-oriented theme and amusement park about 3 miles west of Ligonier on U.S. Highway 30; (724) 238–3666 or (800) 432–9386, www.idlewild.com. Open Tuesday to Sunday 10:00 A.M. to dark, June through August, and some weekends in May. Admission is $16 for children and adults, $11.50 for senior citizens; children under two are admitted free. Idlewild first opened in 1878, and it claims to be the oldest continuously operated amusement park in the country. Many of the old rides are still there, but—faced with competition from parks with ever bigger and faster roller coasters—Idlewild today caters to the younger set.

Favorites at the park for the under-six crowd include the trolley ride through Mr. Rogers' Neighborhood; the Story Book Forest where children meet characters from nursery rhymes; the Jumpin' Jungle, a woodsy state-of-the-art playground; Hootin' Holler, a musical train ride through the Wild West; Raccoon Lagoon, an area with amusement park rides for toddlers; and Little Squirts, a special kids' section in the water park. Older kids will happily spend the whole day on the water slides at the H$_2$Ohhh Zone and the roller coasters of Olde Idlewild.

DINNER: Unless you have a package plan at Hidden Valley that includes dinner, stop on the way home at **Ligonier Country Inn,** an attractive, moderately priced restaurant located on U.S. Highway 30 in Laughlintown, about 3 miles east of Ligonier; (724) 238–3651. There you can get a crab dip appetizer and a great lamb stew or choose from a dozen other steak, seafood, chicken, or pasta dishes. Everyone gets "flowerpot bread"—yeast bread baked on the premises in tiny clay flowerpots. Moderate.

Even if you don't stop in Laughlintown for dinner, you can't pass up the **Pie Shoppe,** U.S. Highway 30, Laughlintown; (724) 238–6621. In addition to pies of all flavors, they sell vegetarian pizzas (the spinach and tomato pizza is great), sandwiches, and mouthwatering doughnuts.

Try the slopes at night or relax in one of Hidden Valley's lounges. The Snowshoe Lounge has a cheerful fire, a pool table, music, and snacks. In winter, Glacier's Pub has serious skiers doing serious relaxing.

LODGING: Hidden Valley Inn.

DAY 3

Morning

BREAKFAST: The Hearthside Restaurant.

After breakfast, have a last ski, hike, mountain-bike ride, or swim before packing up for home. You can pick up sandwiches for the road at the **Mountain Deli** in the main lodge or, if you're on the slopes, grab a burger at the Deck Cafe.

Your drive back to Washington via State Highway 31 east, the Pennsylvania Turnpike east, I–70 east, and I–270 south will take four hours.

THERE'S MORE

Additional Ski Slopes. The nearby Seven Springs Mountain Resort just east of State Highway 711 near Champion has thirty slopes and trails for downhill skiing; (814) 352–7777.

Compass Inn Museum. Restored 1799 stagecoach stop furnished with period pieces and operated by the local historical society. Located in Laughlintown on U.S. Highway 30 about 3 miles east of Ligonier; (724) 238–4983. Open Tuesday to Saturday 11:00 A.M. to 4:00 P.M., Sunday noon to 4:00 P.M., May through October. Admission is $5.00 for adults and $2.00 for students six to sixteen; children under six are admitted free.

Mountain Playhouse. Local theater company performs classic Broadway musicals and comedies at popular Green Gables Restaurant in Jennerstown; the company has been going strong for more than sixty years; (814) 629–9201. Performances June through October. Admission is $12–$25.

SPECIAL EVENTS

April. Annual Pennsylvania Maple Festival in Meyersdale. Food, crafts, and music in Somerset County. (814) 634–0213.

September. Masters Wildlife Art Show. Annual Ligonier event features exhibition and sale of carved and sculpted wildlife. (724) 238–7560.

September. Scottish Highland Games. Games, parades, bagpipes and fiddles, dog shows, food, and more at various sites in or near Ligonier. (724) 851–9900.

September. Mountain Craft Days. Folklife festival in Somerset with dozens of demonstrations of crafts and lots of funnel cakes, fried corn mush with maple syrup, and home-baked pies. (814) 445–6077.

October. Fort Ligonier Days. Annual weekend event featuring food, crafts, a parade, and historical programs. (724) 238–4200.

OTHER RECOMMENDED RESTAURANTS

Baldonieri's Mill Creek Restaurant, Springer Road (west of downtown), Ligonier; (412) 238–3636. Known for its steaks and chops. Moderate.

Oakhurst Tea Room, State Highway 31 west of Somerset; (814) 443–2897. Large smorgasbord and dessert table; bring your appetite and burn off the calories on the slopes. Moderate.

Green Gables, State Highway 985, a half mile north of U.S. Highway 30, Jennerstown; (814) 629–9220. Regional American cuisine in a pleasant setting has made this restaurant popular for more than seventy years. Moderate.

Seven Springs Mountain Resort just east of State Highway 711 near Champion has five restaurants, including Helen's, which offers French, Italian, and continental cuisine in an elegant setting. Reservations are necessary at Helen's; the other restaurants operate on a first-come, first-served basis. Phone (814) 352–7777 or (800) 452–2223. Expensive at Helen's, inexpensive to moderate at the other four.

For additional listings see Other Recommended Lodgings.

OTHER RECOMMENDED LODGINGS

Ligonier Country Inn, U.S. Highway 30, Laughlintown; (724) 238–3651, www.ligoniercountryinn.com. Homey inn with nineteen rooms, all with private baths, air-conditioning, TVs, and telephones; swimming pool; restaurant on premises. Rates: $70–$105.

Trenthouse Inn Bed & Breakfast, Rockwood; (814) 352–8492. Combination Victorian house and general store built in 1884 has four antiques-filled guest rooms, two with private baths; continental breakfast. Rates: $58–$68.

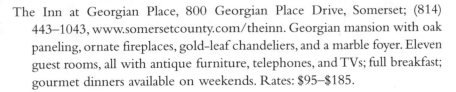
The Inn at Georgian Place, 800 Georgian Place Drive, Somerset; (814) 443–1043, www.somersetcounty.com/theinn. Georgian mansion with oak paneling, ornate fireplaces, gold-leaf chandeliers, and a marble foyer. Eleven guest rooms, all with antique furniture, telephones, and TVs; full breakfast; gourmet dinners available on weekends. Rates: $95–$185.

Glades Pike Inn, 2684 Glades Pike (State Highway 31), Somerset; (814) 443–4978. Once a nineteenth-century stagecoach stop, this recently remodeled redbrick inn has exposed-wood floors and high ceilings. Two of the five guest rooms have fireplaces. Rates: $50–$90.

Mountain View Inn, U.S. Highway 30 east, Greensburg; (724) 834–5300 or (800) 537–8709, www.mountainviewinn.com. Large, comfortable inn with eighty-seven guest rooms and suites furnished with brass beds and antiques. Pleasant gardens, gazebos, and pool; restaurant on premises serves first-rate regional fare. Rates: $69–$129 for rooms, $109–$300 for suites.

Seven Springs Mountain Resort, Champion; (814) 352–7777 or (800) 452–2223, www.7springs.com. Pennsylvania's largest resort, with accommodations for more than 5,000 people in its hotel, cabins, chalets, and condos. Rates: $81–$175 for two people at the hotel; packages available.

FOR MORE INFORMATION

Laurel Highlands, Inc., Town Hall, 120 East Main Street, Ligonier, PA 15658; (724) 238–5661 or (800) 925–7669, www.laurelhighlands.org.

Pittsburgh

GREAT MUSEUMS IN RIVER CITY

---

2 NIGHTS

City tour • Museums • Conservatory
Shopping • Ethnic dining

People have been saying for years that Pittsburgh is one of the most livable cities in the United States. Well, it's a great place to visit too. This old river city shed its smokestack image long ago and is now bursting with art, culture, upscale shopping, new restaurants, Steelers fans, and delighted visitors.

One of the city's many draws is the beauty and variety of its architecture. In the downtown area, you'll see the glittering neo-Gothic spires of Pittsburgh Plate and Glass, the nineteenth-century Mellon Bank building (with its beautifully carved trim looking like a lace handkerchief draped over the roof), the gigantic new rust-red U.S. Steel building, and off in the distance behind a hospital, an angel with outstretched wings atop a church.

Old and new exist side by side all over Pittsburgh. There are old museums with new acquisitions, new restaurants in old neighborhoods, inns and shops springing up in once-blighted enclaves. There are famous attractions that have existed for a hundred years, like the Carnegie Museum of Natural History and the spectacular Phipps Conservatory. And the Frick Estate, built a century ago, is now open for visitors to tour the grand home, grounds, and art gallery and museum.

Your tour won't be confined to the nineteenth century, however. The dazzling Carnegie Science Center on the Allegheny River was completed in 1991, and the Andy Warhol Museum opened in 1993 to showcase the works of this Pittsburgh native, the central figure of pop art. Shops and restaurants

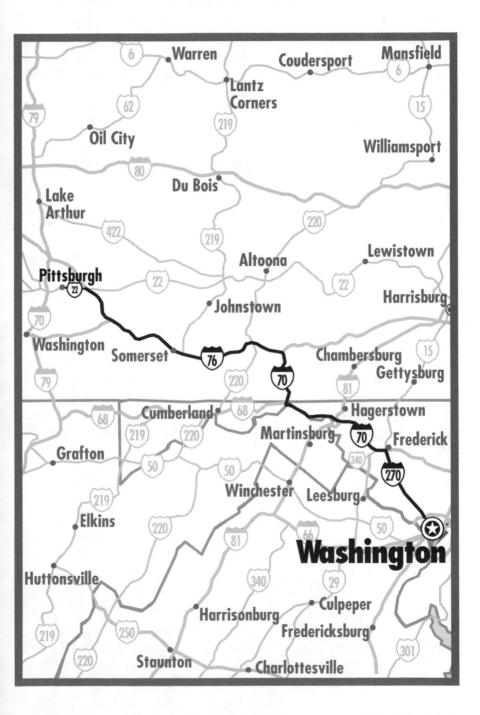

have opened up at the renovated Station Square along the waterfront. And there are hip and lively shopping districts near the University of Pittsburgh and Carnegie Mellon University, where coffee bars, ethnic restaurants, and upscale clothing and gift shops abound.

Your three-day weekend itinerary isn't long enough to do it all, but you'll see enough to fall in love with Pittsburgh and want to return again and again.

DAY 1

Morning

Get an early start—8:00 A.M., if possible—so you'll have a full afternoon in Pittsburgh. Pittsburgh is 220 miles from Washington, but it's a four-and-a-half to five-hour drive via Interstate 270 north to Interstate 70 west to the Pennsylvania Turnpike (Interstate 76) west. Take the turnpike's exit 6 and follow the parkway (Interstate 376 and U.S. Highways 22 and 30) west through the eastern suburbs for 16 miles to the center of the city.

Your first destination is the **Shops at Station Square,** a complex of new stores and restaurants right along the Monongahela River directly across from the Golden Triangle, Pittsburgh's 11-by-11-block spruced-up business district. To get there, exit the parkway at Grant Street, turn left when you can, and go 2 blocks east to Smithfield Street, which runs parallel to Grant. Turn left on Smithfield and follow it a few blocks south straight across the Smithfield Street Bridge. Then make an immediate right turn and find a parking place in the large lots near the Shops at Station Square.

In many ways, the Shops at Station Square are a symbol of the "new" Pittsburgh. A century ago this fifty-acre site was the Pittsburgh and Lake Erie Railroad Yards, and, if the wind was right, the coal-burning, smoke-belching trains could cover downtown Pittsburgh with a dark cloud. Today Station Square is a renovated two-building indoor mall that includes boutiques, upscale apparel chain stores, bookstores, and more than a dozen places to eat. Special events are often held at Station Square or in the spacious parking lots. Station Square is located on West Carson Street; (412) 261–2811, www.stationsquare.com. Shops are open Monday to Saturday 10:00 A.M. to 9:00 P.M., Sunday noon to 5:00 P.M. Restaurant hours vary.

LUNCH: Upon arriving at the Shops at Station Square, your immediate objective is lunch, and there are several choices—from ribs, pizza, or sandwiches to raw bars or ethnic food. One good choice is the very popular **Sesame Inn,** which offers fine Chinese dining in the evening and $6.00 specials for lunch; (412) 281–8282. If you're really in a hurry to begin sight-seeing, try **Jimbo's Specialty Beer and Hot Dog Shop,** where you can wash down hot dogs and pretzels with any of 300 microbrewed and imported beers while you sit in the station court; (412) 765–1543.

Afternoon

After lunch, drive up the hill to the **Mount Washington** section of town. When you reach Grandview Avenue, park your car and stroll west.

Mount Washington itself is worth seeing, with its century-old Victorian homes, peaceful streets, old churches, and new art galleries, but most people make the trip up the hill because Grandview Avenue has, well, a grand view.

You'll see the Allegheny and Monongahela Rivers meet to form the Ohio River. You'll see where tiny Point State Park juts right into the middle of the rivers' intersection, a patch of green with a spewing fountain. Behind it, you'll see the aptly named **Three Rivers Stadium,** home to the Pittsburgh Pirates and Steelers. And, as you stroll along Grandview Avenue, you'll survey all of the Golden Triangle and the vibrant new downtown business and commercial center of Pittsburgh.

As you head west on Grandview Avenue, just past the clutch of restaurants, you'll come to the **Duquesne Incline** station. Don't pass it by. Pittsburgh has two funiculars, or inclines: the **Monongahela Incline,** which climbs Mount Washington from Station Square to the foot of Grandview Avenue, and the Duquesne Incline, which climbs the mountain from a point just west of the Fort Pitt Bridge to the commercial heart of Grandview Avenue.

Take a moment to walk around inside the Duquesne Incline station, which is covered with old pictures and postcards of Pittsburgh in the past. And don't miss the view from the observation deck, where you can see at least sixteen of Pittsburgh's 720 bridges on the Allegheny, Monongahela, and Ohio Rivers.

And, of course, you'll want to ride down and up the Duquesne Incline itself in the original tram car that has been gliding up and down the hill for almost 120 years. It's slightly scary, but that only makes it more fun. The view from the trams at night, when Pittsburgh is all lit up, is especially nice, and the Duquesne Incline has been considered among the most romantic night spots in Pittsburgh for more than a century. Both inclines operate from early morning to 12:45 A.M. Incline rides cost a dollar each way. Phone (412) 381–1665.

Back at the top, a pleasant place for a quick cup of coffee is **City Lights,** 1216 Grandview Avenue (412–431–1101), an espresso shop that also sells pastries and sandwiches. Inexpensive.

Now that you have the big picture, start enjoying some of the individual highlights Pittsburgh has to offer. Collect your car, drive back down the hill from Grandview Avenue, recross the Smithfield Street Bridge, turn left almost immediately onto Fort Pitt Boulevard, and head for **Point State Park,** an 8-block patch of serenity at the confluence of the three rivers. At the tiny park you can cool off in the spray from a 150-foot-high fountain fed by a fourth, pristine underground river; survey the remnants of **Fort Pitt,** built by the British in 1764 to keep an eye on the Ohio River; and study up on the early history of the region at the small museum at 101 Commonwealth Place; (412) 281–9284. The museum is open Wednesday to Saturday 10:00 A.M. to 4:30 P.M., Sunday noon to 4:30 P.M. Admission is $4.00 for adults, $3.50 for senior citizens, and $2.00 for children. A family admission is $10.

There are plenty of parking lots near the park, and, if you haven't written ahead for maps and brochures or if you need help with hotel accommodations or advice about how to get tickets to the ball game or opera, stop at the friendly Visitor Information Bureau near Four Gateway Center; (412) 281–7711. It's worth the 1-block hike to see Gateway Center itself, one of the new skyscrapers that have helped revitalize downtown Pittsburgh. The visitors center is open weekdays 9:00 A.M. to 5:00 P.M., weekends 9:00 A.M. to 3:00 P.M.

When you finish your afternoon's introduction to Pittsburgh, check in at your evening digs, which are located across the Allegheny River from the Golden Triangle. Take the Ninth Street Bridge and you'll see Pressley Street after about 7 blocks. There you'll find **The Priory—A City Inn,** 614 Pressley Street; (412) 231–3338, www.sgi.net/the priory. Built in 1888, this nicely restored European-style inn once was a way station for Benedictine priests traveling to Pittsburgh. The Priory has twenty-four rooms and suites, all of which are large, high-ceilinged, quiet, and handsome, and front-desk staff go out of the way to be helpful. Complimentary sherry, cheese, and crackers are served in the parlor in the afternoon, and there's a self-serve "honor" bar too. Rates: $98–$142.

After sherry and a shower, take in a surprising local attraction that is literally just a couple of blocks from your hotel: the **Andy Warhol Museum,** 117 Sandusky Street; (412) 237–8300, www.warhol.org/warhol. Open Wednesday and Sunday 11:00 A.M. to 6:00 P.M., Thursday to Saturday 11:00 A.M. to 8:00

The Gateway Clipper *and Point State Park*

P.M., closed Monday and Tuesday. Admission is $7.00 for adults, $6.00 for seniors and students, and $4.00 for children over three.

Warhol was a Pittsburgh native who studied art at what is now Carnegie Mellon University. His images of Marilyn Monroe and Campbell's Soup cans became the icons of pop art, and his innovative photographic techniques transformed the modern art world. This interesting gallery, which houses the largest single-artist collection in the world, is one of the Carnegie Museums, in collaboration with the Dia Center for the Arts and the Andy Warhol Foundation.

DINNER: Pittsburgh has lots of nice restaurants to choose from, but for your first night, stay downtown and sample the osso buco, the linguine with fresh clams and mussels, or any of the seafood dishes at **Piccolo Piccolo Ristorante,** 1 Wood Street; (412) 261–7234. Don't overdo it at the complimentary antipasto salad bar before your entree arrives because the servings are generous. Expensive.

LODGING: The Priory Inn.

DAY 2

Morning

BREAKFAST: The Priory Inn serves a buffet continental breakfast that you can eat outdoors on the garden patio in seasonable weather.

After breakfast, head for the east side of Pittsburgh for a morning exploring the wonders of the great **Carnegie Museum** complex. You can't miss the gorgeous century-old building that houses the original structure. Topped with statues, fronted with archways and pillars, and covering an entire city block, the classical Greek building now houses the Carnegie Library, the Museum of Natural History, the Museum of Art, and the Music Hall.

The immense building, expanded in 1903 so that it now covers fourteen acres, is even more wondrous inside than out. The lavish and gleaming foyer, with an arched gold ceiling and immense green marble pillars; the plaster reproductions in the Hall of Architecture and the adjacent Hall of Sculpture (which is modeled after the Parthenon); the brilliant **Music Hall,** with red velvet seats and a beautifully carved ceiling . . . well, you'll have to see them all for yourself.

The **Museum of Art,** which opened in 1896, was designed to bring to Pittsburgh exhibitions of contemporary paintings from Europe and the United States. Today, the Carnegie International (a six-week exhibition of art from around the world held in midwinter) is the biggest international art show in the United States, and the second oldest in the world. It includes old masters, decorative arts, and sculpture.

One complete wing of the Carnegie Museum building is devoted to natural history. **The Museum of Natural History** contains an extraordinary collection of dinosaur skeletons, and fossils; a glittering hall of minerals and gems; anthropological treasures such as Egyptian mummies, jade artifacts, and Native American art; and much, much more. The museum cherishes living creatures too. It is affiliated with a 2,200-acre natural sanctuary in the nearby Laurel Highlands that serves as the base for research on many species.

Be sure to leave time for a visit to the Natural History Museum Gift Shop, which is a treasure trove of posters, imported art objects, masks, dolls, and nature-oriented videos, books, and games.

The **Carnegie Library of Pittsburgh,** at the same location, has an outstanding science and technology collection, one of the nation's best music collections, and an excellent humanities collection. For more than a century it has been a pioneer in defining the true purpose of libraries.

The Carnegie Museum complex is located at 4400 Forbes Avenue; (412) 622–3131, www.clpgh.org or www.cmoa.org. The Museums of Art and Natural History are open Tuesday to Saturday 10:00 A.M. to 5:00 P.M., Sunday 1:00 to 5:00 P.M. The Carnegie Library is open Monday to Thursday 9:00 A.M. to 9:00 P.M., Friday and Saturday 9:00 A.M. to 5:30 P.M., Sunday 1:00 to 5:00 P.M. Admission to the museums is $6.00 for adults, $5.00 for senior citizens, $4.00 for children three and up and for full-time students. (Note: The Carnegie has a six-level parking garage where you can leave your car for $3.00; be sure to have your ticket validated at the museum.)

LUNCH: When you're ready to get off your feet, head for the **Star of India,** a quiet, charming Indian restaurant at 412 South Craig Street, a short walk from the Carnegie; (412) 681–5700. The extensive menu has dozens of meat and vegetarian dishes, including tandoori chicken, lamb, shrimp, biryanis, curries, and wonderful breads, such as puffy pooris and onion nan. This is a "bring your own alcoholic drinks" restaurant, which charges 30 cents for the glass, but cups of hot spiced tea are readily available, and are the perfect accompaniment to the spicy food. Don't forget dessert. The kulfee (cardamom-flavored ice cream) is wonderful. Moderate.

Afternoon

After lunch, stroll along South Craig Street in the pleasant **Oakland** neighborhood and shopping district. There you will see interesting import stores, ethnic restaurants, and coffee bars. Notice Macondo and History, two import stores with beautiful African and Asian arts and crafts, both in the 400 block of South Craig Street, just north of Forbes Avenue.

From South Craig Street, walk or drive a block east on Forbes Avenue to Boundary Street, turn right, and go a few blocks to the Schenley Park Bridge. There turn left and enter **Schenley Park,** an enormous expanse of green where bikers, walkers, and in-line skaters fly up and down the winding drive.

Schenley Park is also home to the **Phipps Conservatory.** The Phipps, built in 1893, has thirteen glass show houses (covering two and a half acres) featuring beautiful and exotic trees, plants, and flowers. Outdoors, there are shade trees, fountains, benches, and more gardens, including a Japanese courtyard. The conservatory is open Tuesday to Sunday 9:00 A.M. to 5:00 P.M. Admission is $5.00 for adults, $3.50 for seniors and students, and $2.00 for children two to twelve; children under two are admitted free. Phone (412) 622–6914, www.phippsconservatory.org.

From the Phipps, drive east about a mile and north about a mile and you'll be in **Shadyside,** another pleasant neighborhood with an interesting shopping area along Walnut Street. There you'll find some fine antiques and clothing stores interspersed with familiar chain store outlets. Don't miss the Four Winds Gallery at 5512 Walnut Street, which has a collection of American Indian artwork, jewelry, pottery, and weavings for sale.

DINNER: Shadyside is also home to lots of ethnic restaurants. You can find Vietnamese, Japanese, Thai, Chinese, and Mexican within just a few blocks. An excellent little Greek restaurant is close by too. **Suzie's,** 1704 Shady Avenue (412–422–8066), is a classic, unassuming, and friendly eatery with a moderately priced selection of homemade soups and stews, great kabobs, phyllo-pastry pies (including spinach and chicken), and lots of good bread, olives, and red wine.

After dinner you should explore what's going on at the **Carnegie Music Hall;** its chamber music series is likely to be featuring an internationally acclaimed group. Call (412) 622–3131 for tickets and program information. Alternatively, check out **Heinz Hall,** where the world-famous Pittsburgh Symphony Orchestra performs, or the **Benedum Center for the Performing Arts,** home of the Pittsburgh Opera and the Pittsburgh Ballet. (See There's More for details.)

LODGING: The Priory Inn.

DAY 3

Morning

BREAKFAST: The Priory Inn.

After breakfast at the Priory, take a walking or a driving tour of downtown Pittsburgh to get a closer look at its many beautiful buildings. (A walking-tour brochure is available at the visitors center and at most hotels.)

Worth a close look are the USX Tower on Grant Street, at 841 feet the tallest building between New York and Chicago; the Alcoa Building on William Penn Place, America's first aluminum skyscraper; Trinity Episcopal Cathedral and the First Presbyterian Church next door to each other on Sixth Avenue, two century-old churches with marvelous stained glass windows; Kaufmann's Department Store on Fifth Avenue, with a large bronze clock that is Pittsburghers' favorite meeting place; and PPG Place, the castle of glass located between Third and Fourth Avenues.

About midmorning, head for the **Carnegie Science Center,** a huge new museum with a four-story domed Omnimax theater, a sophisticated interactive planetarium, a World War II vintage submarine, and 250 more exhibits that make this truly "an amusement park for the mind." You could and should spend days visiting the Science Center. There are special exhibits for preschoolers; three free theaters—the science stage, the kitchen theater, and the works theater—where minidramas illuminate everyday science; a science and sport exhibit; an aquarium; an insect exhibit where you can let insects run up your hands and arms; a weather center; and a creative technology center.

A favorite of visitors of all ages is the miniature railroad and village, which must rank among the top two or three miniature railroads in the world. Yes, there are trains—more than a dozen on the 30-by-90-foot platform. There are also automobiles, bridges, farms, factories, a stone quarry, a baseball field, and inch-high people And they're nearly all moving. Except, of course when the lights dim to simulate nighttime, or winter comes and the snow begins to fall, or. . .well, you get the point. . .when they're not *supposed* to be moving. It's not unusual to see a visitor standing transfixed through two or three rotations of the seasons, watching a tiny portion of the village for fifteen or twenty minutes.

The Carnegie Science Center is located at One Allegheny Drive; (412) 237–3400. It's open Sunday to Friday 10:00 A.M. to 5:00 P.M., Saturday 10:00 A.M. to 9:00 P.M. Admission to the exhibits, the planetarium, or the Omnimax theater is $6.50 for adults, and $4.50 for seniors and children age three to eighteen; children under three get in free. Two-event combination tickets are $10.00 and $6.00. Three-event combination tickets are $12.00 and $8.00. There is an additional charge to tour the submarine.

Your last stop in Pittsburgh will be a visit to the **Frick Art and Historical Center**, which sits in an elegantly landscaped six-acre complex at the edge of Frick Park, Pittsburgh's largest city park. The Frick complex is located at 7227 Reynolds Street in Pittsburgh's fashionable East End; (412) 371–0600.

Open Tuesday to Saturday 10:00 A.M. to 5:00 P.M., Sunday noon to 6:00 P.M. Admission to the art gallery is free, but guided tours of the mansion cost $5.00 for adults, $4.00 for senior citizens, and $3.00 for students. Children under six are admitted free.

LUNCH: Begin your visit to the Frick with lunch at the **Cafe,** located in the middle of the complex. As you eat your sandwich, salad, and pastry, you'll have a panoramic view of the estate. For reservations call (412) 371–0600. Moderate.

Afternoon

After lunch, start your tour of the Frick Art and Historical Center at the **Frick Art Museum,** with its beautiful collection of fourteenth-century icons and Italian, French, and Flemish paintings and examples of the decorative arts. Francesco Ubertini's *Madonna and Child with Saint Elizabeth and John the Baptist* will draw your eyes immediately, with its lush colors and beautifully rendered faces.

Elsewhere in the complex is **Clayton,** Henry Clay Frick's renovated estate, which you can tour if you make an advance reservation; (412) 371–0606. Crowd favorites on the docent-led tour are the leather highchair, the miniature children's entrance, and the tiny sink and coat rack, which show that Clayton was a real family home as well as an elegant mansion where world leaders and wealthy industrialists were entertained.

Also visit the **Carriage Museum,** which displays the Frick's seventeen carriages and automobiles (including a 1914 Rolls Royce Silver Ghost); the **Greenhouse** with thousands of exotic plants and flowers; and the **Children's Playhouse,** which now houses the visitors center and museum shop.

When you finish at the Frick, drive home via the parkway east to the Pennsylvania Turnpike (Interstate 76), I–76 east to Interstate 70, I–70 east to Interstate 270, and I–270 south to Washington. The trip will take you about five hours.

You can stop for dinner on the way home at one of the many fast-food places or diners on, or just off, the Pennsylvania Turnpike. For a more relaxed meal, consider one of the Hagerstown restaurants listed in Maryland Escape Six (see page 128).

THERE'S MORE

Pittsburgh Children's Museum. "Please touch" exhibits, climbing maze, fantastic puppet shows, crafts, a special infant play area with a rice table and peek-a-boo boxes, and exhibits from *Mr. Rogers' Neighborhood*, which is taped in Pittsburgh. Located at 10 Children's Way; (412) 322–5058, www. pittsburghkids.org. Open Tuesday to Saturday 10:00 A.M. to 5:00 P.M., Sunday noon to 5:00 P.M. Admission is $4.50 for everyone over two years old, free for infants.

Kennywood Park. One of the oldest amusement parks in the United States and a National Historic Landmark. Recently updated, it still has some of the old historic rides plus lots of gentle rides for little kids. It also has the Steel Phantom, which may be the world's fastest roller coaster. Located at 4800 Kennywood Boulevard, West Mifflin; (412) 461–0500, www.kenny wood.com. Open daily 11:00 A.M. to midnight, mid-May through Labor Day. General admission is $6.95. To ride all day costs $18 on weekdays and $22 on weekends.

Pittsburgh Zoo. Seventy-five-acre natural-habitat zoo with more than 5,000 animals in the African Savannah, the Asian Forest, and the Tropical Forest; also includes a children's zoo. Located in Highland Park on the Allegheny River about 5 miles east of downtown; (412) 665–3640, www.zoo.pgh.pa.us. Open daily 9:00 A.M. to 4:30 P.M., later in the summer. Admission is $6.50 for adults and $4.75 for seniors and children over age two.

The National Aviary. Your opportunity to see some 450 exotic birds, from egrets to condors to piping plovers to blue-winged kookaburras at the largest freestanding aviary in America. Located at Allegheny Commons West; (412) 323–7235, www.aviary.org. Open daily 9:00 A.M. to 4:30 P.M. Admission is $5.00 for adults, $4.00 for seniors, and $3.50 for children two to twelve; children under two are admitted free.

Professional Sports. Both the Pittsburgh Pirates (600 Stadium Circle; 412–323–5000) and the Pittsburgh Steelers (300 Stadium Circle; 412–323–1200) play at Three Rivers Stadium. You can take a one-hour tour of the stadium by reservation on weekdays between 9:00 A.M. and 1:00 P.M. Call (412) 321–0650. Admission is $3.00 for adults and $2.50 for senior citizens and children. The Pittsburgh Penguins hockey team plays at the Civic Arena, at Auditorium Place downtown; (412) 642–7367.

Gateway Clipper. Five huge riverboat-style cruise ships offer sight-seeing cruises, dinner cruises, family-oriented cruises, and shuttle service to Three Rivers Stadium. Operates from Station Square Dock. There are about thirty different cruises; admission varies. Phone (412) 355–7980, www.gatewayclipper.com.

Pittsburgh Center for the Arts. Pennsylvania's largest community art center has regional, national, and international exhibitions and sells the work of more than 500 local artists. Located at 6300 Fifth Avenue; (412) 361–0873, www.artsnet.org/pghctarts. Open Monday to Saturday 10:00 A.M. to 5:30 P.M., Sunday noon to 5:00 P.M. Donations requested.

Heinz Hall for the Performing Arts. Regular performances by the Pittsburgh Symphony; additional appearances by world-class artists; also home to the Symphony Pops concerts. Located at 600 Penn Avenue. For information on events, times, and prices, call (412) 392–4900; www.pghsym.org.

Benedum Center for the Performing Arts. Home of the Pittsburgh Opera, the Pittsburgh Ballet, the Civic Light Opera, and the Dance Council. Call the box office for events and prices. Located at 719 Liberty Avenue; (412) 456–2600.

Nationality Classrooms. Two dozen classrooms that depict Pittsburgh's diverse ethnic heritage through examples of architecture and decor. Ninety-minute tours available between 9:00 A.M. and 3:00 P.M. Monday to Saturday, between 11:00 A.M. and 3:00 P.M. Sunday. Suggested donation: $2.00 for adults, 50 cents for children. Located at the University of Pittsburgh, 157 Cathedral of Learning Building; (412) 624–6000.

SPECIAL EVENTS

May. Pittsburgh Children's Festival. Week of children's performing arts and family activities. (412) 321–5520.

August. Shadyside Arts Festival. Weekend festival with paintings, sculpture, workshops, and evening jazz draws more than 100,000 people. (412) 681–2809.

August. Three Rivers Regatta. Formula One powerboat racing, water sports, hot-air balloon rides, food, and entertainment at the nation's largest inland regatta. (412) 338–8768.

November–December. Sparkle Season. Begins in November with "Light-Up Night," when all the lights in downtown Pittsburgh are turned on, and ends with "First Night" festival on New Year's Eve; numerous affiliated events. (412) 566–4190.

OTHER RECOMMENDED RESTAURANTS

Poli's, 2607 Murray Avenue, Squirrel Hill; (412) 521–6400. Legendary Italian restaurant that regularly competes for the "best seafood in town" label. Expensive.

Cliffside Restaurant, 1208 Grandview Avenue; (412) 431–6996. Longtime Mount Washington favorite with traditional continental menu and spectacular view of the city from almost every table. Expensive.

Cozumel, 5507 Walnut Street; (412) 621–5100. Unpretentious Mexican eatery with an enormous menu. Old standbys and new dishes, including lots of vegetarian entrees; margaritas and eight brands of Mexican beer. Moderate.

Mallorca Restaurant, 2228 East Carson Street; (412) 488–1818. Popular restaurant on the South Side serving Spanish and Portuguese cuisine. Moderate.

Penn Brewery Restaurant, Troy Hill Road and Vinial Street; (412) 237–9402. Restored North Side brewery serving German specialties and a dozen microbrews in a publike atmosphere. Moderate.

Seventh Street Grille, 130 Seventh Street; (412) 338–0303. New restaurant across from the Benedum and instant contender for top restaurant in town. Steaks, seafood, prime rib, after-the-opera drinks; always crowded. Worth a trip for the warm duck salad or the smoked chicken quesadillas. Expensive.

1902 Landmark Tavern, 24 Market Square; (412) 471–1902. Tin ceilings, tile floors, and hundred-year-old brick walls provide plenty of atmosphere; award-winning chef provides great food; Vodka Bar stocks more than fifty brands of vodka and has thirty-three brands of beer on tap. It's a winning combination. Moderate to expensive.

Top of the Triangle, on the sixty-second floor of the U.S. Steel Building, 600 Grant Street; (412) 471-4100. Continental cuisine in elegant setting with a view of the whole city; great for drinks or lunch on a clear day. Expensive.

Best place for doughnuts: Balcer Bakery, 2126 East Carson Street; (412) 431–6193.

OTHER RECOMMENDED LODGINGS

Shadyside Bed & Breakfast, 5516 Maple Heights Road; (412) 683–6501, www.pittsburgbnb.com/shadyside.html. Very nice B&B with eight rooms, five with private baths. Library with fireplace, billiard room, guest kitchen and dining room; continental breakfast. Rates: $120–$145.

Shadyside Inn, 5405 Fifth Avenue; (412) 441–4444, www.shadysideinn.com. East Side inn with one hundred suites; all have kitchens, cable TV, and telephones. Rates: $99–$129.

Morning Glory Inn, 2119 Sarah Street; (412) 431–1707. Convenient South Side B&B with five guest rooms, all with private bath. Garden, porches, music room with grand piano; full breakfast includes German baked eggs, biscuits, and fruit. Rates: $110–$200.

The Appletree Bed and Breakfast, 703 South Negley Avenue; (412) 661–0631. Shadyside Victorian with five guest rooms, all with private bath. Full country breakfast; afternoon tea. Rates: $99–$140.

Victoria House Bed and Breakfast, 939 Western Avenue; (412) 231–4948, www.victoriahousebb.com. Five-room downtown Victorian B&B that serves full English breakfasts. Rates: $95–$135.

Ramada Plaza, One Bigelow Square; (412) 281–5800 or (800) 225–5858. Chain hotel with 300 rooms, most of them suites; good for families. Rates: $99–$189.

Sheraton Hotel Station Square, 7 Station Square Drive; (412) 261–2000 or (800) 255–7488. Multistory hotel with 292 rooms. Convenient location, good view, indoor pool and fitness facilities; restaurants on premises. Rates: $109–$179.

Westin William Penn, 530 William Penn Place; (412) 281–7100 or (800) 228–3000. Elegant, old downtown hotel with 595 rooms and gracious service; the Palm Court has tea every afternoon. Rates: $120–$260.

FOR MORE INFORMATION

Greater Pittsburgh Convention and Visitors Bureau, Four Gateway Center, Pittsburgh, PA 15222; (412) 281–7711 or (800) 821–1888, www. visitpittsburgh.com.

PENNSYLVANIA

Fayette County

FALLINGWATER AND FALLING WATERS

---
2 NIGHTS

Fallingwater, an architectural masterpiece • Hiking
Biking • White-water rafting • An old-style resort

Four hours from Washington, D.C., is an unspoiled recreational area in south-western Pennsylvania. Wooded and mountainous, Fayette County is bisected by the wild, beautiful Youghiogheny River. (It's pronounced "*Yock*-a-gay-nee," but everyone calls it "the Yock.") Fayette County is also home to Ohiopyle State Park, Pennsylvania's largest state park and the first white-water rafting site east of the Mississippi; miles of secluded hiking and biking trails; several historic sites; and Fallingwater, the cantilevered stone-and-glass home designed by Frank Lloyd Wright that many consider the premier masterpiece of American architecture.

On a long weekend you can see and experience all of the attractions of Fayette County and stay at a century-old resort complete with golf course, swimming pool, tennis courts, and cozy lounge, as well as a spectacular view from the top of Mount Summit.

DAY 1

Morning

Get a midmorning start, and drive to Fayette County via Interstate 270 north to Frederick, Interstate 70 west to Hancock, Interstate 68 west to Grantsville, and U.S. Highway 40 west. The drive through Maryland on the interstate

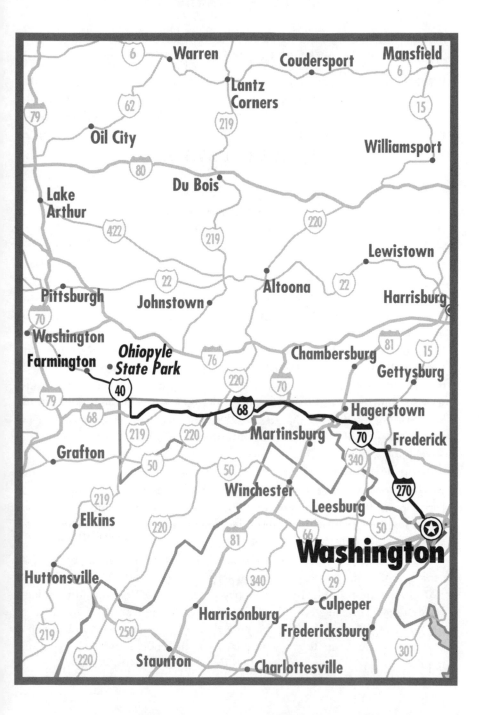

highways will take about three hours; once you leave I–68 at Grantsville (exit 22), you're only 15 miles from Fayette County in Pennsylvania.

LUNCH: Either pack a picnic lunch or stop for a late lunch at the **Hill Top Inn Restaurant,** about three hours into your trip. It's located in Grantsville, Maryland, on U.S. Highway 40 less than a mile west of your exit from Interstate 68; (301) 895–5168. There you can get no-frills, home-style cooking, or you can make your own lunch at the salad bar.

Afternoon

After lunch, continue west on U.S. Highway 40 to the Pennsylvania state line and then west another 5 miles to Fayette County.

Just past the town of Farmington on U.S. Highway 40 are four historic sites maintained by the National Park Service. There's **Fort Necessity National Battlefield,** where the French and Indian War began in 1754 and where the young George Washington fought his first battle (on behalf of the British, who lost); **Mt. Washington Tavern,** a restored 1820s tavern commemorating the early days of the trek west on the Old National Pike; British General **Braddock's Grave,** located 1 mile west of Fort Necessity; and **Jumonville Glen,** where British forces surprised a French troop in a prelude to the battle at Fort Necessity. The attractions are open from 8:00 A.M. to sunset year-round; the visitors center at the fort is open daily from 8:30 A.M. to 5:00 P.M. Admission to all the sites is $2.00 for everyone over age sixteen; children sixteen and younger are admitted free. Phone (724) 329–5512; www.nps.gov/fone.

From Farmington or Fort Necessity, it's only a few miles west to your weekend lodging, the **Summit Inn,** Two Skyline Drive (U.S. Highway 40), Farmington; (724) 438–8594 or (800) 433–8594, www.hhs.net/summit. Note: The Summit Inn has a 4:00 P.M. check-in time, but you can wander around the grounds if you arrive early.

The Summit is a classy old resort at the top of the mountain, with 1,200 acres around it and lots of recreational activities right on the premises. Built in 1907, the Summit Inn boasts that Henry Ford, Thomas Edison, and Presidents Harding and Truman stayed there, and the inn has not changed much since then. The big cool lobby, the huge pink dining room with crystal chandeliers and classical music, the flagstone fireplace, and the enormous porch overlooking the valley feel more like the 1920s than the twenty-first century.

The Summit has added hot tubs and an exercise room as a concession to modern times, but thank goodness they haven't eliminated the shuffleboard, Ping-Pong, badminton, dancing, horseshoes, and board games that hark back to an earlier day. There also are lighted tennis courts, hiking trails, and a beautiful Olympic-size pool to play in.

When you're checked in and comfortably settled, take a drink or a cup of tea out onto the terrace and watch the sun go down behind the mountains.

The Summit Inn's rates are modest: $62–$120 a night for a double. For $109–$163 per night (two-night minimum), you can get the Summit's "classic package," which includes breakfast, dinner, and free use of all the facilities except the golf course. Golf packages, which include unlimited use of the course, start at $126.

DINNER: Dinner at the Summit is as comfortable and traditional as the resort itself. The specialties of the house are prime rib, pork medallions, garlic chicken, spaghetti and meatballs, and penne pasta primavera. For dessert there's homemade bread pudding, bumbleberry pie, and fudge brownies with vanilla ice cream. Moderate.

LODGING: The Summit Inn.

DAY 2

Morning and Afternoon

BREAKFAST: Stoke up for a day of outdoor fun with buttermilk pancakes and sausage or any of the other mountain breakfasts served at the Summit Inn.

After breakfast and perhaps some tennis, head for **Ohiopyle State Park,** the 18,000-acre state park that straddles the Youghiogheny River, site of the first commercial white-water rafting in the East. You reach it by driving 6 miles east on U.S. Highway 40 to Farmington and 6 miles north on State Highway 381.

Numerous rafting companies are located in Ohiopyle, and it's easy to sign up for a trip on the river. Among them are Wilderness Voyageurs (724–329–1000 or 800–272–4141, www.wilderness-voyageurs.com), Laurel Highlands River Tours (724–329–8531 or 800–472–3846, www.laurel highlands.com), and White Water Adventurers (724–329–8850 or 800–992–7238, www.wwaraft.com). For most guided trips, it's necessary to make advance reservations.

If you have kids or are a novice, you might like to start with a guided trip on the middle Youghiogheny. This 9-mile section of the Yough River winds its way around Sugarloaf Mountain from Confluence to Ohiopyle and offers spectacular scenery and easy-to-navigate Class I and II rapids. The guided trip takes three to five hours and includes transportation to the launch site and a picnic lunch. Expect to pay $20–$40 per person for the guided tours.

If you want to launch out on your own, most of the rafting companies will rent you a raft, canoe, kayak, or duckie (a rubber kayak) for use on the middle Yough.

Those with some white-water rafting experience will prefer the lower Yough, whose Class III and IV rapids are moderately difficult. The 7½-mile trip downriver from Ohiopyle to Bruner Run will take you three to five hours. Guided trips vary from $30 to $60 depending on season and day of the week; again, lunch and overland transportation are provided. If you have previous experience on the river, you can (with a permit) tackle the lower Yough on your own in a raft, kayak, or duckie. (Permits cost $2.50 and can be obtained from Ohiopyle State Park; call 724–329–8591 in advance of your trip.)

For the veteran rafter, the upper Yough with its Class V–plus rapids—an hour or so south of Ohiopyle—is the place to be, although trips are sometimes scheduled only on weekdays, when water is released from the upstream dam. Rafting the upper Yough will cost you $100 to $150 for an all-day trip.

If white-water rafting isn't your sport, Ohiopyle State Park is also an ideal spot for hiking and picnicking. You can hike from park headquarters a mile or so to a beautiful spot where the waters of Cucumber Falls cascade into a waterfall bordered by a series of mountain peaks. Or you can cross the river and wander through Ferncliff Peninsula, a hundred-acre nature preserve formed by a horseshoe bend in the river.

Ohiopyle is also a great place to rent a mountain bike and go for a scenic spin along the river on the Allegheny Highlands Trail. The level, gravel bike trail stretches 11 miles upriver to Confluence and 17 miles downriver to Connellsville. Nearly all of the rafting companies also rent mountain bikes for about $5.00 an hour or $16.00 a day.

The truly energetic can arrange an all-day five- or six-hour "pedal and paddle" adventure by biking the 11 miles from Ohiopyle to Confluence and rafting or kayaking back down the middle Yough to the park. All of the outfitters listed above offer the package.

DINNER: Chez Gerard, U.S. Highway 40 (Business Route), Hopwood; (724) 437–9001. You might not expect haute cuisine in the county where the Big

Mac was invented, but Chez Gerard serves French cuisine good enough to earn this small restaurant a national reputation. The restaurant is located in a nineteenth-century stone inn that has a French country–like interior. A prix fixe dinner is $35; lunch is $17. Don't go if you're on a diet; there are more than thirty selections on the cheese board and several "thousand-calorie" desserts.

LODGING: The Summit Inn.

DAY 3

Morning

BREAKFAST: The Summit Inn.

After breakfast and a last round of golf or horseshoes, head for **Fallingwater,** the weekend home of Pittsburgh magnate Edgar J. Kaufman that was designed by Frank Lloyd Wright in 1936.

Fallingwater is located a few miles north of Ohiopyle State Park and is about a half-hour drive from the Summit Inn. It is the only remaining home designed by America's greatest architect that includes the original furnishings, most of which were also designed by Wright. Voted by American architects in 1991 as the "best all-time work of American architecture," Fallingwater has to be seen to be believed. A miracle of concrete, flagstone, steel, and glass, the house is built in layers and cantilevered over a waterfall.

You can see the "perfect marriage between structure and nature" in the massive boulders built right into the house, the highly polished flagstone floors (which Wright meant to resemble the bottom of the riverbed), and the views of the ravine, woods, and waterfall from every angle of the house. Fallingwater cost the fabulous sum of $155,000 when it was built in 1936. Wright's fee for designing the house and furniture was $8,000. There is a wonderful hour-long guided tour of the house, and then you can spend as much time as you like on the forested grounds around it.

Finally, take a moment to visit the gift shop, which offers books and postcards, beautiful pottery and glass, and even a reproduction or two. (A reproduction of a cantilevered wooden lamp designed by Frank Lloyd Wright sells for about $900.) All proceeds go to the Western Pennsylvania Conservancy, to which the Kaufman family gave Fallingwater in the mid-1960s.

Fallingwater is located on State Highway 381, Mill Run; (724) 329–8501, www.paconserve.org. Open Tuesday to Sunday 10:00 A.M. to 4:00 P.M. from

Fallingwater, designed by Frank Lloyd Wright

April 1 through mid-November, otherwise open weekends only. Reservations are required. Admission on weekdays is $8.00, on weekends $12.00. Photography is not permitted on regular tours, but there is a special $30–$35 two-hour tour at 8:30 A.M., during which visitors are allowed to take still photographs.

After your tour, drive a few miles south on State Highway 381 to Ohiopyle. Turn left on State Highway 2012 and drive east 8 miles, then take State Highway 281 north one mile to **Confluence.**

LUNCH: River's Edge Cafe, 203 Yough Street; (814) 395–5059. You can relax and enjoy the beauty of the rippling Yough River from the porch of the cafe as you savor your chef-prepared pasta, salad, or char-grilled chicken sandwich. Moderate.

Afternoon

Begin your return trip to Washington from Confluence by driving about 10 miles southeast on State Highway 523. Then take U.S. Highway 40 east to Keyser's Ridge, I–68 east, I–70 east, and I–270 south. It's a 200-mile trip.

THERE'S MORE

Kentuck Knob. Frank Lloyd Wright–designed home open for public touring is a hexagonal grid constructed entirely of red cypress and fieldstone. Mountainside location with a view of the Youghiogheny River; sculpture park on the grounds. Located near Ohiopyle State Park in Chalk Hill; (4724) 329–1901, www.faywest.com/fayette/kentuckyknob. Prearranged tours are scheduled Tuesday through Sunday between 10:00 A.M. and 4:00 P.M. Admission is $10 on weekdays, $15 on weekends; children must be nine years old or older to tour the house. A two-hour, in-depth tour is offered daily at 8:30 A.M.; it costs $30.

Golf. The Summit's nine-hole course is pleasant, scenic, and not overly difficult. Greens fees are $10 a round for guests; carts rent for $12. (Golf packages are available if you stay at the resort.) If you're looking for a challenge, drive down the road and try Nemacolin Woodlands Links course or its new 6,800-yard, Peter Dye–designed Mystic Rock course, now a regular stop on the PGA tour. Greens fees are $50–$150, including cart rental. Phone (724) 329–8555.

Youghiogheny River Lake Recreation Area. Hiking, swimming, boating, fishing, and camping. Located on State Highway 281 about 4 miles north of U.S. Highway 40 and 4 miles west of Farmington; (814) 395–3242.

Laurel Caverns. Largest cave in Pennsylvania; guided tours and self-guided "explorer" tours available. Located 4 miles west of Farmington and 6 miles south of U.S. Highway 40 on County Route 2001; (724) 438–3003. Open daily May through October from 9:00 A.M. to 5:00 P.M.; open weekends only in March, April, and November. Admission is $9.00 for adults, $8.00 for senior citizens, $7.00 for teenagers, and $6.00 for children six to eleven; children under six admitted free.

SPECIAL EVENTS

May. National Pike Festival. Wagon-train camps with food and entertainment along U.S. Highway 40 (the National Pike) in Fayette and Somerset Counties. (724) 329–1560.

May–June. Pennsylvania Arts and Crafts Country Festival. Fayette County Fairgrounds, U.S. Highway 119 north of Uniontown. (724) 863–4577.

May–September. Wilderness Voyageurs. Series of Saturday concerts, slide shows, and special events, Ohiopyle. (724) 329–5517 or (800) 272–4141.

October. Springs Folk Festival. Annual crafts and music festival that draws artists and crowds from three states. On State Highway 669, just north of U.S. Highway 40, about 15 miles east of Fayette County. (814) 662–4158.

OTHER RECOMMENDED RESTAURANTS

Hopwood

The Sun Porch, U.S. Highway 40; (724) 439–5734. Dinner buffet with huge salad bar; chicken and biscuits every day. Moderate.

Fabrizi's, Jumonville Road; (724) 437–3060. Unpretentious Italian restaurant serving fresh pasta for more than fifty years; spaghetti and meatballs, lasagna, and gnocchi. Inexpensive to moderate.

Chalk Hill

The Stone House Restaurant and Hotel, U.S. Highway 40; (724) 329–8876. Seafood, chicken, beef, and vegetarian choices for lunch and dinner in an attractive renovated dining room. Moderate.

Markleysburg

Glisan's Restaurant, 4 miles east of Farmington on U.S. Highway 40; (724) 329–4636. No-frills, booth-filled diner that opens early for breakfast and bakes its own bread, rolls, and pies on the premises. Inexpensive.

Best place for doughnuts: Country Store, 4 miles east of Farmington on U.S. Highway 40; (724) 329–0700. Freshly made doughnuts, 6:30 A.M. to 9:00 P.M.

Farmington

Nemacolin Woodlands Resort, U.S. Highway 40 East (724–329–8555 or 800–422–2736), has several restaurants. For special occasions, try the Golden Trout; it's formal and expensive. For casual dining, Lautrec and the Tavern are both very good. The newly opened Seasons offers spa cuisine. All three have moderate prices.

For additional listings see Pennsylvania Escape Four (page 235) and Maryland Escape Six (page 128).

OTHER RECOMMENDED LODGINGS

Chalk Hill

The Stone House Restaurant and Hotel, U.S. Highway 40; (724) 329–8876, www.stonehouseinn.com. Circa 1822 inn with eleven nicely furnished, air-conditioned Victorian suites, some of which have private baths. The $99–$159 tariff includes a full breakfast served in a delightful sunroom.

The Lodge at Chalk Hill, U.S. Highway 40; (724) 438–8880 or (800) 833–4283, www.dc1.net/~thelodge. Modern lakeside lodge with sixty-four units, some of them efficiencies. Cable TV, continental breakfast. Rates: $60–$97.

Farmington

Nemacolin Woodlands Resort, U.S. Highway 40 east; (724) 329–8555 or (800) 422–2736, www.nwlr.com. Attractive resort with ninety-eight units in the inn, forty condos, and a 125-room hotel, the Chateau Lafayette, modeled after the Ritz in Paris. Amenities at the resort include two golf courses, downhill skiing, a polo field, a warm-water spa, mud baths, a billiards room, a regulation croquet court, and six restaurants. Rates: $235–$545.

Confluence

River's Edge Cafe Bed and Breakfast, 203 Yough Street; (814) 395–5059. Small, delightful B&B on the banks of the fast-flowing Youghiogheny River. Three rooms with private baths. Rates: $50–$60.

Uniontown

Inn of the Princess and European Bakery, 181 West Main Street; (742) 425–0120. Five deluxe rooms with mission-style furnishings in a large house formerly owned by a Hungarian princess. Large private baths; French linens, English soap, and fresh orchids daily; complimentary tea and breakfast in the European-style bakery on the premises. Rates: $85–$125.

Inn at Watson's Choice, 234 Balsinger Road; (724) 437–4999 or (888) 820–5380, www.watsonschoice.com. Circa 1820 farmhouse with seven guest rooms, all with private baths; full country breakfast. Rates: $89–$125.

Ohiopyle

Ohiopyle State Park Campgrounds; (412) 329–8591. The park has 226 sites for tents and trailers, a couple of dozen of which are walk-in, tent-only sites. Reservations suggested. Rates: $13–$19.

For additional listings see Pennsylvania Escape Four (page 235) and Maryland Escape Six (page 128).

FOR MORE INFORMATION

Central Fayette Chamber of Commerce, P.O. Box 2124, Uniontown, PA 15401; (724) 437–4571 or (800) 916–9365,www.faycham.org.

Ohiopyle State Park, P.O. Box 105, Ohiopyle, PA 15470; (724) 329–8591, www.dcnr.state.pa.us/stateparks/parks/ohio.htm.

DELAWARE AND BEYOND

ESCAPES

DELAWARE AND BEYOND

Wilmington and the Brandywine Valley

BEST HOMES AND GARDENS

2 NIGHTS

Mansions • Gardens • Art museums

The Brandywine Valley, a heavily wooded, rolling stretch of green in Delaware and Pennsylvania, was home to some of America's greatest industrialists, art collectors, gardeners, and artists. A weekend escape here offers the visitor a wonderful range of experiences, from exploring homes and gardens of the very rich and famous, to canoeing the placid Brandywine River.

You see the imprint of Delaware's legendary du Ponts everywhere, from the enormous Italian Renaissance hotel they built in Wilmington to the mansions and gardens at nearby Nemours, Longwood, and Winterthur. Each one of these estates offers a different pleasure: A. I. du Pont's estate, Nemours, reveals the fascinating inventions and enthusiasms of its owner; Longwood Gardens boasts miles of flower trails, fountains, and trees; and Winterthur displays 300 years worth of American decorative arts.

Interestingly, the Brandywine Valley also produced a great dynasty of local artists whose work is the aesthetic polar opposite of the du Ponts' gilded drawing rooms and crystal chandeliers. A highlight of the weekend is a visit to the Brandywine River Museum, which houses the country's greatest collection of works by the three generations of Wyeths—N. C., Andrew, and Jamie—and the landscape artists and illustrators who were their friends and contemporaries in this distinctive movement in nineteenth- and twentieth-century American art, known as the Brandywine School.

DAY 1

Afternoon

It's a two-and-a-half-hour drive to Wilmington and the Brandywine Valley; if you start in the late afternoon or right after work, you'll be there in time for dinner. Follow Interstate 95 north 110 miles to downtown Wilmington. Leave I–95 at exit 7B (State Highway 52 north) and drive north on Pennsylvania Avenue. After a couple of miles, Pennsylvania Avenue becomes Kennett Pike (but it's still Route 52). Drive 5 miles farther north on State Highway 52, and you'll reach your dinner destination in the tiny town of Centreville, Delaware.

DINNER: Buckley's Tavern, located in a house built in 1817, has been greeting and feeding travelers since 1951. Local people unanimously recommend it to visitors, and it is easy to see why. The intimate paneled bar and separate dining rooms are fragrant with wood smoke from the kitchen, and wait staff are friendly, quick, and casual.

Buckley's menu is creative and classy, with unexpected entrees like Thai curry shrimp and peach barbecue pork appearing alongside classics like crab cakes and a mixed grill of beef filet, pork medallion, and chicken breast. Located at 5812 Kennett Pike (State Highway 52) in Centreville; (302) 656–9776. Moderate.

After dinner, continue north on State Highway 52 about 5 miles to U.S. Highway 1; turn left and drive 3 miles west (past Longwood Gardens) to State Highway 82. Turn right on State Highway 82 and drive just over a mile north, then turn right on State Highway 926. If you feel as if you are out in the country, you're right. Your lodgings are on a farm, located at the third driveway on the left.

LODGING: Meadow Spring Farm Bed and Breakfast, 201 East Street Road (Route 926), Kennett Square, Pennsylvania; (610) 444–3903. Meadow Spring Farm is an extremely popular B&B with seven comfortable guest rooms, all with private baths, televisions, and air-conditioning. It's a real farm with chickens, cows, and rabbits. Kids love the animals—and the owner's doll collection, Santa collection, and cow collection. Adults love the peaceful perennial garden, the pool, and the hot tub. Rates: $75–$85 per night, two-night minimum on weekends.

Longwood Gardens

DAY 2

Morning

BREAKFAST: Meadow Spring Farm Bed and Breakfast. Local residents claim that the Brandywine River Valley produces more than 90 percent of the mushrooms consumed in the United States, so it is appropriate that the breakfast specialty at your B&B is a mushroom omelette. But you're also likely to get fruit pancakes or homemade jam and bread alongside, so pack your appetite.

After breakfast, reverse your drive of the night before and take Route 82 south and Route 1 east. Within five minutes, you'll be at the estate of Pierre Samuel du Pont, who served as chairman of the DuPont and General Motors Companies and who was the owner and architect of **Longwood Gardens.**

Said to be the nation's premier public display garden, Longwood Gardens provides visitors literally hours of enchantment with its 11,000 different kinds of plants in a beautifully landscaped park of more than 1,000 acres.

You really should return to Longwood many times, because it is so vast that you could never explore all of it in a single visit. There is a "flower walk" past enormous beds ranging from a deep purple group to the pink family and on to the reds and oranges. There is a garden with dozens of fountains, which on summer and fall evenings are lit for a 9:00 P.M. fountain display, as well as an enormous indoor conservatory with orchids, tropical gardens, a fern grotto, growing houses, and bonsai. Longwood also has huge arching rose arbors, a topiary garden, waterlily ponds, statues, and a lake. Plan to spend the whole morning; there are plenty of benches to rest upon as you tour the gardens.

At the gift shop in the visitors center, shoppers can browse among books, flower prints, gardening tools, whimsical gifts, and live plants. Longwood Gardens is located on U.S. Highway 1 near Kennett Square, Pennsylvania; (610) 388–1000, www.longwoodgardens.org. Open daily 9:00 A.M. to 6:00 P.M. From May through August, the gardens stay open until 10:15 P.M. on Tuesdays, Thursdays, and Saturdays. From November through March, the gardens close at 5:00 P.M. daily except during the Christmas season, when they are open until 9:00 P.M. Admission is $12.00 for adults (except on Tuesdays, when it's $8.00), $6.00 for youths sixteen to twenty, and $2.00 for children six to fifteen; children under six are admitted free.

LUNCH: After you finish touring Longwood, stay for lunch at Longwood's **Terrace Restaurant,** which has a modestly priced cafeteria and a lovely sit-down dining room. Both dining areas have great views of the surrounding gardens. The Terrace's dining-room menu includes fancy sandwiches; local trout; roast chicken stuffed with oysters, mushrooms, and thyme; Caesar salad; and much more. There are boutique beers (including several local brews), mineral water, and espresso to quench your thirst, and chocolate pâté with almonds for dessert. Dining-room prices are moderate.

The Terrace Cafeteria's prices are significantly lower, and the menu is child-friendly. On summer afternoons the cafeteria offers fresh fruit cobblers for afternoon tea from 3:00 to 4:00 P.M. Phone (610) 388–6771.

Afternoon

After lunch, drive a couple of miles east on U.S. Highway 1 and about 5 miles south on State Highway 52. Within ten minutes, you'll be at **Winterthur,** one of the great attractions in the area and—many think—the top decorative arts exhibition in the United States. Winterthur's owner, Henry Francis du Pont, didn't just collect three centuries of priceless American antique furniture, ceramics, and textiles; he literally bought whole rooms—woodwork, plaster, ceilings, wallpaper, and all—and had them installed at his enormous estate.

Happily, his extraordinary 175-room home has been turned into a museum. Du Pont's collection is displayed in dozens of period rooms, showing how antique furniture, furnishings, china, crystal, silver, and textiles from Revolutionary War times to the Shaker period would have been used in daily life, with every detail as historically accurate as possible. A separate building houses galleries where you can take a closer look at treasures from the vast collection.

Because you cannot begin to see it all in one visit, the museum offers a number of ways to view Winterthur, including one-hour introductory tours, and one- or two-hour decorative arts tours. (Note: Children are welcome on introductory tours, but the more specialized decorative arts tours are limited to visitors age twelve and up.) An introductory tour is $13 a person, and the decorative arts tours are $17–$21. General admission, which entitles you to tour the galleries, the "Touch-It Room," and the 900-acre naturalistic garden costs $8.00 for adults, $6.00 for senior citizens and students, and $4.00 for children age five to eleven. If you take one of the tours, Winterthur's enormous garden, wooded grounds, galleries, and gift shop can be seen at no additional charge. The number of people on each tour is limited, so reserve as far in advance as you can. Located on Kennett Pike (State Highway 52) north of Wilmington; (302) 888–4600 or (800) 448–3883, www.winterthur.org. Open Monday to Saturday 9:00 A.M. to 5:00 P.M., Sunday noon to 5:00 P.M.

Before leaving, stop in at the museum's pretty seven-room gift shop, which has reproduction furniture, china, jewelry, books, and plants for sale. And do explore the garden; there's something in bloom nearly year-round.

After your Winterthur tour, drive south 5 miles to downtown Wilmington, where you can tour the original du Pont gunpowder factory, enjoy more art from the Brandywine school, or view a marvelous seashell collection. (See There's More for details.) But, by all means, end up at the **Hotel du Pont,** an enormous old downtown hotel. Built in 1913 and renovated in the early 1990s, the du Pont has the wonderfully luxurious feel of century-old Wilmington. The ceilings are heavily carved, the moldings are gilded, the music is discreetly classical.

DINNER: If you're in Wilmington on a weekend, you must dine in the famous Green Room, the most beautiful of the hotel's several dining areas. A harpist plays on the balcony, the surroundings are glorious, and the menu exquisite (that is to say, expensive). Think French, as in escargot, pheasant, and elegant desserts, and splurge. Located at Eleventh and Market Streets in Wilmington; (302) 594–3154.

While you're at the hotel, poke your head into the Brandywine Room, a smaller wood-paneled dining room where contemporary American cuisine is served. The food is equally as good as it is in the Green Room, and there's a fortune's worth of original Wyeth paintings on the walls. You'll also enjoy wandering through the Lobby Lounge, where a splendid afternoon tea is served from 2:30 to 4:30 P.M.

LODGING: Meadow Spring Farm Bed and Breakfast.

DAY 3

Morning

BREAKFAST: Meadow Spring Farm Bed and Breakfast.

After a leisurely breakfast, drive about 5 miles east to the nearby **Brandywine River Museum,** U.S. Highway 1, Chadds Ford, Pennsylvania; (610) 388–2700, www.brandywinemuseum.org. Open daily 9:30 A.M. to 4:30 P.M. Admission is $5.00 for adults and $2.50 for senior citizens, students, and children over six; children under six get in free.

The museum is housed in a nineteenth-century gristmill and has been designed so that on every floor you get a 180-degree view of the Brandywine River flowing below you. Quiet and unpretentious, the Brandywine River Museum presents a fine collection of nineteenth- and twentieth-century art, with an exceptional group of paintings and drawings by the Wyeth family and other artists and illustrators of the Brandywine School. Be sure to visit the gift shop, which has a large selection of prints, books, and gifts.

LUNCH: The cafeteria-style **Brandywine River Museum Restaurant** is open daily for lunch from 10:00 A.M. to 3:00 P.M., except for Monday and Tuesday from January through March. If the weather is nice, take your sandwich outside for a picnic by the river; otherwise find a table that looks out over the Brandywine and enjoy one of the entrees. Inexpensive.

Afternoon

After lunch, head for **Nemours,** located on Rockland Road north of Wilmington; (302) 651–6912. You can get there in about thirty minutes via the scenic route by taking U.S. Highway 1 east a mile or so to State Highway 100, turning right, and taking State Highway 100 south 9 or 10 miles to State Highway 141. Follow Route 141 north 1½ miles to Rockland Road and turn right.

Nemours is the 300-acre estate of Alfred I. du Pont, who built it in 1909. Modeled after a French château, the hundred-plus rooms are luxuriously decorated with priceless antique furniture, crystal, and tapestries. A beautiful seventeeth-century tapestry hangs from one wall, and a Madonna by Murillo smiles down from another.

Nemours, unlike Winterthur, is not a museum but a family home. The most interesting part is the basement, where some of A. I. du Pont's inventions are on display. For example, in the recreation area (which has its own bowling alley and billiards room), there is a workout room with a mechanical riding machine, topped by a horse's saddle. Du Pont himself designed the contraption, along with an extraordinary roomful of equipment that generated enormous blocks of ice for the refrigeration in the house's kitchens before the invention of Freon (a later du Pont creation).

There are other signs of the owner's creativity throughout the estate. He designed a wind indicator, which hangs on the wall near the upstairs bedrooms, and a Rube Goldbergesque internal vacuuming system. He also had a home-bottling system in one basement room, so that he could take the local Nemours water with him when he was away from home. And the music room houses his violin and Steinway grand, both of which he reportedly played well.

A. I. du Pont was an inventor, musician, chemist, tinkerer, designer, gardener, and philanthropist, and the two-hour tour of his estate introduces you to every facet of this Renaissance man's life.

Note: Tours are limited to small numbers of people; they must be booked well in advance. Tours also require climbing many steps. Open Tuesday to Sunday, May through November. Admission is $10 and visitors must be over sixteen years old.

From Wilmington, it's a 110-mile return trip to Washington on I–95. Allowing for traffic, you'll be home in two and a half hours.

THERE'S MORE

Hagley Museum and Eleutherian Mills. Original du Pont gunpowder factory, which launched the company that became the world's largest arms manufacturer. Also includes the original du Pont family estate and gardens. Located on State Highway 141 north of Wilmington in Greenville, Delaware (follow the signs); (302) 658–2400, www.hagley.lib.de.us. Open daily 9:30 A.M. to 4:30 P.M. April through December, weekends 9:30 A.M. to 4:30 P.M. during the winter months; there is a guided tour at 1:30 P.M. Admission is $9.75 for adults, $7.50 for senior citizens and students, and $3.50 for children six to fourteen; children under six are admitted free. A family admission is $26.50.

Delaware Art Museum. Home to an interesting collection of American art in the Brandywine tradition, and the largest pre-Raphaelite English collection in the country. Located at 2301 Kentmere Parkway, Wilmington; (302) 571–9590, www.delartmus.de.us. Open Tuesday to Saturday 9:00 A.M. to 4:00 P.M., Sunday 10:00 A.M. to 4:00 P.M., sometimes later on Wednesday. Admission is $5.00 for adults, $3.00 for seniors, and $2.50 for students; children under six are admitted free.

Delaware Museum of Natural History. Dozens of exhibits of shells, birds, and mammals; lectures, films, and workshops. Located on Kennett Pike (State Highway 52) in north Wilmington; (302) 658–2601, www.delmnh. org. Open Monday to Saturday 9:30 A.M. to 4:30 P.M., Sunday noon to 4:30 P.M. Admission is $5.00 for adults, $4.00 for seniors, and $3.00 for children three to seventeen; children under three are admitted free.

Canoeing. The gentle Brandywine River is great for canoeing, and rental shops are available at numerous sites, including one near Longwood Gardens: Northbrook Canoe Company, 1810 Beagle Road, West Chester, Pennsylvania; (610) 793–2279. Expect to pay $40–$50 for four hours of canoeing.

Brandywine Battlefield Park. Fifty-acre historical park at the site of one of the most important battles of the Revolutionary War. The gift shop sells a handy map of the park for $1.50. Located on U.S. Highway 1 near Chadds Ford, Pennsylvania; (610) 459–3342. Open Tuesday to Saturday 9:00 A.M. to 5:00 P.M., Sunday noon to 5:00 P.M. Admission to the park is free, but there is a charge to tour Washington's headquarters and Lafayette's headquarters: $3.50 for adults, $2.50 for seniors, $1.50 for children six to twelve. Family admission is $8.50.

Used Books. There are two excellent stores in the area. Baldwin's Book Barn, 865 Lenape Road, West Chester, Pennsylvania (610–696–0816, www.bookbarn.com), has more than 300,000 used and rare books, maps, prints, and paintings in a rustic stone barn. Open Monday to Friday 9:00 A.M. to 9:00 P.M., Saturday and Sunday 10:00 A.M. to 5:00 P.M. Thomas Macaluso Used and Rare Books, 130 South Union Street, Kennett Square, Pennsylvania (610–444–1063), is a charming establishment with six showrooms of books and prints. Open Wednesday to Friday 11:00 A.M. to 5:00 P.M., Saturday 11:00 A.M. to 3:00 P.M.

SPECIAL EVENTS

April–May. Acres of Spring. Spring wildflower exhibits at Longwood Gardens. (610) 388–1000.

June. Delaware Art Museum Craft Fair. Dozens of locals craftspeople display and sell their works. (302) 571–9590.

June–September. Festival of Fountains. Illuminated fountain displays at Longwood Gardens. (610) 388–1000.

July. Ice Cream Festival at the Rockwood Museum, a Victorian English country estate with seventy acres of gardens. Food and crafts; ice cream; admission charged. Located at 610 Shipley Road, Wilmington. (302) 761–4340, www.rockwood.org.

November–December. Yuletide at Winterthur. Enchanting display of antique Christmas decorations. (302) 888–4600 or (800) 448–3883.

OTHER RECOMMENDED RESTAURANTS

The Columbus Inn, 2216 Pennsylvania Avenue, Wilmington; (302) 571–1492. The perfect spot for a twenty-ounce sirloin, prime rib with Yorkshire pudding, or rack of lamb with white bean ragout. Moderate.

Ristorante Carucci, 504 Greenhill Avenue (Wawaset Plaza), Wilmington; (302) 654–2333. Stylish Italian local favorite with artwork and vocal serenades. Moderate to expensive.

Brandywine Brewing Company, 3801 Kennett Pike, Greenville Center (State Highway 52 north of Wilmington); (302) 655–8000. Casual pub with fine sandwiches and a selection of beers brewed on the premises. Inexpensive to moderate.

Mendenhall Inn, Route 52, Mendenhall, Pennsylvania; (610) 388–1181. Candlelight dining in historic mill. Pheasant, lobster, prime rib; harp and piano music. Expensive.

Hank's Place, intersection of U.S. Highway 1 and State Highway 100, Chadd's Ford, Pennsylvania; (610) 388–7061. Diner that is a hangout for artists and staff from the Brandywine River Museum across the road. Pancakes, chipped beef on biscuits, and a three-egg shiitake mushroom omelette that won the praise of *Gourmet* magazine. Inexpensive.

Harry's Savoy Grille, 2020 Naamans Road, Wilmington; (302) 475–3000. Prime rib and crème brûlée make this a favorite of locals. Elegant and expensive.

Feby's Fishery Restaurant, 3701 Lancaster Pike (State Highway 48), Wilmington; (302) 998–9501. Top spot for lobster and seafood. Moderate.

Dilworthtown Inn, 1390 Old Wilmington Pike, West Chester, Pennsylvania; (610) 399–1390. Duck terrine for starters, followed by baby organic lettuce with shaved portobello mushrooms and truffle vinaigrette, and chateaubriand. Expensive.

OTHER RECOMMENDED LODGINGS

Hotel du Pont, Eleventh and Market Streets, Wilmington; (302) 594–3100 or (800) 441–9019, www.dupont.com/hotel. Century-old luxury hotel in downtown Wilmington. More than 200 guest rooms, all recently renovated and decorated with antique reproductions. Rooms range from $189 to $239 per night; suites from $499 to $599. Packages available.

Fairville Inn, Kennett Pike (State Highway 52), Mendenhall, Pennsylvania; (610) 388–5900, www.innbook.com/inns/fair. Centrally located inn with fifteen individually decorated rooms. All have antiques and flowers, some have fireplaces. Complimentary breakfast and afternoon tea served. Rates: $140 and up for a room, $195–$200 for a two-room suite.

Inn at Montchanin Village, State Highway 100 and Kirk Road, Montchanin; (302) 888–2133 or (800) 269–2473, www.montchanin.com. Luxurious Delaware inn with thirty-seven rooms and suites (all with private baths) in eleven buildings; gardens. Fireplaces, coffee makings, and newspapers in the rooms; upscale restaurant on the grounds. Rates: $160–$180 for rooms and $190–$500 for suites, breakfast included.

Brandywine River Hotel, intersection of U.S. Highway 1 and State Highway 100, Chadds Ford, Pennsylvania; (610) 388–1200, www.virtualcities.com. Renovated country Victorian hotel with forty guest rooms and suites; restaurant and fitness room on the premises. Large contintental breakfast; complimentary wine and cheese in the afternoon. Rates: $125–$169.

Pennsbury Inn, 883 Baltimore Pike (U.S. Highway 1); Chadds Ford, Pennsylvania; (610) 388–1435, www.pennsbury.com. Two-hundred-year-old coach house with original fireplaces and uneven floors and six renovated guest rooms with feather beds and antique furnishings; private baths, telephones and cable TV in rooms. Pleasant grounds; full country breakfast. Rates: $140–$225.

Pace One Restaurant and Country Inn, Thornton and Glen Mills Road; Thornton, Pennsylvania; (610) 459–3702. A 250-year-old barn restored to a comfortable six-room country inn with a first-rate restaurant. The $75–$95 tariff includes continental breakfast.

Whitewing Farm Bed and Breakfast, 370 Valley Road, West Chester, Pennsylvania; (610) 388–2664, www.whitewingfarm.com. Beautiful B&B on forty-three acres adjacent to Longwood Gardens; seven guest rooms and two suites. Tennis court and pitch–and–putt golf course; full country breakfast on the terrace; afternoon tea. Rates: $125–$249.

Bed and Breakfasts of Delaware, 2701 Landon Drive, Suite 200, Wilmington (302–479–9500), will make reservations for you at one of dozens of B&Bs in the area. Rates range from $65 to $175 per night.

FOR MORE INFORMATION

Greater Wilmington Convention and Visitors Bureau, 100 West Tenth Street, Suite 20, Wilmington, DE 19801; (302) 652–4088 or (800) 422–1181, www.wilmcvb.org.

Brandywine Valley Tourist Information Center, U.S. Highway 1, Kennett
Square, PA 19348; (610) 388–2900 or (800) 228–9933, www.
brandwinevalley.com.

DELAWARE AND BEYOND

Bethany Beach and Rehoboth Beach

OCEANS OF FUN

---

2 NIGHTS

Swimming • Beachcombing • Fine dining
Picnicking • Museums • Shopping

One of the quickest and most complete escapes from Washington is "the beach," which to many city dwellers means Delaware's Bethany and Rehoboth Beaches. They are the closest ocean beaches to Washington, and have everything a classic summer escape requires: soft sand, T-shirt shops and saltwater taffy stalls, and crashing, rolling, glorious surf.

These once-sleepy beach towns have experienced something of a boom in recent years, and Rehoboth, in particular, is home to an increasing number of upscale shops, restaurants, condos, and outlet malls. But an unspoiled stretch of national seashore is just a few miles away when you want to escape the crowds.

Your weekend escape to the shore is an enjoyable mix of old and new. You'll lunch on boardwalk fries and pizza, then have dinner at one of the fanciest restaurants at the beach. There will be a luxurious stay at a fine old inn that has lace curtains in the Victorian parlor and afternoon iced tea and cookies on the big front porch directly facing the ocean.

But the main reason for escaping to the Atlantic shore is the ocean itself, with the the beautiful white sand beaches of Delaware stretching before you. Spread out a beach blanket and watch the waves roll in and out and the kids whoop and tumble as they bodysurf the big ones. Walk next to the water as the sand slips away under your feet and the gulls shriek overhead. Then give

in and joyously splash into the spray, while the sun warms and the water chills. It's the beach, and it's all yours, absolutely free of charge.

DAY 1

Morning

Leave Washington early, especially on a Friday or a Saturday, so you can beat the considerable weekend beach traffic. Although the ocean is only about 125 miles from Washington, count on a three-hour drive. Take U.S. Highway 50 east from Washington. About 16 miles after you cross the Chesapeake Bay Bridge, turn east on State Route 404, where the route becomes scenic and enjoyable. The terrain is flat and level with fields of corn, roadside fruit stands, and pleasant little towns along the way. To avoid the worst of the beach traffic, just before you reach Georgetown, turn south on State Highway 113 and drive 11 miles to Dagsboro, then east on State Highway 20 a mile or so to State Highway 24 east, which you follow about 10 miles to **Bethany Beach.** As you get close to the shore, you'll smell the sea and sense the change in the air even before you see the ocean.

Bethany Beach is a small and friendly town with a devoted summer crowd that returns every year. Garfield Parkway, the town's main drag, is lined with shops selling candy, T-shirts, and beach paraphernalia. There are also a number of casual restaurants on Garfield Parkway and on the short boardwalk, but a picnic is a better choice for lunch your first day.

LUNCH: Di Febo's Restaurant, 789 Garfield Parkway (302–539–4914), located on State Highway 24 about a mile before you reach the beach, is a first-class restaurant with an attached carryout. It has a great selection of deli sandwiches and Italian subs, as well as buffalo wings, cheesesteaks, and pasta specialties. If you're picnicking, be sure to take lots of cold drinks and napkins. Inexpensive to moderate.

Afternoon

Bethany is a much quieter town than nearby Rehoboth. One of its charms is the **Addy Sea Bed and Breakfast,** a century-old house where you will be staying. You'll want to dump your suitcases and change into your swimsuit before your picnic, so check in as soon as you pick up your provisions for lunch. The Addy Sea has five rooms with curtains waving in the breeze in the

Bethany Beach

open windows, and a lovely Victorian parlor with an antique pressed-tin ceiling. Rocking chairs on the porch face the sea, and in the afternoon there's sure to be a big pitcher of lemonade or iced tea. Located at the corner of Atlantic Avenue and Ocean View Parkway, 5 blocks north of Garfield Parkway; (302) 539–3707 or (800) 418–6764, www.beachnet.com/addysea.html. Rooms range from $170 to $235 during the summer for single or double occupancy, with a $20 surcharge for each additional guest. Call well in advance for summer weekend reservations.

The Addy Sea is slightly off the beaten track of Bethany's commercial area, and the beach in front of the inn is less congested than other sections of Bethany Beach. Once you're settled in, the first order of business, of course, is to race to the ocean for a long look at the waves and some deep gulps of clean, salty sea air.

If you're a walker, there are miles of immaculate white beach to explore— walk right along the water where it's hard packed, and watch the shorebirds skitter and race. Kids will love to collect the rounded stones and purplish bits of shells, rubbed smooth by the sand and water. If you're a water baby yourself, this section of the Atlantic Ocean is perfect for floating and swimming, with waves just big enough to give you a good ride all the way up to the beach if you jump on them at the right moment.

After you get cleaned up back at the Addy Sea, take a short drive to Fenwick Island for dinner. Go 6 miles south on State Highway 1, turn right (west) on State Highway 54, and drive about a mile and a half to a bright pink building just past the bridge.

DINNER: Your dinner destination is **Tom and Terry's.** Don't let the flamingo-colored exterior deter you. This is a beautiful, casual, upscale restaurant. Seafood is fresh, and all the classics are there: clams casino (with bacon and cheese), sea scallops, flounder topped with crab imperial, softshell crabs, catch of the day, and more. For those who prefer turf to surf, there are hand-cut Angus beef steaks char-grilled to order, as well as a handful of chicken and pasta selections. Even if the food at Tom and Terry's were only half as good, you should go anyway for the view. The pale pink walls indoors match the color of the sky as the sun sets over the marshy inlets of Assawoman Bay. It's a perfect end to a perfect day. Located on State Highway 54 in Fenwick Island; (302) 436–4161. Moderate.

LODGING: The Addy Sea Bed and Breakfast.

DAY 2

Morning

BREAKFAST: The Addy Sea Bed and Breakfast.

After a breakfast of homemade muffins, juice, and coffee at the Addy Sea, go for a morning dip or long walk by the ocean. If you are interested in boating, surf fishing, or parasailing, see the listings under There's More.

Midmorning, take a short drive to the nearby town of **Rehoboth Beach.** There, the 10-block boardwalk is lined with shops and fast food, and the beach is crowded with umbrellas, bikinied and Speedo-clad young beauties gliding along the sand, toddlers in sun hats with their pails and shovels, and kids with boogie boards, racing for the waves.

LUNCH: If you want lunch before a swim, you won't have to go far. Do what everybody seems to do, and stroll up and down Rehoboth Avenue and the boardwalk, collecting junk food as you go. A favorite in the area is **Grotto Pizza,** where $2.25 will get you a greasy, pepperoni-studded slice of pure pleasure. (Grotto has eight locations in the Delaware beach towns, including three on the boardwalk in Rehoboth; 302–227–3278.) Then it's on to **Thrashers French Fries** for a large cupful of the best fries made anywhere. They're best straight from the deep-fat fryer, sprinkled with salt and vinegar. Stands are located at 7 Rehoboth Avenue and several other spots; (302) 227–8994.

Afternoon

Just in case you haven't had enough beach food, there's plenty more harm to be done. Rehoboth has made some concessions to the changing times: There are now espresso bars and Italian lemon ice shops. But the gigantic salt water taffy sign that reads DOLLE'S SALTWATER TAFFY still hangs in the most prominent spot on the boardwalk. Located on the boardwalk at Rehoboth Avenue; (302) 227–0757.

As you cruise Rehoboth's extensive shopping area, don't limit yourself to the T-shirt shops along Rehoboth Avenue. Be sure to explore the flanking streets, Baltimore and Wilmington Avenues, and the short connecting side streets. Here you'll find several interesting stores, and renovated Cape Cod homes that have been painted in Crayola colors—melon with spruce trim, periwinkle with egg-yolk yellow trim, and purple everywhere.

As you explore Rehobeth, consider renting a bike or a hilarious "team trike," a cumbersome monster that will seat two people side by side. Team trikes rent for $6.00–$8.00 an hour, regular bikes for $4.00–$5.00 an hour at several beach locations.

Or take a short drive north to Henlopen Acres, the beautiful residential section of Rehoboth, and stop in at the **Rehoboth Art League,** 12 Dodds Lane, Henlopen Acres, just north of Rehoboth; (302) 227–8408. Open Monday to Saturday 10:00 A.M. to 4:00 P.M., Sunday 1:00 to 4:00 P.M. You'll know it by the bizarre cement couch and matching archway in the yard, painted to resemble old-fashioned upholstery. The Art League exhibition center is located in a quiet, cool clapboard home filled with juried works by local artists. There are watercolors, sculpture, oil paintings, and prints for sale. The exhibit center also includes a small museum, the 1743 **Homestead House,** which has an interesting history and some lovely art and antiques as well.

DINNER: Plan to stay in Rehoboth for dinner at the **Blue Moon Restaurant,** a chic beach house decorated in myriad shades of blue. It's a serious competitor for best restaurant at the beach, located at 35 Baltimore Avenue; (302)

227–6515. The Blue Moon, which has been earning kudos from the beach crowd for more than twenty years, specializes in Pacific Rim cuisine. Look for seafood lasagna or baked salmon stuffed with scallops and leeks. Expensive.

LODGING: The Addy Sea Bed and Breakfast.

DAY 3

Morning

BREAKFAST: The Addy Sea Bed and Breakfast.

After a light breakfast at the Addy Sea, take a long walk on the beach or a morning swim. If you're interested in a truly unspoiled beach area, drive a few miles north to **Delaware Seashore State Park** (302–227–2800), or a few miles south to **Fenwick Island State Park** (302–539–9060, www. destateparks.com). Swimming, wave-jumping, and sand-castle building are even better there, because the crowds are smaller. And the sand is the same immaculate white quartz. Both state parks have showers and bathhouses for changing. An entrance fee of $5.00 a car ($2.50 for Delaware residents) is charged. The fee entitles you to enter any state park on the day of purchase.

LUNCH: When you're hungry, head back to Bethany and **Mango's,** Garfield Parkway and the Boardwalk; (302) 537–6226, www.mangomikes.com. You can fill up on appetizers (black bean hummus; crab cakes stuffed with cheddar, jack, and goat cheese; lime-seasoned crab fritters) or opt for one of the many seafood specials. Moderate.

As you head toward home, you might want to take an hour or so to explore some of the dozens of outlet shops that have sprung up just north of Rehoboth Beach. Most of the stores are open from 10:00 A.M. to at least 9:00 P.M. daily, except Sundays, when they close at 6:00 P.M.

The fastest route home from Rehoboth Beach is to take State Highway 1 about 8 miles north to State Highway 9 heading west, which quickly runs straight into State Highway 404. As you drive through the Delaware countryside, you will notice several barbecue chicken signs, announcing roadside stands run by fire departments, civic organizations, and struggling entrepreneurs battling the fast-food giants. Most have picnic tables for the really hungry, or, better yet, rearrange your cooler and enjoy a late supper at home.

THERE'S MORE

Amusement Rides and Arcade. At the corner of Delaware Avenue and the Boardwalk in Rehoboth, there are several amusement park rides and arcades; the latter are especially crowded on rainy days.

Indian River Lifesaving Station. Lovers of shipwreck lore will be fascinated by the state-of-the-art learning center devoted to lifesaving techniques and the museum of shipwrecks, situated in a newly renovated century-old building. Located on State Highway 1 a mile north of Indian River Inlet in Bethany Beach; (302) 227–0478, www.dspf.org. Open daily 10:00 A.M. to 5:00 P.M. Admission is $3.00 for adults, $2.50 for seniors, and $1.00 for children age five to twelve; children under five are admitted free.

Surf fishing. No fishing license is required in tidal waters. For deepwater fishing, contact the *Judy V,* North Indian River Marina, Indian River Inlet, Rehoboth Beach; (302) 226–2214. For $24, you spend a half day trying your luck with rod and reel. Rods and bait provided.

Anna Hazzard Museum. 17 Christian Street; (302) 226–1119. Artifacts and memorabilia from Rehoboth's early days as a Methodist camp-meeting ground. Open in season on Wednesdays and Saturdays from 10:00 A.M. to 2:00 P.M. Admission is free.

SPECIAL EVENTS

March or April. Easter Egg Hunt on the Beach, Bethany Beach. (302) 539–8011.

April. Ocean to Bay Bike Tour: 20- or 50-mile bike ride over fairly level terrain with manageable traffic. Starts from Bethany Beach. (302) 539–2100.

June–August. Summer concert series at the Bethany Beach Bandstand features free family entertainment. Call for scheduled events. (302) 539–8011.

August–September. Boardwalk Arts Festival in Bethany Beach includes paintings, sculpture, pottery, photographs, and amazing sand castles. (302) 539–2100.

October. Annual Sea Witch Halloween Festival and Fiddler's Convention. Parade, entertainment, broom-throwing contests at Rehoboth Beach. (302) 227–2233.

OTHER RECOMMENDED RESTAURANTS

Bethany Beach

Sedona, 26 Pennsylvania Avenue; (302) 539–1200. Bethany's top dining spot features new Southwest cuisine and desert decor. Expensive.

McCabe's Gourmet Market, York Beach Mall, State Highway 1, South Bethany; (302) 539–8550. Fresh baked bread, cheeses, salads, specialty foods; great for picnic supplies.

Magnolia's Restaurant and Pub, Cedar Neck Road, Ocean View (a half mile west of Bethany Beach on State Highway 26 and 1½ miles north on Central Avenue); (302) 539–5671 or (888) 415–3474. The restaurant's menu and ambience are old South; seafood, prime rib, and corn muffins are featured. The pub has nice salads, hearty sandwiches, and a dance floor. Moderate.

Old Mill Restaurant and Crab House, Cedar Neck Road, Ocean View; (302) 537–1290. The best reason to choose this informal restaurant is the steamed crabs, and scores do so nightly. Moderate.

Gary's Beach Cafe, Marketplace at Sea Colony; (302) 539–2131. Casual spot and good choice for vegetarian fare; whole-grain breads and soy cheese featured. Inexpensive.

Cottage Cafe, State Highway 1 (across from Sea Colony); (302) 539–8710. The place to go if you get the urge for pot roast or liver and onions at the beach. Inexpensive.

Rehoboth Beach

Camel's Hump, 21 Baltimore Avenue; (302) 227–0947. If sand makes you hungry for Middle Eastern food, you're in luck; the tabbouleh, hummus, and kebabs here are excellent. Moderate.

La La Land, 22 Wilmington Avenue; (302) 227–3887. Glittery California-style restaurant that is a favorite of locals and critics. Expensive.

Back Porch Cafe, 59 Rehoboth Avenue; (302) 227–3674. Excellent seafood, generous portions, outside dining. Moderate to expensive.

Planet X Cafe, 35 Wilmington Avenue; (302) 226–1928. Cheery purple beach house restaurant that serves no red meat, which is not surprising in a place that stocks beet, celery, and carrot juice as before-dinner drinks. Moderate.

Sydney's Blues and Jazz, 25 Christian Street; (302) 227–1339. Dine on New Orleans specialties as you listen. Moderate.

Fran O'Brien's Beach House, 59 Lake Avenue; (302) 227–6121. A Rehoboth attraction for more than twenty years. Steak and fresh seafood until 1:00 A.M. Many go for the piano bar. Moderate.

The Avenue Restaurant, 110 Rehoboth Avenue; (302) 226–0132. Family favorite on the main drag. Moderate.

Ann Marie's Italian Restaurant, Second Street and Wilmington Avenue; (302) 227–9902. Lasagna, steaks, family fare. Moderate.

Best place for doughnuts: Bethany Beach Bake Shoppe, Lem Hickman Beach Plaza (State Highway 1), Bethany Beach; (302) 539–8879.

OTHER RECOMMENDED LODGINGS

Bethany Beach

Blue Surf, Oceanfront at Garfield Parkway; (302) 539–7531. No-frills oceanfront rooms and efficiencies ideal for families. All units have refrigerators and microwaves; some have full cooking facilities. Rates: $68–$145.

Bethany Arms, Oceanfront, a half block from Garfield Parkway; (302) 539–9603, www.beach-net.com/bethanyarms.html. Rooms and efficiencies on the beach. Rates: $45–$155, depending on season and view.

Westward Pines Motel, Kent Avenue; (302) 539–7426. Small, inexpensive motel located 4 blocks from the beach. All units have air-conditioning, TV, and refrigerators. Rates: $55–$80. Fireplace and Jacuzzi units cost $15 extra.

Rehoboth Beach

The Delaware Inn Bed and Breakfast, 55 Delaware Avenue; (302) 227–6031 or (800) 246–5244, www.delawareinn.com. Pleasant, conveniently located eight-room inn open year-round. Beach chairs, bicycles, box lunches, continental breakfast. Rates: $95-$190 in the summer; up to 60 percent off other seasons.

Dinner Bell Inn, 2 Christian Street; (302) 227–2561 or (800) 425–2355, www.beach-net.com/dinnerbell.html. Among the best in Rehoboth. A pleasant inn only 2 blocks from the beach. All thirty-two rooms and two cottages are air-conditioned and all have private baths, telephone service, and cable TV; continental breakfast served. Rooms are $59–$199; cottages are $145–$350.

Royal Rose Inn, 41 Baltimore Avenue; (302) 226–2535. Delightful eight-bedroom B&B close to the beach. You can get a room off-season on a weekday for as little as $45. Summer weekend rates: $85–$140.

Corner Cupboard Inn, 50 Park Avenue; (302) 227–8553, www.corner cupboard.com. Eighteen guest rooms, comfortably furnished. Rates: $145–$260; breakfast and dinner in the inn's superb restaurant are included.

Camping. Delaware Seashore State Park, Indian River Inlet, between Rehoboth Beach and Bethany Beach; (302) 539–7202. Bayside campground with 439 sites. No reservations accepted. Rates: $16–$26.

FOR MORE INFORMATION

Bethany-Fenwick Area Chamber of Commerce, P.O. Box 1450, Bethany Beach, DE 19930; (302) 539–2100 or (800) 962–7873, www.bethany-fenwick.org. Located on State Highway 1 south of Bethany Beach on the ocean side of the road.

Rehoboth Beach–Dewey Beach Chamber of Commerce, 501 Rehoboth Avenue, P.O. Box 216, Rehoboth Beach, DE 19971; (302) 227–2233 or (800) 441–1329 (outside Delaware), www.beach-fun.com.

Lewes and Cape May

VICTORIAN SECRET

2 NIGHTS

Victorian house tour • Ferry ride
Shopping • Biking • Ocean beaches

A funny thing about the reign of good Queen Victoria in the final sixty years of the nineteenth century: The dictionary refers to the era that bears her name as prudish, repressed, narrow-minded, and exceedingly fastidious. Yet the Victorian era was also a time of exuberant artistic expression, best reflected in architecture that was as colorful, lush, and playful as Queen Vicky (in her stiff black satin and jet beads) was not.

There is no better way to explore the delights of the Victorian era than to visit Cape May, New Jersey, a beautifully preserved and restored little town right alongside the Atlantic Ocean. In the nineteenth century, Cape May was the summer playground of the Philadelphia rich. Today it's a village that is bent on pleasing its doting visitors. Its inns, tea shops, and magnificently restored Victorian homes are strewn through town as thickly as currants in an English scone.

When you combine some 600 candy-colored, extravagantly beautiful Victorian homes with the fresh, cool breezes off the ocean, and add superb restaurants to linger in, flower gardens to admire, a gorgeous beach, and the surf to play in, you have the makings for a heavenly weekend escape.

Being so small, Cape May is easy to explore, and its unique attractions—the Victorian "painted lady" homes—are impossible to miss. The itinerary outlined here contains some hints, though, about how to see and do the most if you have only a few days to spend in Cape May and in the delightful town of Lewes, Delaware, where you'll catch the ferry to Cape May.

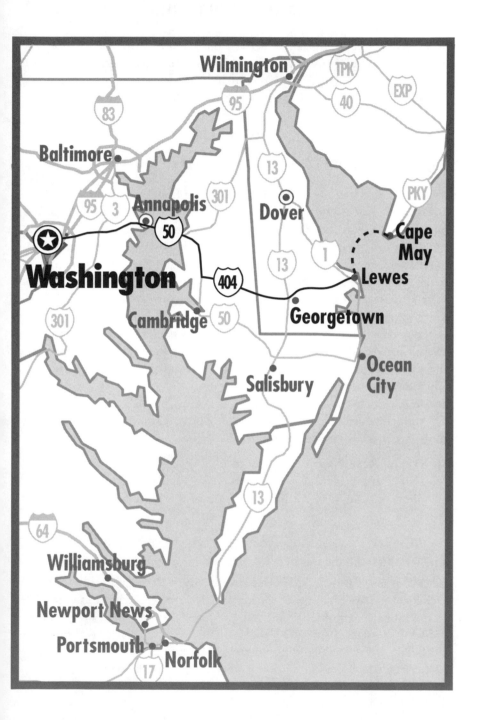

Be sure to bring your camera, because the whole area is so special that you'll want some proof when you brag about it later. And don't forget swimsuits; the beach is clean and inviting. As for picture hats, flowing skirts, lace handkerchiefs, handlebar mustaches, waistcoats, and pocket watches—that's up to you!

DAY 1

Morning

As always when heading for the Atlantic Ocean from Washington on a weekend, an early start is a smart start. Pack a thermos of coffee and a bag of doughnuts, and hit the road before 8:00 A.M. if you can, especially in the summer.

To get to Lewes from Washington, take U.S. Highway 50 east. Twenty-eight miles after you cross the Bay Bridge, take State Highway 404 east through Maryland into Delaware. Just before you reach the ocean, follow the signs (and State Highway 9) east to **Lewes.** The 125-mile trip will take you nearly three hours even if traffic is light.

Lewes has the feel of a real fishing town, and has fewer Victorian trappings than Cape May. But you will find some shopping opportunities, especially in the attractive historic area along Second Street and Market Street. There are antiques shops, art galleries, and gift stores, as well as coffee bars, bakeries, and restaurants.

After an hour or so of strolling and shopping, stop at one of Lewes's many pleasant restaurants for lunch.

LUNCH: La Rosa Negra, at 128 Second Street (302–645–1980) has a menu filled with tasty delights. You can easily make a splendid meal of the focaccia and soup or salad, or opt instead for one of the sophisticated pasta dishes. Moderate.

Afternoon

Lewes has one must-see: **Cape Henlopen State Park,** just east of the ferry terminal on State Highway 9; (302) 645–8983, www.destateparks.com. This beautiful state park has 4 miles of unspoiled beaches that are much less crowded than the beaches to the south. Here, the "walking" sand dunes (including Great Dune, the largest sand dune between Cape Cod and Cape Hatteras) are loved and protected, and several areas of the park are set aside as sanctuaries for nesting birds.

A map that you can pick up at the entrance to the park will show you where to find marked trails through the dunes and brush. There's also the ocean beach for strolling and swimming, as well as a nature center and a World War II observation tower for a great view of the whole area. Open daily 8:00 A.M. to sunset. Admission varies by season, but it is usually $5.00 a car for out-of-staters and $2.50 for Delaware residents.

As you leave the park, you'll see the ferry dock, which is located about a half mile east of downtown Lewes, almost immediately. The **Cape May–Lewes Ferry** makes six to fifteen trips a day between 6:00 A.M. and 9:30 P.M., depending on season and day of the week. For ferry schedule information, call (302) 426–1155 or (609) 886–1725; www.capemay-lewesferry.com. To make a reservation, call (800) 643–3779. (Note: Reservations are not accepted on many busy weekends; instead, the ferry operates on a first-come, first-served basis. On those weekends, count on a two-hour wait.) The one-way fare is $20.00 for a car and driver, an additional $6.50 for each passenger over six years old, and $2.00 for children under six. It will cost you $6.50 if you go on foot, $7.00 if you take your bike. The ferry ride itself is a very pleasant seventy-minute trip across the Delaware Bay.

When you arrive in Cape May, you will find yourself instantly drawn to the historic area of town. If you arrive before 5:00 P.M., head first for the **Cape May Welcome Center** at 405 Lafayette Street (609–884–9562), where you can obtain additional information about most of the area's attractions, lodgings, and restaurants. There are lots of evening activities in Cape May; if you are interested in theater or chamber music, you can pick up a calendar of events while you're there. Also look for a free copy of *The Gaslight Review*, which is a complete guide to nightclubs, live music, cabarets, dinner theater, live comedy, movies, and dockside entertainment.

Then, check in at the **Queen Victoria,** the bed-and-breakfast inn where you will be staying, to relax for a while and change for dinner. They serve a very nice complimentary tea that will perk you up after your day's travel.

The Queen Victoria is near the top of everyone's list of most beautiful and romantic B&Bs in the country. There you will find classical music, quilts on the beds, ceiling fans, a cozy fireplace, a player piano, a popcorn maker, a library, a game room, bicycles you can borrow, and juice and soda available all day. The Queen has expanded to three buildings and now has seventeen guest rooms (each with a private bath) and six suites. Located at 102 Ocean Street; (609) 884–8702, www.queenvictoria.com. Rooms are $80–$205, suites are $95–$280.

DINNER: One of Cape May's attractions is its many fine restaurants. Among the best is **410 Bank Street**, located at 410 Bank Street; (609) 884–2127. It's a very pretty little Victorian restaurant with mint-green trim, ceiling moldings, and a tiny lamp with a pink frosted globe on every table. Here the specialty is French, New Orleans, and Caribbean cuisine, and the offerings include baby rack of lamb with demi glaze and foie gras, and catfish fillet in lime-jalapeño sauce with bananas and fresh tomatoes. Expensive. (Note: Most of Cape May's restaurants do not have liquor licenses and operate as "bring your own bottle" establishments.)

Follow dinner with one of the plays or concerts in town or turn in early after a long day.

LODGING: The Queen Victoria.

DAY 2

Morning

BREAKFAST: The Queen Victoria serves a bounteous buffet breakfast that includes fruit, cereal, an egg dish, pastries, and plenty of coffee.

There are many good ways to tour Cape May. If you walk up and down the streets running perpendicular to the ocean boardwalk, from Windsor to Howard, and the cross streets between them in a 10-by-4-block area along the ocean, you will see most of the beautiful Victorian houses. Alternately, you can borrow a bike from your B&B or rent a bicycle, a tandem, or a four-person bicycle surrey at any of a half dozen convenient shops or stands in town. Bikes rent for $4.00 an hour or $10.00 a day, surreys for about $30.00 a day.

But perhaps the best way to see the town is to head for the east end of the Washington Street Mall, where you can purchase a combination ticket that allows you to take a forty-five-minute guided trolley tour of the downtown residential area and spend an equal amount of time touring the beautiful Emlen Physick estate The $15 cost of the ticket benefits the Mid-Atlantic Center for the Arts (MAC), which conducts the tour. For tour times phone (609) 884–5404; no reservations accepted for individual tickets.

No matter how much you have heard about the more than 600 "painted ladies" of Cape May, nothing quite prepares you for your first visit. With their pastel colors, exquisitely elaborate porches, gingerbread trim, and stained glass windows, the Victorian homes are absolutely ravishing. Each inn seems to be trying to outdo the others with its beautiful colors and trim, and even mod-

Physick House, Cape May

est private homes are decked out in sherbet colors and have flowers peeping from window boxes.

As you creep along through the tree-lined streets of Cape May on the jolly red MAC trolley, you'll see Gothic cottages, Italianate villas, and mansard and Stick Style homes. Keep your eyes open for cupolas and captain's walks, wide verandas, gazebos, fancy wrought-iron fences, horse ties and carriage steps, and beautiful stained glass windows. You'll want to keep your camera handy.

Cape May residents are proud of the little town's uniquely decorative architecture. Even a tiny, portable kiosk that sells church bingo tickets recently was painted three shades of lavender, with lots of fancy gingerbread trim. And the tiny 12-by-24-foot **Old Firehouse Museum** at the corner of Washington and Franklin Streets looks like an overgrown Victorian dollhouse. Children will love the gleaming fifty-year-old American La France fire engine inside; admission is free.

At the end of the trolley tour, you get to tour the marvelous **Emlen Physick House and Estate**, located at 1048 Washington Street; (609) 884–5404. In many ways, the Emlen Physick House is Cape May's most authentically restored house. Designed by renowned architect Frank Furness and built in 1879, the fifteen rooms of the Stick Style house have all been restored to their original grandeur. The house also contains Cape May's most extensive collection of Victorian furniture, clothing, toys, tools, and artifacts. MAC also sponsors special seasonal exhibits, such as "A Physick Family Christmas," portraying Victorian life.

Take a few minutes while you're at the Physick Estate to visit the two museum shops there. The Sun Porch Museum Shop has books, cards, Victorian home furnishings, and thousands of Victorian-style Christmas ornaments. The Carriage House Gallery Shop specializes in teapots and tea accessories. Should you need a restorative, they've recently opened a tearoom that serves tea sandwiches and scones.

The Physick Estate offers tours from 10:00 A.M. to 3:00 P.M. daily from mid-May through October 31. During the off-season, tours are offered two or three days a week. Call (609) 884–5404 for information and reservations. Admission is $7.00 for adults and $3.50 for children three through twelve. Children two and under are admitted free.

Before lunch, try to fit in a visit to a second beautiful Cape May mansion, the **Mainstay Inn,** 635 Columbia Avenue; (609) 884–8690. Originally built as a gambling club in 1872 for $7,000, the inn is famous today for its elegant interior, although the exterior, with its gleaming white columns, extra-wide veranda, and 13-foot-high windows, is pretty spectacular as well. Only the downstairs is open for touring (and only from 11:00 A.M. to 1:30 P.M.); the upstairs houses the inn's guests. But you can see the grand parlor with its several sofas and love seats, Oriental carpets, gleaming chandeliers, and ornate ceiling. You can also see the luxurious dining room and library with their walnut furnishings. Many consider the Mainstay to be the most lovingly and beautifully restored period house in America. The self-guided tour costs $3.00, which goes to support the Mid-Atlantic Center for the Arts.

LUNCH: Have a late lunch at the **Mad Batter,** 19 Jackson Street; (609) 884–5970. This marvelous restaurant somehow manages to be young, Victorian, decadent, and health conscious all at the same time, and it could easily become your favorite place to eat in Cape May. For lunch, the grilled chicken breast salad is a standout, as is the spinach quesadilla served on a bed of greens Wash lunch down with a fresh fruit smoothie or one of the special blends of coffee. And take seriously the sign outside that says LIFE IS UNCERTAIN . . . EAT DESSERTS FIRST! Desserts at the Mad Batter are fabulous (try the triple-layer chocolate cake), and the sumptuous choices on the menu are augmented with daily specials. Moderate.

Afternoon

After lunch, spend the rest of the afternoon shopping. The **Washington Street Mall** is a 2-block pedestrian shopping mall in the heart of Cape May between Perry Street and Decatur Street. There, several nice shops offer chocolates, antiques, jewelry, and gifts. **Swede Things in America,** 307 Washington Street Mall (609–884–5811), has beautiful Scandinavian crystal and pottery and lots of Christmas selections. **The Toy Shop of Cape May,** 510 Washington Street Mall (609–884–0442), has kites, beach toys, travel games, and children's arts-and-crafts kits.

There are also several upscale shops that sell clothing, jewelry, antiques, arts and crafts, and kitchen items at **The Shops at Congress Hall,** located between Perry Street and Congress Place, just adjacent to the Washington Street Mall. Phone (609) 884–8421.

After your shopping, give your feet a rest and enjoy tea or a soda on the porch of the Queen Victoria. If you've had a late lunch, you might want to plan a late dinner as well; it would be in keeping with Victorian tradition.

DINNER: For a special experience, try the romantic but informal **Peaches at Sunset,** One Sunset Boulevard; (609) 898-0100. The menu is eclectic and international. Here's where to come for Thai mussels with coconut-curry sauce followed by oven-roasted Chilean sea bass with an orange and chipotle glaze or filet mignon with peppercorn and cognac sauce. Peaches is a pretty restaurant too, with pastel walls, fresh flowers, a tropical fish aquarium, and ceiling murals. Moderate.

LODGING: The Queen Victoria.

DAY 3

Morning

BREAKFAST: The Queen Victoria.

Begin with a long, leisurely stroll up and down the promenade along the beach. There you'll find some elegant shops and more amazing Victorian homes and inns. If you've brought your suit, spend the morning playing on the oceanfront. The narrow beach is clean and pretty, and it's dotted with umbrellas, children with sand pails, and couples strolling by the water's edge. There is a beach admission charge of $4.00 a person.

LUNCH: Zoe's, located right on the beach at 715 Beach Drive (609–884–1233), has generous fresh-roasted turkey or roast beef sandwiches, burgers, hoagies, salads, vegetarian specials, cheese fries, potato salad, coleslaw, and desserts. If you skipped the beach scene and want to get an early start home, Zoe's will pack your lunch to go. Inexpensive.

Afternoon

Before you leave the area, consider a visit to the **Cape May Lighthouse** at Cape May Point State Park; (609) 884–5404. There you can climb the 199 steps of this 140-year-old structure and get a panoramic view of the whole area, including, on a clear day, the Delaware coast. The lighthouse is still in the process of reconstruction but it has been repainted in its original colors and the lantern has been finished. The Mid-Atlantic Center for the Arts conducts living-history events at the lighthouse, and you're sure to learn much about the lighthouse's history and the lives of its keepers on your visit. Open 9:00 A.M. to 5:00 P.M. daily from April through November, weekends only December through March. Admission is $3.00 for adults, $1.50 for children five through twelve; children under five are admitted free.

To return to Washington, you can retrace your route, using the ferry and driving home through Delaware. Or you can take State Highway 47 north about 50 miles to Millville, State Highway 49 west 40 miles to Interstate 295, I–295 west a few miles across the Delaware Memorial Bridge to Wilmington, and Interstate 95 south to Washington. Either option will take a little more than four hours.

THERE'S MORE

Ocean Cruise. The **Cape May Whale Watcher** offers two- or three-hour cruises on the ocean in search of either whales or dolphins. Three trips daily April through December. The three-hour whale-watch cruise costs $26 for adults, $23 for seniors, and $15 for children age seven through twelve. There is no charge for children under seven. The two-hour dolphin-watching cruise is about $8.00 cheaper. Located at Miss Chris Marina, Third Avenue and Wilson Drive; (609) 884–5445 or (800) 786–5445, www.capemaywhalewatcher.com.

Historic Cold Spring Village. Nineteenth-century farm village with country store, restaurant, bakery, and daily craft demonstrations of pottery, basketry, ironware, and more. Located at 720 Route 9 about 3 miles north of downtown Cape May; (609) 898–2300, www.hcsv.org. Open daily 10:00 A.M. to 4:30 P.M. in July and August, weekends 10:00 A.M. to 4:30 P.M. from May 15 to July 1 and in September. Admission is $5.00 for adults, $4.00 for seniors, and $3.00 for children five to twelve; children under five are admitted free.

Golf. Cape May National Golf Club, located on State Highway 9 about 2 miles south of State Highway 47; (609) 884–1563. Beautiful eighteen-hole course built around a fifty-acre wetlands nature preserve. Greens fees and cart rental cost $35–$80 depending on day and season.

Wildwood. Just north of Cape May is the widest and among the most popular beaches in New Jersey. Wildwood has a mile-and-a-half-long boardwalk with four amusement piers, hundreds of souvenir and novelty shops, and tons of saltwater taffy.

SPECIAL EVENTS

March–April. Annual Delaware Kite Festival. Kite-flying at Cape Henlopen State Park; festival events at the park and in Lewes; area attraction for more than thirty years. (302) 645–8073.

April. Cape May Jazz Festival. Regional and national artists perform at the ferry terminal. (609) 884–7277.

May–June. Annual Cape May Music Festival. Chamber music, jazz, opera, and pops. (609) 884–5404.

October. Victorian Week. With all the tours, craft shows, food, and entertainment, everyone has so much fun that Victorian Week now lasts ten days. (609) 884–5404 or (800) 275–4278.

December. Christmas Season in Cape May. Candlelight house tours, holiday crafts fair, gingerbread house workshops, heated trolley tours with complimentary wassail punch. (609) 884–5404 or (800) 275–4278.

OTHER RECOMMENDED RESTAURANTS

Cape May

Axelsson's Blue Claw, 991 Ocean Drive (north of dowtown); (609) 884–5878. Seafood, beef, veal; piano bar; waterfront dining. Moderate to expensive.

Vanscoy's Restaurant and Bakery, Carpenter's Square Mall (downtown); (609) 898–9898. Pleasant bistro with many vegetarian selections; also nice for dessert and cappuccino. Moderate.

Dock Mike's Pancake House, South Jersey Marina (on Lafayette Street 1 mile north of downtown area); (609) 884–2855. First choice for huge, inexpensive breakfasts.

Louisa's Cafe, 104 Jackson Street; (609) 884–5882. Small, upscale restaurant specializing in innovative vegetarian and seafood entrees and great desserts; open for dinner Wednesday through Saturday. Moderate to expensive.

Elaine's Dinner Theater, 513 Lafayette Street; (609) 884–4358. Cape May tourist attraction gets you dinner at 7:30 P.M. (choice of a dozen entrees) and entertainment along with your coffee for $36.95 ($20.00 for seniors, $13.00 for children). Reservations are necessary.

The Lobster House Restaurant, on Fisherman's Wharf; (609) 884–8296. Ultra-fresh seafood (they have their own fleet of boats). Make the catch of the day your choice after you've had a bowl of the crab soup. Moderate to expensive.

Fresco's, 412 Bank Street; (609) 884–0366. Attractive, upscale Italian restaurant that serves both old and new Italian cuisine. Try the four-cheese lasagna, the osso buco, or the veal chops with crabmeat, asparagus, and garlic. Expensive.

Best place for doughnuts: Cape May Bakers, 482 West Perry Street; (609) 884–7454.

Lewes

Rose & Crown Restaurant and Pub, 108 Second Street; (302) 645–2373. Sandwiches and pub food for lunch; seafood, pasta, poultry for dinner; large selection of beers. Moderate.

The Lighthouse Restaurant, Savannah Street and Anglers Road, by the Draw-bridge on Lewes Harbor; (302) 645–6271. Seafood and great view make for a pleasant lunch spot. Moderate.

Gilligan's Restaurant and Harborside Bar, Front and Market Streets; (302) 645–7866. New-American seafood and more; dine inside or outside. Moderate to expensive.

OTHER RECOMMENDED LODGINGS

Cape May

Angel of the Sea, 5 Trenton Avenue; (609) 884-3369 or (800) 848-3369, www.angelofthesea.com. One of Cape May's most popular inns, with twenty-six guest rooms, all with private baths. Close to the beach; full breakfast, complimentary afternoon tea, use of bicycles and beach equipment. Rates: $95–$285 depending on season and size of the room.

The Mainstay Inn, 635 Columbia Avenue; (609) 884–8690, www.mainstayinn.com. Exquisite Italianate villa considered by many to be the top B&B in Cape May, has nine guest rooms, all with private bath. Beautiful grand parlor, spacious veranda with swings and hammocks; full breakfast served. Rates: $195–$295.

Victorian Rose, 715 Columbia Avenue; (609) 884–2497, www.victorianroseinn.com. Former tearoom, now a romantic B&B with seven guest rooms, two suites, and a cottage. Most of the rooms have private baths; the suites and cottage have fully equipped kitchens. It also has a large porch with rockers, and a rose garden. The $90–$165 tariff includes a full breakfast.

Carroll Villa, 19 Jackson Street; (609) 884–9619, www.carrollvilla.com. Family-run 1882 bed-and-breakfast hotel with twenty-one guest rooms. Private baths, air-conditioning, phones, period antiques; full breakfast at the Mad Batter. Rates: $66–$160.

The Brass Bed Inn, 719 Columbia Avenue; (609) 884–8075. Lace curtains, wall coverings, Oriental rugs, and brass beds adorn the nine airy guest rooms in this nicely restored 1872 home; full breakfast served. Rates: $75–$180.

The Abbey, 34 Gurney Street at Columbia Avenue; (609) 884–4506. Very pleasant inn with fourteen large, antiques-filled rooms, all with private baths. The draw here is the owners, who entertain you with songs, hats, and snappy patter. Rates: $100–$275. Minimum two-night stay on weekends.

Lewes

New Devon Inn, Second and Market Streets; (302) 645–6466 or (800) 824–8754, www.beach-net.com/newdevoninn.html. Nicely restored inn with twenty-four elegant guest rooms and lots of warm hospitality; continental breakfast included. First-rate restaurant on premises. Rates: $50–$150.

Inn at Canal Square, 122 Market Street; (302) 645–8499, www.beach-net.com/canalsquare.html. Downtown inn on the canal with nineteen rooms. All the rooms are large and tastefully furnished; all have private baths, phones, and cable TV, and nearly all have balconies overlooking the scenic canal. Continental breakfast is served. Rates: $85–$185.

FOR MORE INFORMATION

Lewes Chamber of Commerce and Visitors Bureau, P.O. Box 1, Lewes, DE 19958; (302) 645–8073, www.leweschamber.com.

Chamber of Commerce of Greater Cape May, P.O. Box 109, Cape May, NJ 08204; (609) 884–5508 or (800) 275–4278.

Cape May County Department of Tourism, P.O. Box 365, Cape May Courthouse, NJ 08210; (609) 463–6415 or (800) 227–2297, www.beachcomber.com/capemay/capemay.html.

For more information visit www.lewesde.com.

INDEX

A

Abby Aldrich Rockefeller Folk Art
Center, 56
Addy Sea Bed and Breakfast, 287–89
Admiral Fell Inn, 108
Afro-American Historical and
Cultural Museum, 202
Agecroft Hall, 37
Alexander Dobbin Dining
Rooms, 226
America's Railroads on Parade, 64
Amish Farm and House, 217
Amusement parks, 60, 240, 255
Andy Warhol Museum, 248–49
Angler Restaurant, 96
Anna Hazzard Museum, 292
Annapolis, 70–79
Annapolis City Dock, 74
Antietam National Battlefield,
117–121, 125
Antique Row (Baltimore), 107
Antique Row (Philadelphia), 197
Antiques shopping, 10, 24, 37, 107,
124, 146, 150, 197, 239
Art festivals, 11, 25, 49, 64, 77, 114,
125, 163, 187, 198, 204, 220,
256, 268, 281
Art galleries, 21, 33, 74, 88, 110, 131,
135, 160, 172, 213, 215, 256, 290
Art Gallery of Fell's Point, 110
Artists at Work Gallery, 160

Artworks at Doneckers, 215
Ashby Inn & Restaurant, The, 5
Ash Lawn–Highland, 18, 21
Aspen Dining Room, 161
Assateague Island National Seashore,
92, 96–98, 102
Atlantic Hotel, 98
Augusta Festival, 160
Augusta Heritage Arts Workshops,
160
Aurora Gallery, 74

B

Babe Ruth Birthplace and Baltimore
Orioles Museum, 113
Baltimore, 103–16
Baltimore Maritime Museum, 113
Baltimore Museum of Art, 111
Baltimore Orioles, 111
Baltimore's Inner Harbor, 108
Baltimore Zoo, 112
B&O Railroad Museum, 113
Banneker-Douglass Museum of Afro-
American Life and Culture, 76
Barboursville Vineyards and Ruins, 25
Barrier Island Visitor Center, 96
Basilica of the Assumption, 107
Bassetts Ice Cream, 194
Bath House, 146
Bath Street Open Air Market, 150
Beans and Bagels, 119

Beartown State Park, 170
Beckley, West Virginia, 185–86, 188
Beckley Exhibition Coal Mine, 185
Bellevue, Maryland, 84
Belmont, 48
Benedum Center for the Performing
    Arts, 252, 256
Benjamin Franklin Bridge, 202
Berger's Bakery, 106
Berkeley Castle, 148–49
Berkeley Plantation, 62–63
Berkeley Springs, West Virginia,
    142–53
Berkeley Springs Antique Mall, 146
Berkeley Springs State Park,
    142–47, 149
Berlin, Maryland, 92, 94
Bethany Beach, Delaware, 285–95
Betsy Ross House, 196
Bicycling, 64, 83, 161, 172, 175, 201,
    264, 290, 292, 300
Big Meadows, 9
Big Meadows Lodge, 10
Bird-in-Hand, Pennsylvania, 211–12
Bird-in-Hand Bakery, 212
Bishop White House, 197
Black Bear Snack Bar, 182
Black History Museum and Cultural
    Center of Virginia, 34
Blackwater Brewing Company, 158
Blackwater Falls State Park, 158–59
Blackwater National Wildlife
    Refuge, 99
Blue Moon Restaurant, 290
Bluestone Dining Room, 181
Bluestone State Park, 182–83
boardwalk, Ocean City,

Maryland, 94–95
Boating, 75, 85, 99, 162, 183, 257, 267
Bookpress, 63
Bookstores, 124, 281
Boonsboro, Maryland, 124, 130, 138
Braddock Heights, 130
Braddock's Grave, 262
Brandywine Battlefield Park, 280–81
Brandywine River Museum, 272, 278
Brandywine River Museum
    Restaurant, 278
Brandywine Valley, 272–84
Broadway Market, 110
Bruton Parish Church, 55
Buck Hollow Overlook, 4
Buckley's Tavern, 274
Buggy rides, 219
Busch Gardens, 60
Byrd Visitor Center, 10

C

Cabin Club, 172
Cacapon Resort State Park, 142,
    147–50
Cacapon Restaurant, 148
Caledon Natural Area, 45
Camp Hoover, 9, 10
Camping, 12, 122, 151, 164, 181, 188,
    267, 295
Canaan Valley Resort Park, 154,
    156–58
Canal Walk (Richmond), 35
C&O Canal, 132
Canoeing, 25, 85, 122, 148, 175, 182,
    186, 237, 263, 280
Canyon Rim Center (Pipestem), 181

Canyon Rim Visitors Center (New River), 185

Cape Henlopen State Park, 298

Cape May, 296–308

Cape May–Lewes Ferry, 299

Cape May Lighthouse, 304

Cape May National Golf Club, 305

Cape May Welcome Center, 299

Capitol Building in Colonial Williamsburg, 55

Captain Dan Vaughn's Decoy Shop, 85

Carnegie Hall, 171, 174

Carnegie Library of Pittsburgh, 251

Carnegie Museum of Art, 250

Carnegie Museum of Natural History, 244, 250–51

Carnegie Music Hall, 250, 252

Carnegie Science Center, 244, 253

Caroline Street, Fredericksburg, 44

Carriage Museum, 254

Carrol's Creek Cafe, 75

Carter's Grove, 58

Carytown, 37

Casselman Hotel, 134

Casselman River Bridge, 135

Cass Scenic Railroad State Park, 168

Catoctin Mountain Park, 122

Catoctin Wildlife Preserve and Zoo, 122

Central Market (Lancaster), 211

Chadds Ford, 278

Chalk Hill, 268

Charlottesville, 16–28

Chase-Lloyd House, 76

Cheat River Inn, The, 160–61

Cheese Shop, 57

Chesapeake Bay Maritime Museum, 82, 86

Chestertown, 87

Chez Gerard, 264–65

Chez Trinh, 61

Childrens Museum of Rose Hill Manor Park, 119, 125

Children's Playhouse, 254

China Sea Marine Trading Company, 110

Chocolate World, 227–28

Chowning's Tavern, 54

Christ Church, 196

Circular Dining Room at the Hotel Hershey, 229

City Dock Cafe, 75

City Lights, 248

City Park, Hagerstown, 131

City Tavern, 198

Civil War sites, 11, 37, 48, 117, 225, 230

Clayton, 254

Clayworks, 172

Colonial Beach, Virginia, 45, 50

Colonial Parkway, 57

Colonial Williamsburg Visitor Information Center, 54

Columbia, Pennsylvania, 218

Compass Inn Museum, 241

Confluence, Pennsylvania, 266, 269

Congress Hall, 195

Coolfont Resort, 147

Country Inn, 149

Country Store Antique Mall, 24

Covered bridges, 124

Cozy Restaurant, 123

Crab Claw, The, 82

Craft festivals, 11, 49, 89, 125,
137–38, 150, 160, 163, 187,
242, 268, 305
Cross-country skiing, 122, 158, 166,
182, 237
Cruises, 76, 88, 256, 304
Crystal Grottoes Cavern, 124
Cumberland, Maryland, 128,
133, 138
Cumberland Narrows, 133
Cunningham Falls State Park,
117, 122
Curtis Center of Norman Rockwell
Art, 198
Customs House, 87
Cyclorama Center, 225

D

Dante's and Luigi's, 200
Dark Hollow Falls, 10
Davis, West Virginia, 159
Davis and Elkins College, 159
Declaration House, 196
Deep Creek Lake, 137
Delaware Art Museum, 280
Delaware Museum of Natural
History, 280
Delaware Seashore State Park, 291
Deli, The, (Frederick), 119
Del Sol Cafe and Market, 171
DeWitt Wallace Decorative Arts
Gallery, 56
Di Febo's Restaurant, 287
Dickey Ridge Visitor Center, 6
Dobbin House, 226–27
Dolle's Saltwater Taffy, 290

Dolly Sods Scenic Area and
Wilderness Area, 158, 161
Doughnuts, 12, 26, 39, 50, 65, 78, 89,
101, 106, 133, 144, 160, 174,
188, 206, 221, 232, 240, 268,
294, 306
Draper's Cafe, 174
Duquesne Incline, 247

E

Eastern Shore, Maryland, 80–91
Eastern State Penitentiary, 203
Easton, Maryland, 88, 91
Eastport, 75
Edgar Allan Poe Museum, 38
Einstein Books and Toys that
Matter, 204
Eisenhower National Historic
Site, 230
Eldreth Pottery, 220
Elkins, West Virginia, 154–56,
159, 163
Elkwallow Wayside, 7
Emlen Physick House and
Estate, 301
Ephrata, Pennsylvania, 214–16
Ephrata Cloister, 215
Expressions, 160

F

Faidley's, 105
Failingers Hotel Gunter, 136
Fairmount Park, 201
Fallingwater, 260, 265
Family Recreation Park, 124

Fan District, 36–37
Farmhouse Restaurant, The, 8
Farmington, Pennsylvania, 262, 269
Fawcett's Boat Supplies, 75
Fayette County, Pennsylvania, 260–70
Fayette Theater, 187
Fayetteville, West Virginia, 183
Fell's Point, 110
Fenwick Island State Park, 291
Fisher's, 212
Fishing, 80, 88, 148, 182, 237,
    267, 292
Flint Hill, Virginia, 11
Food and Friends, 172
Ford's Colony Country Club Golf
    Course, 59
Fort Ligonier, 239–40
Fort McHenry, 105
Fort Necessity National
    Battlefield, 262
Fort Pitt, 248
410 Bank Street, 299–300
Fox Hollow Nature Trail, 6–7
Franklin Institute Science
    Museum, 202
Frederick, Maryland, 119–20, 125
Fredericksburg, Virginia, 41–44
Fredericksburg/Spotsylvania
    National Military Park, 48
Frick Art and Historical Center, 253
Frick Art and Historical Center
    Cafe, 254
Frick Art Museum, 254
Frick Art Museum Cafe, 254
Frog and the Redneck, The, 34–35
Front Porch Restaurant, 156
Front Royal, Virginia, 5, 12, 14

Frost Mansion, 136
Frostburg, Maryland, 130, 136

G

Gardens, 17, 55, 74, 111, 229, 275
Gateway Clipper, 256
Geddes-Piper House, 87
General Lewis Inn, 170
General Sutter Inn, 212
George Washington's Birthplace
    National Monument, 45
Gettysburg, Pennsylvania, 223–27,
    230–31
Gettysburg National Military Park,
    223, 225–26
Gettysburg Railroad, 230
Gettystown Inn, 227
Gibson's Lodgings, 72
Glassmeyers Restaurant, 213
Globe Theatre, Berlin, 94
Golden Horseshoe Golf
    Courses, 59
Golden Triangle, 246
Golfing, 59, 149, 156, 230, 263, 305
Gourmet Shop, 174
Governor's Palace, 55
Grandview Avenue, Pittsburgh, 247
Grantsville, Maryland, 134, 139–40
Greenbrier, 173–74
Greenbrier River Trail, 172
Greenbrier Valley Theatre, 173
Greenhouse, 254
Greene House Shops, 24
Groff's Farm Restaurant, 210–11
Grotto Pizza, 289

H

Hagerstown, Maryland, 121, 130, 138
Hagley Museum and Eleutherian
    Mills, 280
Halliehurst Mansion, 159
Hammond-Harwood House, 76
Hancock, Maryland, 132–33
Hanover Street, Fredericksburg, 45
Hans Herr House, 218
Harborplace, 103, 109
Hardware Store Restaurant, 22
Harpers Ferry, West Virginia, 149
Harrison's Chesapeake House, 85
Harry Browne's, 74
Hearthside Restaurant, 238
Heinz Hall for the Performing
    Arts, 252, 256
Helmand, 110
Heritage Repertory Theatre, 25
Hershey, Pennsylvania, 227–34
Hershey Gardens, 229
Hershey Museum, 230
Hersheypark, 228
Hidden Valley Four Seasons
    Resort, 237–43
Hiking, 6, 7, 8, 99, 120, 158, 172,
    178, 182
Hill Top Inn Restaurant, 262
Historic Annapolis Foundation
    Museum Store and Welcome
    Center, 73
Historic Cold Spring Village, 305
Homestead House, 290
Hopwood, Pennsylvania, 268
Horse racing, 114
Horseback riding, 10, 152, 182, 189

Hotel du Pont, 277
Hotel Hershey, 233

I

Ice House Art and Community
    Center, 150
Idlewild Park, 240
Imperial Hotel, 87
Independence Hall, 192–95
Independence National Historical
    Park, 195
Indian Fields Tavern, 62
Indian River Lifesaving Station, 292
Ingleside Plantation Vineyard, 47
Inspiration Bakery and Cafe, 147
Intercourse, Pennsylvania, 211–12
Island Kayak, 85-86
Italian Market, 199

J

Jamestown Colonial National
    Historical Park, 58
Jamestown Settlement, 58
Japonaji, 110
Jefferson Hotel, 36, 39
Jewelers' Row, Philadelphia, 198
Jewish Museum of Maryland, 113
J. Fenton Gallery/Quilts
    Unlimited, 171
Jimbo's Specialty Beer and Hot Dog
    Shop, 247
Jimmy's Restaurant, 110
John Marshall House, 37
Jolly Roger Amusement Park, 95
Jonathan Hager House and

Museum, 131
Jordan Hollow Farm Inn, 8
Joseph Meyerhoff Symphony
    Hall, 110–11
J's Gourmet, 6
Jumonville Glen, 262
Junction 808, 121

K

Kanawha Cruises, 35
Keedysville, Maryland, 127
Kenmore, 43–44
Kenmore Inn, 44
Kennett Square, Pennsylvania, 274
Kennywood Park, 255
Kentuck Knob, 267
King of France Tavern, 72
Kingsmill Resort Golf Courses, 59
Konstant's Candy, 105
Kooser State Park, 238
Kowerski Gallery, 213
KrackerJack's Cafe and Spirits,
    225–26

L

Ladew Topiary Gardens, 111–12
Lancaster, Pennsylvania, 211
Lancaster County, Pennsylvania,
    208–22
Lancaster Visitors Information
    Center, 211
La Rosa Negra, 298
Laughlintown, Pennsylvania, 240
Laurel Caverns, 267
Laurel Highlands,

Pennsylvania, 235–43
LaVale Toll Gate House, 133–34
League of Maryland Craftsmen, 74
Lewes, Delaware, 296, 308
Lewisburg, West Virginia, 166–77
Lewisburg Visitors Center, 171
Lewrene Farm B&B, 121
Lexington Market, 105
Le Yaca, 59
Liberty Bell, 192, 195
Ligonier, Pennsylvania, 239–40,
    242–43
Ligonier Country Inn, 240, 242
Ligonier Tavern, 239
Linden Row Inn, 32
Lititz, Pennsylvania, 213–14
Little Devils Stairs, 7
Little Hogback Overlook, 7
Little Italy (Philadelphia), 192, 199
Lodge Restaurant, 158
Logan Circle, Philadelphia, 201
Log Cabin Restaurant, 216
Longwood Gardens, 275–76
Lovely Lane Church and Museum,
    Baltimore, 113
Luray Caverns, 10
Lyric Opera House, 111

M

Mad Batter, 302
Made in Virginia Store, 44
Maggie Walker National Historic
    Site, 34
Mainstay Inn, 302, 307
Main Street Grill, 32
Maison Marconi, 103, 107

Mango's, 291
Manor Inn, 147
Mansion House Art Center, 131
Martinsburg, West Virginia, 149
Maryland Avenue, Annapolis, 74
Maryland Science Center, 112–13
Maryland State House, 73
Maymont, 35
McGuffey Art Center, 21
McKeever Lodge, 180
Meadow Spring Farm Bed and
    Breakfast, 274
Merchants Square, 56
Merry Sherwood Plantation, 94, 96
Metropolitain, 22
Michie Tavern, 21
Middleton Tavern, 72
Middletown, 130
Miller House, 136
Miller's Smorgasbord Dinner, 217
Mitchell Art Gallery, 74
Model Railroad Museums, 64, 219
Monongahela Incline, 247
Monticello, 16, 18, 19
Montpelier, 18, 23
Montross, Virginia, 45, 50
Moravian Church, Lititz, 213
Morris A. Mechanic Theater, 111
Mountain Creek Lodge and Dining
    Room, 181–82
Mountain Deli, 241
Mountain Laurel Crafts, 146
Mountain Playhouse, 241
Mount Holly Steamboat Inn, 45
Mount Vernon Methodist
    Church, 107
Mount Vernon neighborhood,

Baltimore, 107
Mount Washington, 247
Mt. Washington Tavern, 262
Mueller House and Museum, 213
Mummers Museum, 198–99
Museum of the Berkeley
    Springs, 145
Museum of the Civil War, 225
Museum of the Confederacy, 33
Museums, art, 34, 59, 106, 111, 137,
    192, 202, 248, 254, 272, 279, 280
Museums, children's, 37, 119, 185,
    203
Museums, culture, 33, 34, 38, 56, 58,
    73, 76, 88, 99, 113, 135, 137,
    145, 160, 175, 185, 197, 198,
    213, 215, 218, 230, 241, 276, 278
Museums, history, 10, 33, 37, 45, 48,
    58, 62, 73, 88, 105, 171, 195,
    225, 239, 248, 253, 262, 280
Museums, natural history, 86, 96,
    113, 133, 183, 244, 250, 280, 305
Museums, science, 112, 202, 244, 253
Music festivals, 38, 64, 100, 114, 160,
    187, 205, 231, 241, 268, 292, 305
Mystic Rock Golf Course, 267

N

Nancy's Corner, 212
National Aquarium, 103, 108
National Aviary, 255
Nationality Classrooms, 256
National Pike, 128–30
National Toy Train Museum,
    The, 219
National Watch and Clock

Museum, 218

Nav Jiwan International Tea
Room, 214

Nelson Beal House, 136

Nemours, 272, 279

New Jersey State Aquarium, 203

New Market, Virginia, 14

New Market Battlefield State
Historical Park, 11

New River, 183–84

New River Gorge, 178, 183–84, 188

O

Oak Supper Club, 182–83

Oakencroft Vineyard, 23

Oakland (Pittsburgh), 251

O. C. Parasail, 99

Ocean City, Maryland, 94–96

Ohiopyle State Park, 260, 263–64

Old City Hall, Philadelphia, 195

Olde Towne Cafe, 144

Old Factory Antique Mall, 150

Old Firehouse Museum, 301

Old Hardware Gallery, 172

Orange, Virginia, 27

Orchards, 5, 47

Ordinary at Michie Tavern, The, 21

Oriole Park at Camden Yards, 111

Orrell's Maryland Beaten
Biscuits, 86

Outdoor Amphitheater, 182

Outlet shopping, 60, 150, 219, 291

Oxford, Maryland, 84, 89

Oxford-Bellevue Ferry (Tred-Avon
Ferry), 84

P

Paper Moon Diner, 111

Park's Fried Chicken, 105

Peabody Conservatory of
Music, 107, 111

Peabody Library, 103, 107

Peaches at Sunset, 303

Pearl S. Buck Museum, 175

Penn Alps Craft Shop, 135

Penn Alps Restaurant, 135

Pennsylvania Dutch Country, 208–22

People's Place Country Store and
Museum, 211

Philadelphia, 192–207

Philadelphia City Hall, 194

Philadelphia Museum of Art,
192, 200

Philadelphia Orchestra, 200

Philadelphia Zoological Gardens, 202

Phipps Conservatory, 244, 252

Physick House, 197

Piccolo Piccolo Ristorante, 249

Pie Shoppe, 240

Pipestem Drive-In Theater, 183

Pipestem Resort State Park, 178–90

Pittsburgh, 244–59

Pittsburgh Ballet, 252, 256

Pittsburgh Center for the Arts, 256

Pittsburgh Children's Museum, 255

Pittsburgh Opera, 252, 256

Pittsburgh Symphony Orchestra,
252, 256

Pittsburgh Zoo, 255

P.J.'s Place, 110

Planet Maze, 100

Please Touch Museum, 203

Point State Park, 247, 248
Polock Johnny's Sausage, 105
Pottery, The, 60–61
Priory–A City Inn, 248
Professional sports, 111, 113,
    204, 255
Prospect Peak, 147
Pusser's Landing, 72

Q

Queen Victoria, 299

R

Railroad Museum of
    Pennsylvania, 219
Railroad museums, 113, 219
Railroad rides, 137, 168, 219, 230
Randolph County Convention and
    Visitors Bureau, 159
Raynes Reef, 96
Reading Terminal Market, 194
Rebecca T. Ruark, 88
Rehoboth Art League, 290
Rehoboth Beach, Delaware, 285–95
Richmond, Virginia, 29–40
Richmond Children's Museum, 37
Richmond National Battlefield
    Park, 37
Rick's Steaks, 194
Rittenhouse Square,
    Philadelphia, 201
Riverby Books, 44
River's Edge Cafe, 266
Rock climbing, 156, 162
Rodin Museum, 192, 200

Rose Hill Manor, 119, 125
Royal Oak Bookshop, 6
Ruckersville, Virginia, 24

S

Sailing, Etc., 99
St. John's College, 74
St. John's Church, Richmond, 32
St. Mary's Square Museum, 84
St. Michaels, Maryland, 82–83,
    86, 89
St. Michael's Church, 136
Salisbury, Maryland, 98–99
Schenley Park, 251
Schmankerl Stube, 131
Schooner Woodwind, 72, 75
Sea Rocket, 99–100
Seasons Cafe, 60
Second Bank of the United
    States, 195
Second Bank Portrait Gallery, 195
Sedona Grille, 184
Seneca Rocks, 156
Sesame Inn, 247
1764 House, 212
Shadyside, 252
Sharpsburg, Maryland, 126
Shenandoah National Park, 2–15
Shenandoah Valley Overlook, 6
Shepherdstown, West Virginia, 149
Shockoe Bottom, 33
Shockoe Bottom Arts Center, 33
Shockoe Slip, 33
Shops at Congress Hall, 303
Shops at Station Square, 246–47
Shops by the Depot, 136

Sideling Hill Exhibit Center, 133

Silver Thatch Inn, 18

Sirianni's Pizza Cafe, 159

Skiing, 157, 237

Skyline Drive, 2–15

Smoke Hole Caverns, 162

Snow Hill, Maryland, 98

Snow Hill Inn, 98

Society Hill, Philadelphia, 197

Somerset, Pennsylvania, 237, 242, 243

South Street, Philadelphia, 198

Southern Culture Cafe and Restaurant, 23

Southern Inn, 180

Splash Mountain Water Park, 95

Sports Club, 239

Spruce Knob, 168

Spruce Forest Artisans Village, 135

Star of India, 251

Star Theater, 148

Strasburg, Pennsylvania, 219

Strasburg Rail Road, 219

Stratford Hall Plantation, 46

Stribling Orchard, 5

Sturgis Pretzel House, 213

Summit Diner, 237

Summit Inn, 262

Susanna Foo, 196

Suzie's, 252

Swede Things in America, 303

T

Talbot Street, St. Michaels, 83

Tari's Premier Cafe and Inn, 148

Ten Thousand Villages, 215

Tennis Club, 239

Termini Brothers Bakery, 194

Terrace Restaurant, 276

Theater West Virginia, 187

Thomas Bond House, 194, 196

Thornton Gap, 8

Thrasher Carriage Museum, 137

Thrasher's French Fries, 95, 290

Three Rivers Stadium, 247

Thurmont, Maryland, 126

Tilghman Island Inn, 85

Tilghman Island, Maryland, 84, 89

Timberline Four Seasons Resort, 157

Todd House, 197

Tom and Terry's, 289

Town Dock Marina, St. Michaels, 83

Toy Shop of Cape May, 303

Treetop House Restaurant, 147

Trellis, The, 55

Trimper's Rides of Ocean City, 95

200 South Street Inn, 19, 22

U

Union Canal House, 228–29

United States Mint, 196

University of Virginia, 16, 22

Upper Crust, 144

Upstairs Emporium, 132

U.S. Naval Academy, 70, 76

V

Valentine Museum, 33

Victualling Warehouse Maritime Museum, 73

Vineyards, 23, 25, 47
Virginia Discovery Musuem, 24
Virginia Museum of Fine Arts, 36
Virginia State Capitol, 34

W

Walters Art Gallery, 106
Ward Museum of Wildfowl
    Art, 98
Washington Avenue,
    Fredericksburg, 43
Washington County Museum of
    Fine Arts, 137
Washington Monument
    (Baltimore), 107
Washington Monument State
    Park, 119–20
Washington Square,
    Philadelphia, 198
Washington Street Mall,
    Cape May, 303
Washington, Virginia, 10
Water Country USA, 60
Weaver's Restaurant and
    Bakery, 133
Western Maryland Scenic
    Railroad, 137
Westmoreland Berry Farm and
    Orchard, 47
Westmoreland County,
    Virginia, 41–51
Westmoreland County
    Museum, 45
Westmoreland State Park, 47
Whistle Stop Cafe, 136

White Dog Cafe, 201
White House of the
    Confederacy, 33–34
White Sulfur Springs, West
    Virginia, 173–74
White Swan Tavern, 87
White-water rafting, 38, 162,
    183, 263
Whiteoak Canyon, 10
Wickham House, 33
Wilbur Chocolate Company's
    Candy Americana Museum
    and Store, 213
Wildflowers B&B, 131
William Paca House and Garden, 74
William and Mary College, 59
Williamsburg, Virginia, 52–67
Williamsburg Sampler Bed and
    Breakfast, 56
Wilmington, Delaware, 272–84
Wilson's General Store, 132
Winchester, Virginia, 144
Winterthur, 272, 276–77
Winthrop Rockefeller Archaeology
    Museum, 59
Witmer's Quilts, 214
Woman's Industrial
    Exchange, 103, 106
Wye Gristmill, 86
Wye Oak State Park, 86

Y

Ye Olde Doughnut Shop, 160
Yorktown Victory Center and
    Battlefield, 61–62

Youghiogheny River, 260
Youghiogheny River Lake
    Recreation Area, 267

Z

Zanzibar Blue, 196

Zoe's, 304
ZooAmerica, 229
Zoos, 112, 122, 202, 212, 229, 255

ABOUT THE AUTHORS

JOHN FITZPATRICK teaches political science and is the Director of the State University of New York at Brockport's Washington Semester Program. John is a graduate of Georgetown University and has a Ph.D. from the State University of New York at Buffalo. He worked as a Congressional staffer for ten years and ran a political consulting firm for eight years.

HOLLY J. BURKHALTER is Advocacy Director of Physicians for Human Rights, an international human rights monitoring organization. Holly is a graduate of Iowa State University and a recipient of one of its Distinguished Young Alumni awards. She is the author of numerous articles and op-ed pieces, and she frequently appears on radio and televison discussing foreign policy. She is also the author of a cookbook/memoir, *Four Midwestern Sisters Christmas Book* (Viking Penguin, 1991).

John and Holly have been married since 1984. They have two daughters, Grace Bofa Fitzpatrick and Jo Bao-Ngan Fitzpatrick.